BEYOND THE CALL

THREE WOMEN on the FRONT LINES in AFGHANISTAN

EILEEN RIVERS

DA CAPO PRESS

Da Capo Press
Hachette Book Group
1290 Avenue of the Americas, New York, NY 10104
www.dacapopress.com
@DaCapoPress

Printed in the United States of America
First Edition: November 2018

Published by Da Capo Press, an imprint of Perseus Books, LLC, a subsidiary of Hachette Book Group, Inc.

The publisher is not responsible for websites (or their content) that are not owned by the publisher.

Editorial production by Christine Marra, *Marrathon* Production Services. www.marrathoneditorial.org

Book design by Jane Raese
Set in 12-point Dante

Cataloging-in-Publication Data is available from the Library of Congress.
ISBN 978-0-306-90307-6 (hardcover)
ISBN 978-0-306-90309-0 (ebook)

LSC-C

10 9 8 7 6 5 4 3 2 1

TO BESSIE COLEMAN, WILLA BROWN,

AND ALL THE OTHER GROUNDBREAKING FEMALES,

PAST AND PRESENT,

WHOSE STORIES ARE TOO RARELY TOLD

CONTENTS

PART TWO. THE WARS AT HOME

CHRONOLOGY

A HISTORY OF WOMEN
IN THE MILITARY

Cannonball fire burst through the trees, and Private Robert Shurtleff felt the ground shake.

It was dark. Shurtleff ducked and lifted his arms to shield his face from the mounds of dirt flying through the air. He looked quickly to his left and watched Diston, a man he had grown close to in just a few months, begin to fall. Shurtleff wanted to lunge across the mud to save him, but enemy fire stopped the private from moving. Instead, he watched Diston's lifeless body fall atop one of many others, Continental and British alike, scattered across the Revolutionary War battlefield.

Shurtleff was tough—lauded as one of the fastest, strongest, and most capable men in his scouting unit. He could read, a rarity in eighteenth-century America. He was the first to volunteer for dangerous missions. His fellow soldiers playfully called him Molly because of what they thought were slightly feminine characteristics—he had no facial hair and tended to shy away from the wrestling and roughhousing that other men participated in during brief moments of free time in the field.

It was 1782.

And what none of those soldiers knew was that the man everyone called Shurtleff, the one they loyally and fiercely followed into battle, was actually a woman.

Deborah Sampson was the first female known to have fought in an American war. She tried, but failed, to enlist twice (under different male monikers) before she perfected her ability to pass under the name Robert Shurtleff. Her work during the Revolutionary War proves that women have been capable of fighting in combat for the United States since the first group of men set boots to muddy ground for American freedom.

REVOLUTIONARY WAR

1775–1783: Although women are not allowed to join the military, not all females who believe in the quest for America's freedom are as extreme in their desire for combat as Deborah Sampson. Hundreds of women serve openly during the American Revolution—not as soldiers but as civilian nurses, water carriers, cooks, spies, and in other support roles. Some follow their husbands to battle. Sampson's actions, passing as a man, are illegal during the Revolution, and dozens of women are jailed for attempting it. A doctor discovers that Sampson is a woman after the private is shot and requires a long hospital stay. She is kicked out of the military and has to fight for years, with the help of her husband and other men, to get acknowledged for her service through a military pension.

CIVIL WAR

1861–1865: Still unable to serve in the military but surely having heard about the work and accolades of Deborah Sampson (who became a brand, was the subject of at least one book, and toured the country lecturing about her experiences as a soldier), hundreds of women disguise themselves as men to fight in combat for both the Union and the Confederacy. As slave men sign up to fight for their freedom, slave women follow. Cathay Williams, a slave from Missouri, is forced to serve the Union Army as a cook. After her service was over, she disguises herself as a man (under the name William Cathay) and becomes a Buffalo Soldier. She is the only known ex-slave woman to have done so. She fought successfully for two years before a doctor discovered she was a woman and she was discharged. The Army refused to recognize her service or give her a pension.

NURSE CORPS

1901: After three years of hiring female nurses as government contractors, the Army finally enlists its first group of women. In 1901 nurses become part of the regular Army. They are hired for three-year stints but are not allowed to become officers.

1908: The Navy establishes a nurse corps.

WORLD WAR I

1914–1918: Some estimate more than thirty-five thousand women serve in the military during the war, with more than twenty-five thousand serving overseas throughout Europe as, among other things, nurses, secretaries, and phone operators.

WORLD WAR II

1939–1945: These years saw some of the most significant advancements in military service for women. More than one hundred thousand women enlist in the Army, and roles for women expand for the first time under the Women's Army Auxiliary Corps, created in 1942. Some female pilots take on stateside missions usually reserved for men through the newly created Women's Airforce Service Pilots (WASPs). But nursing is still by far the most popular military occupation for women. More than sixty thousand nurses serve during the war. Black women, who had been fighting for years to serve as nurses, are finally allowed to join the Army Nurse Corps in greater numbers. African American women also make other strides during the war. Heard of the Tuskegee Airmen? A woman, Willa Brown, aids the group. Brown started an aviation school with her husband and trained male pilots to qualify for advanced flying school at the Tuskegee Institute. Another black female pilot, Janet Bragg, trained at the Tuskegee Institute with male pilots. She was the only woman there and experienced a tremendous amount of discrimination from white and black men alike. A white male instructor failed her on the flight examination, Bragg said much later when recounting the experience during an interview with the Smithsonian Institution. She said the instructor told her after she landed the plane that she'd done as well as any man, but that he'd never given a colored woman a license to fly, and he didn't intend to start that day. A racially segregated Army also denied the commercial pilot entry into the WASPs.

1948: Three years after the war ended, regular and reserve Army status is officially opened to all women.

The Women's Armed Service Integration Act creates a female reserve for the Army, Air Force, and Marines. Six years earlier, the Navy Women's Reserve Act created the WAVES (Women Accepted for Volunteer Emergency Service).

KOREAN WAR

1950: Female soldiers enter a combat theater for the first time as Army nurses, the only women allowed to do so during the war.

1951: Female reservists are forced into active duty for the first time.

1953: Fae M. Adams becomes the first female physician commissioned as an officer in the regular Army Medical Corps, as a first lieutenant.

VIETNAM WAR

1960–1973: Women serve in Vietnam as nurses training the South Vietnamese as early as 1956. By 1967 some five hundred thousand American troops, men and women, are on the ground in Vietnam. But the first female officer from the Women's Army Corps actually landed in the country five years before that. By the end of the war about eleven thousand women (mostly nurses) had been stationed in the conflict zone. Just as during World War II decades earlier, the need for troops forces a boon in progress for women in the armed forces. By 1972 all noncombat jobs are opened to women, and women are allowed, for the first time, to command men. Nearly sixty thousand troops died as a result of the Vietnam War and eight of them were women. In 1967 rules for retirement and promotion are opened to female officers in all branches.

1970S AND 1980S

1976: Enlistment age is reduced for women.

1979: For the first time men and women have the same qualifications for enlistment. The Women's Army Corps, no longer needed, was officially disbanded the year before. Women have been integrated into the regular Army and reserves for about thirty years.

1980: First women graduate from West Point.

1983: Four female military police officers deploy to an active combat zone; eventually one hundred women serve in Grenada. Females fly for the first time in conflict.

1988: Secretary of Defense Frank C. Carlucci issues a Standard Risk Rule that "excluded women from noncombat units or missions if the risks of exposure to direct combat, hostile fire or capture were equal to or greater than the risk in the units they supported." Six years later Defense Secretary Les Aspin rescinds the rule, allowing women to serve in any units except those "below brigade level whose primary mission is to engage in direct combat on the ground." This 1994 directive sets women up to serve in combat zones without acknowledging their combat roles through pay or title.

1989: Captain Linda Bray leads her military police unit on what is supposed to be a routine mission to capture a kennel of guard dogs in Panama. But when her unit arrives, members of the Panamanian Defense Forces (PDF), which had been using the location as barracks, open fire. Bray tells her soldiers to return fire, becoming the first woman to command and lead a unit into battle. Bray and her thirty soldiers (both men and women) of the 988th Military Police Company fight for three hours during the December battle, which was on day one of the US invasion of Panama. The unit kills three PDF soldiers. Bray's work, although applauded (not one American soldier died), forces public discussion about whether there is still a distinction between combat and noncombat units (tactical military police companies are supposed to fall into the latter category) during conflict. It is the first time the military questions whether "frontlines" still exist or shield women from direct combat.

GULF WAR

1990–1991: The first war after which military commanders admitted that women were critical to combat readiness, the Persian Gulf War is also the first that openly diverges from conventional definitions of *frontlines.* Guerilla warfare puts the forty thousand women who serve at greater risk of injury and death. It is the first modern-day war in which women were held hostage—Major Rhonda Cornum and Specialist Melissa Coleman are held for a week and thirty-three days, respectively, as Iraqi prisoners of war. For the first time women take on virtually all combat roles in every way but name. They fly helicopters into combat, launch missiles, and command male soldiers.

1990S

1993: President Bill Clinton officially ends the exclusion of women on aircraft and ships that carry out combat missions, though women had already flown aircraft into combat zones.

1994: A shift in Department of Defense (DOD) assignment policy—one that had given units some leeway in assigning women based on billeting availability and physical requirements—opens some thirty-two thousand Army and forty-eight thousand Marine positions to women.

The Army chief of staff announces that all Army basic training will fully gender integrate. A gender-integration steering committee begins making recommendations for smooth transitions of all basic training units.

1994–1995: The Army once again begins experimenting with gender integration in basic training after initial experiments in the 1980s failed. Men and women participate in mixed-gender basic training classes for the first time in Fort Jackson, South Carolina, and Fort Leonard Wood, Missouri.

1998: The first woman takes command of a Navy combat ship.

THE WARS IN IRAQ AND AFGHANISTAN

2001–PRESENT: As combat roles for women have expanded, so has the necessity for women to fight. More than 11 percent of the forces deployed to Iraq and Afghanistan have been women, and most of these women have served more than one tour.

2003–2004: The first group of women, known as Team Lioness, form a female engagement team that serves in Ar Ramadi, Iraq. The women, with little to no combat training, engage in firefights and are assigned to combat missions with male infantry units. The group of twenty women follow infantry units into battle to search and question Iraqi females, becoming an integral part of intelligence collection.

2005: Two women establish themselves as early heroes of the war in Iraq. Sergeant Leigh Ann Hester, of the Kentucky National Guard 617th Military Police Company, earns a Silver Star for valor in combat after leading military police officers in a counterattack against fifty insurgents who attacked their convoy. Specialist Ashley J. Pullen, of the same Kentucky National Guard unit, earns a Bronze Star for bravery.

2007: RAND National Defense Research Institute releases a report in which it states that both the Army and DOD policies that delineate when and how women can serve in combat and noncombat units are ambiguous and hard to understand. In Iraq, the report says, it seemed as if the Army was complying with some policies and not others and that some personnel were concerned that strictly following protocol would keep women out of operations in Iraq and hurt the Army's mission. In other words, military personnel on all levels were defying the rules of engagement to use women in combat, as they knew women were mission critical. But without an official rules change, women are still not getting credit for combat duty. The RAND report states, "In many ways, the language and concepts in the current policy for assigning women do not seem well suited to the type of operations taking place in Iraq. The focus on a defined enemy and the linear battlefield . . . is inappropriate to Iraq."

2009: The Marine Corps adopts the US Army's Team Lioness program, renaming the groups of women who attach to infantry units *female engagement teams* (FETs). One of the earliest iterations of the FET program occurs with the 3rd Battalion, 8th Marine Regiment in Farah Province, Afghanistan.

2010: The Defense Advisory Committee on Women in the Services and the Military Leadership Diversity Commission recommend eliminating combat exclusion policies and opening all military career fields and schools to women.

FEBRUARY 2012: The Department of Defense opens thousands of positions to women in all branches of service after striking down a 1990s policy that banned women from collocating with combat units and opening battalion-level positions to women in ground combat units.

NOVEMBER 2012: Marine Captain Zoe Bedell, Marine First Lieutenant Colleen Farrell, Air Force Major Mary Jennings Hegar, and Army Staff Sergeant Jennifer Hunt sue Defense Secretary Leon Panetta to open all combat positions to women.

2013: Chairman of the Joint Chiefs of Staff encourages Panetta to end combat exclusion for women.

JANUARY 2015: The Army misses its deadline to open all combat roles to women set by the Obama administration in 2012, though the Navy and Air Force have already opened nearly all combat positions.

AUGUST 2015: First Lieutenant Shaye Haver and Captain Kristen Griest become the first women to graduate from the Army Ranger School.

DECEMBER 2015: Secretary of Defense Ashton Carter announces that the Pentagon will open all combat jobs to women by early 2016.

MAY 2017: More than two hundred years after Deborah Sampson, the first American woman to fight in combat, broke the law to defend American independence, eighteen women graduate from the U.S. Army's infantry basic training, the first women to do so. They meet the same gender-neutral standards as their male counterparts. In a *New York Times* report Drill Sergeant Joseph Sapp referred to one of his female recruits as a "hoss"—a high compliment. "Forget male-female," he said. "She's one of the best in the company. She's one you're happy to have."

PREFACE

FINDING WOMEN'S STORIES
OF WAR

If all that has been said by orators and poets since the creation of
the world in praise of women were applied to the women of America,
it would not do them justice for their conduct during this war.

—ABRAHAM LINCOLN

CHANGING ROLES FOR WOMEN

CAMP DOHA, KUWAIT, 1997, 9 A.M.—A man's voice—deep, panicked, choppy—cut through the static, and I pressed an old pair of headphones firmly against my ears, straining to catch every word. I translated his Arabic into English as quickly as my pen would allow.

My workstation, a narrow table, sat in front of a large whiteboard that was covered in a jumble of numbers and hurriedly scribbled notes. What looked like random text to most was the vital data that kept our military intelligence mission going—frequencies that allowed us to listen in on the phone conversations of enemy targets and potential terrorist networks.

I was one of five Arabic linguists the Army deployed to Kuwait to gather information. It was years after Desert Storm but only months after Operation Desert Strike—President Bill Clinton's late 1996 cruise missile and air attack that hit Iraqi radar and communications sites in retaliation for the country's threats against Kurds to the north. My deployment supported one of many operations that followed Clinton's decision—operations that gave the US Army the chance to work with and train Kuwaiti forces. Notes from listeners like me were passed on to analysts, and their reports helped infantry units develop missions on the ground. The information could, among other things, give fellow soldiers warnings about the plots and locations of terror suspects. The goal was to help combat fighters head off attacks before they happened.

And until the most recent wars in Iraq and Afghanistan, those frontline combat missions would have been carried out almost exclusively by men.

But in 2010 an International Security Assistance Force directive ensured that infantry units brought a key group of women with them. The bands of combat fighters were known as *female engagement teams* (FETs), and their work has been among the most important in the modern-day campaigns to push insurgent forces out of Iraq and Afghanistan. Although women had been putting their lives on the line during previous wars, they generally fought as part of the second wave (troops that helped battle residual forces after the most dangerous frontline combat missions were over).

But for FET women, combat was much more gruesome. Improvised explosive devices (IEDs) and surprise village attacks meant that the frontlines were everywhere. The days of formal standoffs during which nations faced one another on a designated field of battle and fought until one side surrendered were long gone. Battle ready meant that everyone had to be prepared to fight at any time, any place. By 2010, the year female engagement and training became ubiquitous, nearly 130 women had already died as a result of direct combat. Yet there are men who still deny that women can and do fulfill combat missions. That repudiation is like a punch in the gut. It attempts to erase the work and the smarts and the perseverance that sometimes made female contributions harder fought than those of their male colleagues.

In the ground war to win over the hearts, minds, and trust of communities overrun by terrorists, FET women fought in a way that even the most skilled infantrymen in restrictive Muslim countries couldn't—by gaining intelligence from the countries' women. Before the FET, attempts by infantrymen to frisk and interrogate Iraqi and Afghan women breached cultural and religious norms and turned friendly villages into enemies.

At the start of both the war in Iraq and the war in Afghanistan, members of Iraqi terror networks along with the Taliban and other insurgent groups in Afghanistan took advantage of religious restrictions, hiding important documents—bomb plots and enemy names and phone numbers—on their mothers, sisters, wives, and daughters. They used female bodies as objects to harbor terror, slowing down efforts by American troops to pinpoint and destroy enemy targets.

FET women became the American military's secret—and, in many cases, most effective—weapon.

I spent a year and a half learning Arabic at the military's Defense Language Institute (DLI) in Monterey, California. Other service members spent six months learning Spanish, nearly a year learning Russian. We did it so we could listen to targets all over the world. But even in the 1990s my classmates and I knew that methods of intelligence collection desperately needed to evolve. Using radio frequencies to intercept enemy communications was a practice that dated back to World War I. As technology advanced, so did the equipment, but the fundamental practice hadn't changed: information gathering was mainly conducted by linguists at a distance and focused on listening to enemy combatants. I was often based miles away from my targets and the towns and villages in which the targets operated.

When I entered DLI in 1995 the internet was already being used as a means of terrorism recruitment. Guerilla tactics (a common approach among fractured, nonstate actors) meant that attack plans changed quickly. And that technology to share those plans was no longer limited to phones and radio frequencies. It was clear even then that strategies used by terror networks were shifting much more rapidly than long-held means of amassing and disseminating information about our enemies could handle.

But the FETs circumvented traditional means of intelligence collection used by linguists. With minimal language training (they used translators), they were able to gain information by doing what scientists say for women comes much more naturally than for men—having intimate conversations. They gathered information about terrorist activity not by listening to the enemy but by talking to the people who had observed the enemy most—the women who lived among them, were victims of their violence, and had spent years watching insurgents' day-to-day activities.

FET members had tea with local village mothers and talked to them about their children and their medical needs. They brought them blankets, clothing, and feminine hygiene products, and they talked to women about when and where insurgents were infiltrating their neighborhoods. They asked whether their children or their neighbors' children were in danger of recruitment. And in a matter of weeks they would have collected more immediate and actionable information than I would have in months as an Arabic linguist. As a listener, my job was a bit like throwing darts in the dark. I could spend hours, even days listening to targets who yielded no actionable information. Sometimes frequencies that appeared to belong to targets actually didn't. Other times they did.

But in Afghanistan and Iraq the faces of FET women became the faces of trust. And trusting communities were willing to share information—the most important weapon for defeating any insurgency. Village women who had previously looked at soldiers with suspicion started welcoming FET women into their homes. Unlike their husbands, local women were willing to spill all they knew about the insurgents for fear that their sons would be recruited by them. Most Afghan women didn't work. They spent days and weeks at a stretch inside their homes watching insurgent groups travel in and out of their communities. They had a wealth of information that their husbands lacked.

FETs picked up vital data about patterns of behavior—the roads insurgents used to enter villages, how long they stayed, when they regularly traveled through towns and when they left, and which boys insurgents attempted to recruit and their methods for doing so. FETs could tell, by observing the women, in which towns the American fight against the insurgents was working and where it wasn't. Those were details that regular listeners couldn't always provide. And field interrogators who didn't have access to women in these Middle Eastern nations were having difficulty gathering the same kinds of information from men.

The moment FET members turned an old model of intelligence collection on its head marked a crucial turning point for the fight against terrorist insurgencies. The women helped build loyalty among villagers who, in some cases, picked up arms to assist the military in driving out terrorist groups. Some village elders went out of their way to help FET members once they saw the positive impact American women were having on local women. Experts in the intelligence community lauded the FETs as one of the primary examples for reshaping methods of information gathering.

FETs were among the last females to fight sexism under an American military system that refused to recognize women as combat soldiers. It was the FETs' groundbreaking work that ultimately forced the Pentagon to end its big lie: one that denied women had been crossing into enemy territory and fighting US ground wars for decades.

But FET successes came with struggles.

FET programs were *clearly* making a difference, yet FET women struggled for equal rights and recognition among infantrymen. The military's hypocritical approach to female recruits—its big lie—has haunted the institution for more than a century. Officers on the ground have always wanted to use the vital skills females provided, but the institution has rarely given women the protection, credit, and compensation they deserve. Even after the government opened full enlistment to females in the regular Army in 1948, it took another twenty years for women to get equal promotion and retirement benefits. By that time women had served as Army nurses and worked overseas as bilingual telephone operators as part of the Army Signal Corps. They went to Vietnam as early as 1956 but weren't required to learn to shoot weapons for another two decades.

Military hypocrisy has gotten worse as the roles of women have expanded beyond operating rooms and onto battlefields. By the time FETs landed in Iraq and Afghanistan, institutional hypocrisy had reached its climax. FET women endured public comments that denied women were in combat and exclaimed they didn't deserve to be. All the while women were committing acts of heroism that saved fellow soldiers from the rubble of IED blasts and defended men in infantry units during days-long firefights. And after the battles were over, some FETs were still denied the supplies needed to fulfill female engagement missions.

BEGINNING THE SEARCH

CAMP DOHA, KUWAIT, 1997, 6 A.M.—Flooding had begun on Camp Doha.

I made my way down the front steps of the warehouse where my team slept and headed toward the shower trailers located about a hundred feet away. The faint desert sun broke the coolness of the morning, and I felt a rush of warmth hit my skin as floodwaters bounced against my calves.

I looked to the right where, miles away, soldiers lived and worked in the *kabal*—a place that, as an Army linguist, I had only heard about and witnessed secondhand. I learned, since my arrival on the base, that it was rough: an area where men and women regularly got caught in sandstorms and fought harsh fifty-seven-mile-per-hour winds. The soldiers conducted training missions with Kuwaiti forces just fifty miles from Iraq's border.

I had made the same morning trek from warehouse to trailer every day for weeks. But three days after the floods, the trek ended differently.

As usual, when I opened the narrow trailer door, the bright fluorescent ceiling lights made the floor look mottled. The rough surface made me long even more for the barracks in Fort Gordon, Georgia, where I had been stationed for only a few months when I got called up for the desert mission. To my left were three toilet stalls, each sitting across from a sink and mirror. I waved hello, as always, to the quiet woman from India who entered the latrines daily to clean them. To my right I also expected to see the usual: three empty wooden benches, flanked on either side by narrow shower stalls. At that early hour I was usually the only soldier in the trailer. But that morning, when I looked to my right, there was a woman sitting on the first bench.

She was hunched over, resting her arms on her thighs. Beige desert boots, covered in sand, sat only inches from her feet. Her frame was small and tired, and thick sand covered her uniform, which was strewn across the floor. Sand arched a trail from the door to her bench and spread around her area, popping against the floor's surface. She had come in from the kabal. Wrapped in a towel, hair wet, she looked up and flashed a smile. I responded with a quick hello, jumped in the shower, and fifteen minutes later, when I emerged, she was still there, primping, pruning. "Sorry, I'm taking so long," she said as she saw me trying to eke out an inch of space on a nearby bench. She moved some of her stuff out of the way, then went back to clipping her toenails. "Horrible sandstorm. Sundays are my days for doing everything from head to toe."

I stared blankly at her for a few seconds. "It can't be storming out there," I said. "It's been flooding for the past few days here. There are sandstorms out there now?"

"I don't know what it's been doing here," she tilted her head toward her dust-covered boots, "but it's storming out there."

I was reminded of that experience thirteen years later while working on an interactive reporting project I had started in 2009 for *USA TODAY* on the wars in Iraq and Afghanistan. We were eight years into our fight against terrorism, and I had been out of the Army for ten. I left the military holding on to one of my childhood goals of investigating political corruption, exposing wrongdoers, and bringing the stories of hard-working Americans to life as a journalist. By the time I got to *USA TODAY* I had covered, for the *Washington Post*, the problems faced by veterans returning from war and an alternative treatment used at Walter Reed medical center to help them. In Georgia I had written about corruption and incompetence within the Augusta/Richmond County government and its police department. I had received an award for investigating the challenges of the first female firefighters allowed to join the county's fire department. But despite everything I had read and written about the military, as an Army veteran I was still unsatisfied with the coverage of the Iraq and Afghan wars. In my mind it was spotty (by 2009 stories about the wars had significantly slowed down), and the little that was published focused mainly on the extremes (desertions, rogue soldiers who took out communities, others who released classified documents)—and extremes never tell the most important parts of any story. There were plenty of silent heroes who, just as I and many other soldiers had done in Kuwait, woke up early every morning to navigate harsh floods and painful sandstorms without complaint. There were hundreds of soldiers in Iraq and Afghanistan who struggled to make the right decisions in the middle of firefights, surrounded by crumbling homes full of innocent women, screaming babies, and the elderly. Sometimes they made the right calls; sometimes battle fatigue and lack of sleep forced them to make the wrong ones. Sometimes luck or prayer or the thin, subjective line between morality and political victory were the only things that put soldiers on the right side of history. There were plenty of heroic efforts that the public wasn't hearing about.

The biggest problem: stories about the wars weren't being told by the soldiers who were fighting them. Instead, those stories were being written by journalists who, in some cases, were stationed far from the troops and battles being waged. The *Washington Post*'s Iraq correspondents were handing in stories from a house near the Hamra Hotel in Baghdad. Their primary connections to the battlefield came in the form of faxed updates, press releases, local television news, and tips from sources. They also got help from Iraqi stringers to get access to stories. And although they were good, few if any of those journalists had extensive military or combat experience.

Journalists embedded within military units (and print-publication budget cuts combined with worries about danger allowed this to happen less and less) had a slight advantage. They saw battles and military life up close and could provide incredible amounts of detail. But far too often limited stints with combat units didn't give them the time or intimacy required to really understand what it was like to be a soldier. The ravages of combat and deployment could best be told by those who were living it. Troops were using their cell phones to photograph newly forged relationships with local Afghan and Iraqi communities, make short films while on patrol, and catch the looks of fear and exhaustion on the faces of fellow Marines after dangerous encounters. I wanted to show the wars from the perspective of the troops fighting them.

I reached out to every military *Times* newspaper Gannett (*USA TODAY*'s parent company) then owned—the *Army Times*, the *Navy Times*, the *Air Force Times*, and the *Marine Corps Times*—in order to place the following promo in print and online "From the home front to the frontlines: As action in Iraq begins to unwind, send us your stories of war from Iraq and Afghanistan through photos and words." I also modified an already existing online tool so that troops could easily upload their photos for publication and I could quickly display them on the web.

Within a week we had received dozens of photos: black-and-white pictures of final good-byes between men leaving for Iraq and their families—little girls hugging their father's necks as wives and mothers looked on with tears in their eyes, color shots of tankers headed down desolate desert roads, a photo of an American Marine surrounded by smiling Afghan children. But among all the photos of hope and disaster, among the tragic faces and smiling ones, I encountered nothing that documented the experiences of females fighting in either war. I knew women were there and in as much danger as their male counterparts.

A few weeks later I started my work day as usual: I arrived at the office around 11 A.M. and attended a meeting, during which I and about ten other Editorial Board members debated issues such as abortion, Supreme Court decisions, and the performance of the Obama administration to hash out what *USA TODAY*'s opinions would be in our next series of editorials. I settled in at my desk by 1 P.M., ready to brainstorm ways to bring *USA TODAY*'s opinion content to life online. But first I navigated to the project URL to flip through the newest photo submissions.

Five had come in that day. The first, a sunset in Iraq, was striking. Deep orange and red hues surrounded a radio tower that stood in an isolated part of the desert. The second was of a Marine standing next to an Afghan man who was wearing a tan turban and a light blue shirt; both men smiled into the camera. I flipped through the senders' information to find their e-mail addresses. I sent them both messages requesting answers to the following: Did you send this photo exclusively to *USA TODAY*? Taken by you? Can you verify your first and last name? Address? Any more details we can use in the caption?

It often took several days to hear back from service members in the field, but they all invariably, enthusiastically answered. As soon as they did, I posted the best of their submissions into the project's photo gallery on *USA TODAY*'s opinion site.

Great photos. All very telling.

None of them of women.

Until the third photo.

Liz Carlin, a Marine combat photographer, stood in front of a desert-colored tanker. She had an M4 rifle in her right hand and a huge smile planted on her face. A thick layer of desert dust covered her uniform. I rushed to catalog her photos (there were three) and experiences with those I had collected from men. I was about to click away from that first photo to look up the sender's contact information when the expression on Carlin's face caught my attention: there was something slightly familiar about her smile. Had I, at some point, served with a Liz Carlin? No. She looked too young to have been in the military for more than two or three years. Was she the friend of a friend? Not likely. I clicked on the sender's information. It was submitted by an editor from a Delaware newspaper who had published a feature story on Carlin. There were two other photos attached. One was of Carlin standing in the living room of her family home with her sisters. They were wearing short-sleeved shirts and silly hats. The story, published in May 2010, explained that Carlin was celebrating Christmas with her family because she had been in Iraq and then Afghanistan during the holidays. I flipped back to the main photo and looked at Carlin's desert uniform. Sand dusted her weapon. My mind flashed back to that morning in Kuwait. Desert dust popping off a bathroom floor. And a woman trying desperately to rid her body of any memory of the harsh sandstorm she had encountered. Carlin had that same smile. The same tell-tale signs of a sandstorm covered her body.

I tracked down Carlin's number (she had left the war zone and was by then stationed in North Carolina) and called her a week later to get more information for the caption to go with her photo. When I asked her about her experiences, one of the first things she described were Iraq's sandstorms. I was reminded of the kabal on the outskirts of Kuwait's Camp Doha. I had tried, thirteen years earlier, to imagine what it would have been like to withstand those fifty-seven-mile-per-hour winds and the thick clouds of dust they kicked up. Now, listening to a fellow service member recount her life during a different war in the same region of the world, I was finally getting my answers. Carlin called the layers of sand that had swirled around her "moon dust." She often encountered it as she sought shelter in blown-out buildings away from her forward operating base (FOB) during combat missions.

By the end of the frontlines/home front photo project, I had collected more than one hundred photos and had given some of those who served a platform through which to tell their stories of war. But the photos felt like just a beginning. I wanted to know more about the experiences of the Marines, airmen, and soldiers who sent them. And I was sure our readers did as well. The few words contained in the captions that accompanied their photos weren't enough. My desire to learn more was the first incarnation of this book. My goal was to interview all the folks who had sent their photos of war and get the deeper stories. I wanted to find out what caused them to join the military, how they felt about serving their country in a time of war, what led up to the snapshots they sent to us, and what happened after.

I knew after that first conversation with Carlin that I wanted to hear more from her. I called her again and reached out to several of the men who sent photos so I could begin collecting their narratives. But the more I talked to Carlin about the work of American women in Iraq and Afghanistan, the more I realized there was a much bigger story of females in combat that I, a woman who had served after an earlier war, wasn't familiar with. She mentioned that American women reached out to women in Afghanistan as part of a new mission using *female engagement teams*. American women also collected information. I asked her for more details. She seemed shocked.

"Wait, you've never heard of the FET?" she questioned.

"No. I really haven't."

She recounted stories of missions that prioritized humanitarian aid for abused and impoverished women that I'd never encountered in any narrative I'd heard or read about the wars in Iraq and Afghanistan. They participated in combat missions.

I scrambled to make note of every detail.

Women working in intelligence was nothing new.

But the addition of tactics that relied on combat skills to collect intelligence far surpassed anything I had done in Kuwait.

PLENTY HAD STORIES TO TELL

LAUREL, MARYLAND, 2011—The book began in earnest on a late morning in October. I sat down at the dining room table in my small Maryland condo and opened my laptop. It was the first official call I would make to Carlin for the new version of the book and the first time I would hear the more intense details about the FET. I pulled out my cell phone and dialed her number. As she spoke from her home in North Carolina, I heard a freedom in her voice that hadn't been present before. Her tone was soft, calm. She had traded in her desert togs and combat camera for a paintbrush and canvas. Months after she left Afghanistan she started working on a painting, the cushier side of a combat photographer's role that most people never hear about.

A violent storm began rolling into Laurel, Maryland. As I asked my first question, a strong gust of wind pushed its way through the open windows of my home and forced my bedroom door to slam shut. I jumped slightly out of my chair, startled by the sound that echoed through the condo. I thought briefly about the sandstorms she and I had previously discussed and told myself that a storm at this exact moment must have been a good sign.

My anxiety dissipated.

"So when you think back to your time in Iraq and Afghanistan," I asked, throwing out a softball question just to break the ice, "what's the thing that sticks out in your mind the most?"

"The FET," Carlin said. "Out there it was women helping women."

A short statement that speaks to tremendous power. Both Afghan and American women were fighting multiple wars—ones that were entangled in rights to work, to be recognized as combat fighters, to be protected from abuse, to strengthen families, to protect young boys from becoming terrorists. Accomplishing those things hinged on catching and defeating insurgents—and Afghan and American women were helping each other do that in ways no one had expected.

As I listened to Carlin talk about the significant work the FET had done, I realized this book had the potential to convey to the public what I already knew: women are vital when it comes to intelligence collection in the Middle East. My work in Kuwait proved it thirteen years earlier, and the multiple roles women played in fighting insurgents in Iraq and Afghanistan were proving it again.

Her words inspired me to hunt for the stories of other women who have served on FETs throughout Afghanistan.

In this book I tell the story of Jamila Abbas, one of many Afghan women who benefitted from the work of the FET. Jamila spent most of her young married years running—first with her husband to escape the Mujahedeen and the Taliban and then away from her husband's killers. I also tell the story of FET leaders like Army Captain Johanna Smoke, who helped women register to vote in Afghanistan; Army Major Maria Rodriguez, who headed American military police operations and fought to find and train Afghan Female Police (AFP) officers to take over when American forces moved out; and Sergeant Sheena Adams, a Marine helicopter mechanic from California who faced a Kevlar ceiling that hindered her ability to get promoted after she returned from battle.

The FET program was powerful. Their gender alone was, in many cases, the biggest asset the US military had. For them, dedication to and belief in the mission went well beyond the teams' practical beginnings.

These are the stories of everyday women who exhibited extraordinary amounts of courage in the face of danger. Even as they fought, military policies denied their combat existence.

They were on the frontlines of war. Their stories are important.

PROLOGUE

Very learned women are to be found in
the same manner as female warriors.
—VOLTAIRE

ZABUL, AFGHANISTAN, JUNE 2011—Major Maria Rodriguez jumped to the
ground from the back of the armored vehicle.

The rocky soil that surrounded the truck made a light crunching
noise under the weight of her desert boots, but even that smallest of
sounds made her cringe. As her feet hit the ground, Rodriguez's knees
buckled slightly under the weight of the forty-pound rucksack on the
back of her petite frame. It was pitch black on the streets of Afghanistan. Rodriguez pulled night-vision goggles from the top of her Kevlar
helmet over her eyes. She waited a few seconds for her pupils to adjust
to the hazy green that tinted everything around her, then held her M4
rifle at the ready, her forefinger grazing the trigger. Quietly, briskly,
Rodriguez crossed the dirt road to approach the family home of the
wanted terrorist.

She and her team of three women were helping C Company of
the 1st Battalion, 24th Infantry Regiment find the suspect, and every
move they made had been calculated, mapped out, and discussed in
detail only days before. The entire unit reviewed the mission again in
the morning hours before they left on the mission. They stood at attention, Rodriguez's team of four women making up a skimpy squad
behind the group of about fifteen men, as the convoy commander

1

walked back and forth relaying the plan one last time. He closed the briefing by warning that timing was everything, that it was imperative they not be heard, and that safety was their first priority. So by the time Rodriguez was standing beside her vehicle in this small village in Zabul, she knew, in a very cold, detached way, exactly what to expect: she would follow the men of the 24th out of the vehicle and across the street (even though she outranked most of them, men always entered homes first during a mission). Then she would wait for the okay and push her way into the building, her team members in tow, to inspect the Afghan women. They would catalog everything they found and tag it for military intelligence.

It was her first cordon and search mission—one that would leave some of her soldiers guarding the street and place her and others on searches inside the home. But none of that training—not the days of planning, or the week of morning meetings that she, as the officer in charge of police operations in the brigade battle space in Afghanistan, was required to attend, or the afternoon briefings that she participated in as head of the all-female team needed for this mission—had readied her for what she was about to see.

The brigade had been monitoring the house—a small, mud, cave-like structure with an open courtyard behind it—since receiving intelligence that a suspected member of the Taliban, who was part of a cell specializing in making IEDs, had been living there. The two-room mud cave also had a cache of weapons, according to intelligence reports, and was surrounded by four similar dwellings, all built behind the mud walls of a housing compound.

The night of the mission the engines of the six military vehicles across the street from the compound had been turned off as soon as the unit arrived so their invasion could take place in silence. Within moments of dismounting the armored vehicle Rodriguez stood against the outside of the compound wall. She watched the green-tinted shadows of men quickly disappear behind it—the first wave of soldiers to run into the home. "Hands up!" she heard one of the American soldiers yell. It sounded as if the family had been startled from sleep to action. Chaos unfolded.

A baby wailed, and what sounded like an older Afghan man yelled for the soldiers to leave. A woman screamed hysterically for Allah through violent sobs. Toddlers and young children cried for their mothers. She heard several teenage girls and young women trying to corral and quiet the children. But she didn't dare move until she got the all-clear.

After about fifteen minutes she saw another shadowy figure, a young private, take two steps out of the compound, turn to her, and signal for her to enter. The men in the home had been checked for weapons, and the home was safe enough for her crew to enter.

She turned to her three female charges and signaled for them to follow.

Once inside she lowered her M4, raised her night-vision goggles, and got to work. The only furniture inside the two-room dwelling aside from a wood-burning stove and a table were a few blankets used as mattresses strewn across the dirt floor. An older man with a gray beard was sitting with his legs crossed on one of them. He was eye level to an M9 handgun. His hands were behind his head. Though he wasn't, he looked like he was begging for his life. Beside him stood a small group of Afghan men surrounded by American soldiers with their weapons drawn. The soldiers were questioning the men. One of the men looked the soldier guarding him straight in the eyes and kept asking why he was in their home, spit flying with each question.

Rodriguez and her soldiers walked past them to a group of women and children huddled together near the back of the home. The children were shaking, their eyes wide and full of tears, their faces red. She started searching the women first.

Rodriguez loved her job and fought to get female members of the American military the chance to have an impact on the Iraq and Afghanistan wars. What she and her female engagement team were doing, she knew, was vital. But she struggled with the idea of forcefully entering someone's home and, more than that, violating someone's personal space.

Rodriguez put on her plastic gloves, which all soldiers used when patting down a potential threat. She described in detail to the woman each step of what she was doing before she began. "I'm going to start by touching your arms." Her translator repeated the phrase in Pashtu and then asked the woman to hold her arms out to her sides. Rodriguez started by feeling the woman's left wrist. During the inspection the youngest member of the FET stood beside Rodriguez, plastic baggie in hand, ready to seal and tag each item Rodriguez found. Each piece of evidence would be bagged separately, and the female soldier, who got special permission to leave her job to go on the mission, would carefully label each bag using a black magic marker: "June 2011, Zabul Cordon and Search."

Another FET member, the oldest and most experienced of the three women in Rodriguez's charge, stood guard over the women and children left huddled in the corner of the cave. She held her rifle waist high and pointed it toward the middle of the group in case one of the women attacked or revealed a weapon that had gone undetected. The fourth member, the most outgoing member of the FET, was about thirty feet behind Rodriquez. She was crouched on the floor, her M4 strapped across her back, repeating the words "calm down" in Pashtu. She had been instructed to quiet the woman who had been yelling for "allahu" and crying the entire time the military unit had been in the home. The tiny woman was kneeling on a blanket in the middle of the room. Her constant swaying was punctuated by moments when she would go silent, look up at the cave's ceiling and raise her arms in prayer. Tears ran from the corners of her eyes and down her cheeks, falling onto the blanket near her knees. The strength of her movement seemed in direct contrast to her tiny frame. Her flailing arms had pushed her headscarf away from her face, revealing sun-damaged skin and deep-set wrinkles around her mouth and eyes and across her forehead. She looked sixty but, as the FET would later learn from their translator, was only forty-two. The women in areas hardest hit by the Taliban and, as a consequence, by the American military, often looked tired, worn by life, much older than their years.

By the time Rodriguez approached the last woman to be searched, all was quiet. The women and children watched as Rodriguez pulled the young mother out of the group, off to the side, and slightly out of view. Again she turned to her translator and nodded, "I'm going to start by touching your arms."

The man they were looking for, the member of the Taliban, had been tipped off at the last minute about the mission. Either that or he had seen the convoy drive up across the road, figured they were coming for him, and fled. In either case, Rodriguez could tell from the interrogations that had been going on with the men at the front of the house that the man they had been looking for had left in a hurry, potentially leaving important documents behind. She had been briefed about members of the Taliban using their wives, daughters, and children as holding pens to stash incriminating evidence while they escaped potential arrest. The women were left holding the proof and hiding it in intimate places. The Taliban wrongly assumed that their women wouldn't be questioned or frisked. At one point in the course of the war they would have been right.

The woman avoided eye contact as Rodriguez started her search, patting every inch of the woman's right arm, then her left. Near the woman's left shoulder, tucked under her dingy brown tunic dress, Rodriguez felt a stiff piece of paper. The woman's gaze remained to the right of Rodriguez's face, focused on one of two windows in the room. Rodriguez shifted her gaze to meet the woman's and tugged at the document, which was covered in Pashtu script. In the squiggly lines of foreign writing, Rodriguez recognized bits of American English text: a few street names and numbers and what appeared to be Anglo-Saxon surnames. She bagged the evidence.

Rodriguez placed her hands on the woman's waist, "I'm going to pat down your midsection now," she said. The woman nodded as the translator explained. Rodriguez dragged her hands along the woman's waist and felt a small plastic tube on the left side of her lanky frame. The woman's mouth was twisted in an awkward frown. Her eyes briefly locked with Rodriguez's, then darted away. Tucked in the waistband of the woman's underwear were two rolls of film. Rodriguez removed both of them.

She felt under the woman's breasts to make sure that nothing was hidden in the crevice where the underside of her breasts met the top of her ribcage. She swiped the inside of the young woman's buttocks. The search revealed another hidden piece of evidence, a cell phone SIM card.

After she was done, Rodriguez removed her gloves. "Please put your burqa on," she instructed.

After the woman slipped the burqa over her head, Rodriguez told the woman what would happen next. Her name would be noted— Rodriguez turned to the translator to make sure she was keeping up with the instruction—and the information would be turned over to the provincial governor and police chief. Even with this much evidence, the unit was not authorized to arrest or apprehend Afghan women. If a woman is arrested by the American military and returned to her village, her life could be in danger—if not at the hands of her family (who might think she's been violated somehow) then at the hands of the Taliban.

Rodriguez searched the children next. With her interpreter she knelt down in front of a six-year-old boy. She gently pushed his dark hair off his damp forehead and out of his eyes. Rodriguez had a seven-year-old boy at home in California waiting for her to come back to him. She could relate to the child's fear. She wanted to say something comforting. She whispered, "Don't worry. Everything is going to be okay. We're going to check your clothes to make sure you don't have anything we need." The boy listened to the translator, then turned back to Rodriguez and shook his head to show her that he understood.

He was calm as she started at the top of his head and moved her hands in slow, gentle strokes around his ears and down his neck. Then she worked her way down to his legs, feeling the cuff of his left leg and then slowly felt his right. Without being too invasive, in the cold, dank corner of the musty cave, with the boy's mother watching, she felt for any information that could be passed along to intelligence. She found nothing.

In the adjoining room, a soldier instructed one of the Afghan men to put his hands behind his back. The suspected operative was hand-cuffed. Blackout goggles were slipped over the man's eyes and thick headphones were placed over his ears so that he couldn't hear or see the route back to the forward operating base. The suspect would be taken in for questioning.

As Rodriguez moved her team out the door, she looked back and caught a glimpse of the six-year-old boy. He looked back at her, his eyes blank and unflinching, his mouth closed so tight that wrinkles formed over his thin lips, his fists clenched as if ready to strike. For a flash he again reminded her of her little boy waiting in California for her return. Yet something about him looked different to her now. He appeared cold, angry, no longer innocent, no longer trusting—a six-year-old hardened to the ways of an unforgiving world. She fought back tears as the prisoner was guided to the military vehicle parked just across the street.

PART ONE
BATTLE

JAMILA ABBAS
1996–1998

CHAPTER 1

THE FIRST RUN

A good woman is one who loves passionately; has guts, seriousness
and passionate convictions; takes responsibility; and shapes society.
—BETTY FRIEDAN

Slowly, one by one, her neighbors began to disappear from the Macroyan community she had come to think of as a safe haven, the place where she had moved after fleeing the attacks and infighting of militants in a Mujahedeen-controlled area of Kandahar a few years earlier.

It was 1996, and for days the streets of Kabul had been building into a chaos that looked all too familiar as the Taliban rolled in to seize control of Afghanistan's capital. The militant group's arcane rules had reduced women like Jamila, who, days before, had been working as a schoolteacher, to an oblivion in which she barely recognized herself. She was trapped in her own home, unable to work, forced to watch (along with her children, the youngest of whom was still in diapers) the takeover unfold. The mood of the city had been shifting for months, but the gruesome death of former president Mohammad Najibullah shrouded the city and her remaining neighbors in a fear and oppression from which it would take years to recover.

The posh neighborhood of Macroyan was full of government workers hated by the Taliban. The military officers (Jamila's husband was a general), high-ranking administration officials, schoolteachers, and rank-and-file bureaucrats represented a link to and loyalty for the old Soviet system, under which Najib had been the last president.

The insurgent group's first political move was to assassinate Najib.

On September 27, 1996, a small, beat-up truck crept beside the gate surrounding the United Nations (UN) compound where Najib had been hiding since 1992 when the Mujahedeen—a terror group once supported by the United States—pushed him out of office. It was 1 A.M. The truck slowed to a stop as it reached the gated entrance. Two Taliban members jumped out of the front while a third climbed out of the small truck bed in the back. The three militants walked the narrow strip of concrete leading to the front door of the compound.

In a matter of hours thousands of Taliban, who were marching to the heart of the city from southern suburbs, would join them in Kabul.

Najib's assassination was key to the Taliban solidifying control over the nation's capital and, by extension, the political and religious direction of the entire country. The group had already taken control of the northern provinces; Kabul was the last domino to tumble. Before the raid Pakistan—a powerful ally that supported Najib's destruction and the defeat of the Mujahedeen insurgency—had warned the insurgents to keep the assassination away from the UN compound. So, to draw as little attention to themselves as possible, the men had to move quickly.

Three of them entered the compound. The fourth kept the truck's engine running. The details of what happened next are in question. According to some reports, the Taliban played into Najib's ego, coercing him out of the building by kneeling before him, kissing his hand, complimenting him, and giving him the impression that his life would be spared. That idea—the thought of being saved by the Taliban—is what kept Najib alive during four years of isolation from his wife and children. In all that time the former leader never left the UN compound and had only his brother, a guard, and a personal assistant for company. In the first scenario Najib willingly followed the Taliban, unwittingly moving out of the guarded compound and toward the neglected presidential palace. He rode the dilapidated truck toward his death with the misguided confidence that the Taliban, some of whom hailed from Najib's home town, would fly him to India to be reunited with his family. Confident of his safety, the ex-president told his body-guard and assistant to stay behind.

More than likely, however, Najib's kidnapping was much worse, as gruesome as the final blows that ended his life. Some report that his capture was brutal and full of the kind of violence intended to instill fear in the hearts of citizens still loyal to the old Soviet order and who might have considered fighting back, including women like Jamila.

After entering the compound the three men likely pushed their way into an upstairs bedroom where Najib and his brother Shah had been cautiously waiting for the insurgents to arrive. They knew the Taliban was coming. The ex-president had earlier thrown away three chances to get out of the country, one of which had come to him just hours before the Taliban arrived when Afghanistan's interim president—a political rival but also childhood friend—had sent a member of his administration, a general, to the compound with both a warning and a plea. The general knocked on the door of the residence to find Najib playing cards with his brother, bodyguard, and assistant. The general walked into the living quarters and broke up the game. He had a message from the interim president: there was space for Najib, his brother Shah, his bodyguard, and the general who was his personal assistant on a plane booked to leave the country. The Taliban, the general said, was an enemy not just to the interim government but also to the Soviet-backed regime under which Najib had served. But Najib refused to go. The politician's refusal showed how politically out of touch he had become and how little knowledge he had of the inner workings of the insurgency.

By the time the Taliban had cornered the leader and his brother, Najib's bodyguard and personal assistant, who had faithfully served the former president throughout his exile, had deserted the compound. They ran from the only home they had known for four years into a territory that had changed significantly. No one was willing to provide a place for the men to hide. Everyone who had served under Najib's administration was either gone, planning an escape, or too scared to help. Two days later the Taliban found both men and killed them.

Najib and his brother were left unprotected.

Blood splattered across the bedroom walls of the compound as one insurgent hit Najib with the butt of his rifle. The former president was reputed to have once been as cruel as the Taliban. Perhaps, because of his past, Najib should have predicted what would happen to him. In the 1980s, when the future president was head of the Afghan secret police, he was known for abusing and torturing Afghan citizens.

The three men took turns kicking the former president and his brother in the stomach, shoulders, and back. Najib leaned on the men who had beaten him, barely able to walk, as the insurgents dragged the leader down the stairs and to the waiting truck. The former president's brother was thrown into the truck bed beside Najib. The insurgents drove them toward the now-empty presidential palace.

Behind the thick walls of the presidential complex the insurgents castrated the former president. They tied him, while he was still alive, to the back of their pickup and dragged him along the dirt road that surrounded the palace. When they were done, dust covered Najib's lifeless body.

As the sun was just beginning to push through the early morning darkness, the Taliban had hung the former leader's body from the remains of a pylon that stood in front of the palace out of which Najib once ruled all of Afghanistan. His brother's body hung only a few inches away. Twenty-four hours later the same insurgents who had tortured the former president tied thick ropes around the necks of the president's former bodyguard and assistant, adding their bodies to the long, metal pole protruding from the muddy tower.

For the next two days members of the Taliban, now well entrenched inside the city, shot bullets into the four corpses as they drove by. Money, which had been tucked between the dead man's fingers, fell to the ground. His face, caked with dried blood, began to bloat. Men stuffed cigarettes in the dead leader's nose. Some Kabul residents cheered in the streets, glad that the once cruel leader was gone, according to reports. A few years later some of those same people would long for the former leader's return. Under the Taliban those cheering crowds would no longer have control over what they wore, how they worshipped, or whether they could even leave their homes. The infrastructure of Kabul would, for the first time, become unstable. Rural areas of Afghanistan, which were already hurting for things like clean water and electricity, would fall even further into decay.

But most people in Kabul weren't celebrating the fall of Najib. Former government employees were forced to walk by his corpse, fearing that they would be next. Jamila was among them. It was in those days, as the Taliban grew stronger in the nation's capital, that Jamila and her husband began plotting their escape. If the Taliban could so grotesquely torture and hang a former president, the young teacher thought, what was the insurgency planning to do to average citizens who had been loyal to the administration?

Within weeks of the former president's death Jamila and her husband would join the ranks of the vanished.

IT WAS MIDNIGHT, and Jamila had spent the entire day deciding what she, her husband, and their children had to take to survive the long trip to Kabul Gate and what they could leave behind. It was important that the children didn't know they were leaving. No one who was left in her small neighborhood could find out. No trace of where they were headed could be left behind.

Quietly she followed her husband out the front door of their home.

Jamila softly bounced her newborn daughter in her arms, rocking the small, silent baby gently against her chest to ensure she remained quiet. Her husband led the family past the doors of other apartments in the complex—some of which had emptied long ago. Jamila shifted awkwardly underneath her new burqa as she followed her husband down the stairs that led to the complex's front walkway and through the gate that surrounded her small neighborhood.

She leaned over periodically to shush her youngest boy, the gentle, sensitive one who had always been too attached to her to deal with change. The mere inkling that they could be separated made him emotional. Crying on this night, at this moment, could be dire for them all.

They left with nearly nothing. They had the clothes on their backs, diapers for their daughter, and very little food. Jamila knew that wherever they stopped she would need to fill the bags she had brought with snacks and meals for her children. She was breastfeeding her infant, but the boys—young, rambunctious, active—would need real sustenance. She had no idea where it would come from.

By 4 A.M. they had arrived at Kabul Gate, the last exit out of the city. A small car sat near the curb, engine running, waiting for them to climb in. Her husband had arranged for a driver to meet them there and carry them through the next leg of their journey—the forty-mile drive to Charikar, where they would switch cars again along the corridor that connected southern Afghan provinces to ones that were generally safer and much more rural further north.

At Kabul Gate Jamila opened the back door of the compact car, pulled the seatbelt out of the way, and placed her oldest son on the far end of the passenger seat. Her second oldest filed in behind him, and the youngest boy sat in the middle. She sat behind the driver, and her husband sat beside him in the front. Her daughter lay sleeping on her lap. It wasn't until she scooted back in the seat and allowed her neck to sink back into the slightly springy cushion of the headrest behind her that she realized how painful the ache in her legs actually was. During the four-hour journey over hard pavement, dirt roads, and rocky soil, she hadn't stopped to think about how unpleasant the trip was or how difficult it had been to keep her children quiet. Escape was about survival. Thinking about pain—or slowing down because of it—wasn't an option.

Jamila lost track of time.

As the car slowed down she opened her eyes and looked out the window to her right. Once her baby had stopped crying, the young mother had leaned back to get some sleep. Now she looked up at the stars shining back at her and realized it was still night, or perhaps it was night again—she wasn't sure. She looked to the front seat and heard her husband directing the driver to pull up to the right of a van parked underneath a bridge. She looked out of the window to her left, past her oldest son's closed eyes, his head leaning against the glass, and realized that they were in Charikar. She nudged her three boys to wake them and told them to follow their father to the van. Her boys climbed into the back, and she followed, taking care not to wake her daughter.

Her husband again sat in the front and this time instructed the driver to take them to a hostel.

The building was large, had very few windows, and was the first place the family could lay their heads for an uninterrupted night's rest. The rooms in the makeshift inn were small; there was one bathroom per floor. The next morning Jamila was relieved to see the unimpressive cafeteria on the first floor; her children had been surviving on bread, water, and small snacks since they left their home in Kabul. As her husband paid for the family's breakfast, Jamila added to the tab, placing milk and bread and fruit on the counter. Her husband paid for each item as she stuffed it into one of two plastic bags she had brought with her for the trip. She filled one thermos with water and the other with milk.

As she walked out of the building she noticed in the distance the van they had ridden to the hostel the night before. It was sitting in the far corner of the grounds that surrounded the building. The engine was running, and the driver waved them over. She piled into the vehicle and prepared for the next leg of the journey, the one that would take them to Sheghnan, the area where her husband was raised. She would be surrounded by family, a tribe that loved and understood them, and, she hoped, for the first time in a long time, peace.

SHEGHNAN, AFGHANISTAN, 1998—The mother of four felt the cold morning air hit her cheeks—the only part of her body that wasn't covered—as she walked out of the mosque and toward her husband, who was surrounded by other men, all slaughtering goats for the Mawlid al-Sharif holiday. It was Jamila's turn to bring in the meat to be cooked. The festival, celebrating the birth of Muhammad, was unfolding just as it had the year before. Jamila had spent the entire week collecting money for the poor. The goat that Amir was taking care to slaughter as Muslim halal rules dictated and that Jamila would cook to perfection with other wives in the mosque kitchen would be shared with the families who had been invited to the religious ceremony—the poorest of the village's poor. They would distribute the rest to the husbands they knew were out of work and widows raising several children.

Amir was rarely home. His work as a military officer—in what was left of the country's fledgling army—kept him away during the week and traveling long distances to spend weekends with his family. They had to make the few days they had together count, trying to pack in multiple activities for themselves, their children, and their community.

They had been living in Sheghnan, a remote area that bordered Tajikistan, for two years now, and there was no reason for them to think that this holiday celebration would be different from any of the others.

Jamila had walked along the community's dirt roads, passing its low-slung, simple stone homes, to the mosque with her husband that morning. In this rural neighborhood, nestled along the Panj River, the couple walked everywhere. They left their four children—now ages two through ten—at home with her husband's niece. She passed only a few neighbors on her way, mostly family members. Many of them would soon follow to their place of worship the twenty-nine-year-old mother and the man her parents arranged for her to marry when she was only seventeen.

Since they had fled the high-end Kabul neighborhood of Macroyan, the couple had taken their family through at least three different districts in two provinces but thought they would be safest in Sheghnan, one of the northernmost districts in the country. The community was much more rural and mountainous than Kabul. Its reputable school system allowed Jamila to play up her strengths. The teacher fit well into an area known for pumping out top-notch educators—some of whom would eventually be forced by the Taliban to work in neighboring provinces for free. Unlike residents in Afghanistan's southernmost provinces who practiced a highly conservative form of Islam, most Sheghnan residents were Ismaili Muslims, a part of the Shia sect, which emphasizes higher education and charity. Women in the village were well educated, and many wore scarves to cover their hair instead of the burqas that covered their faces from public view.

Rules instituted by the Mujahedeen in 1992 changed life for women throughout the country. And, although it took longer for those rules to reach remote areas like Sheghnan, by 1996, when Jamila and her husband moved there, small changes could be seen. Some women, afraid to walk the streets without their husbands, had stopped working before the Taliban made it illegal for women to do so. Other women covered from head to toe in burqas after hearing about females being raped in the streets by members of the Mujahedeen. But Jamila, who wore just a head scarf, and her husband traveled faster than the newly established Taliban edicts did. So for two years life was good in Sheghnan for the schoolteacher and her officer husband.

They had established a routine that worked.

Jamila, determined to keep working after losing her job in Kabul, rose early every morning to cook for her children. She did housework and caught up on last-minute planning for the day's lessons. She kissed her youngest good-bye and walked to the local school, where she taught history and mathematics to second through fourth graders. She was home every day by early afternoon, which gave her the chance to cook and spend the evenings with her children. Their home was humble: one large room with mattresses in the back, a kitchen that consisted of a small stove and countertop near the front, and an outhouse. The family owned goats and chickens, which they kept just behind the house. They also owned farmland not far from their home, which Jamila tended as regularly as she could.

Inside the mosque, during Mawlid al-Sharif, Jamila moved through the kitchen with the speed of a professional. The women meticulously organized their work. They gracefully maneuvered across the wooden floors, lightly brushing shoulders with one another as they traversed the small room from the corner where they seasoned freshly butchered meat and cut onions and sliced garlic to the other where they slowly stewed it all.

And just as the women slowed down, as they put the last bits of meat into the bubbling broth, Jamila saw a strange man, wearing a black turban, approach Amir behind the mosque. Her husband was preparing to slit the throat of another goat so his wife and the wives of the other men around him could cook more food. Amir stopped as soon as he saw the man, who had a beard and was wearing a long kaftan that indicated he was a strictly conservative Muslim. Amir stood to listen as the man began speaking to him, and then he turned to lead the turbaned stranger away from the mosque.

Out of the small kitchen window Jamila watched them walk further and further out of her line of sight. Before they had gotten too far she ran out the back door to catch up with her husband. He was returning to the house, Amir told her. He would only be a moment. He had just been informed that someone was there waiting for him. It was unusual for him to get such a request. Jamila stuck by him. The couple walked the same dirt path they had taken earlier that morning. The man who had delivered the message walked behind them.

As the group approached the couple's home, another turbaned man stepped into the walkway. Amir stopped and waited, expecting the stranger to explain himself. As the officer opened his mouth to speak, he felt a pair of hands grab his wrists and pull his arms behind his back. Jamila jumped to the right as the man who had come to the mosque tried harder to restrain her husband, who was now twisting his shoulders and leaning forward in an attempt to free himself.

Jamila saw a machete on the right hip of the man who had been waiting at their house. The long blade rested on his right thigh, the tip of the knife stopped at his right knee, with its black handle held in place by a black belt tied snugly around the man's waist. One man held Amir as another punched him in the stomach and across the face. As soon as Jamila realized the men were Mujahedeen, she began to scream.

Amir's knees buckled, his head fell forward. Blood dripped from his nose into the dirt around his feet. Metal handcuffs held his wrists tightly behind him.

Jamila's screams had brought her children to their front door. They watched as their father was beaten; the baby, now two years old, was too young to understand what was happening. The youngest boy began to wail as the insurgents dragged his father away. The Mujahedeen had found out that Amir had worked for the government, that he had been a Soviet-era general under Najib. The Mujahedeen were also fighting with the Taliban to maintain control of provinces they had ruled long before the Taliban rolled into Kabul and killed the former president. Jamila and Amir had run from one insurgency only to be victimized by another.

The young mother watched as the militants dragged her husband away.

At the top of a hill not far from the Abbas family home, three small figures, slightly blurry in the distance, appeared. One man was hand-cuffed; two wore black turbans. One stood in front, the other still holding the man's arms near the shoulder, stood behind him. They forced Amir to his knees. Jamila and her four children stood where the insurgents had left them. They were frozen with shock, fear. Jamila watched as one man drew his machete and slowly raised it into the air. He swung the sword quickly, slicing through Amir's neck. Then she watched as they dumped her husband's body in a nearby river.

Eventually Jamila's screaming subsided. She didn't try to stop. She wasn't even aware she had stopped. Her voice could produce nothing more. She watched through blurred vision as the men walked away as if nothing had happened. She raised her right hand and wiped tears, still streaming, from her face. She stared in the distance at nothing.

She would have to run again. But right now she had nowhere to go and no idea what to do.

CHAPTER 2

REVOLT

A week after her husband's death the terrorists returned. Someone had told local Mujahedeen fighters that the Abbas family had hidden on their property rifles, handguns, and other items that could be powerful in the struggling insurgent group's fight to wrestle the country back from Taliban control.

The men burst through the front door of Jamila's home. They tore apart her kitchen, ripped up floorboards in the sleeping area, and turned over what little furniture she had—damaging her windows and the tall wooden pillars that supported her roof and loosely divided the small, one-room house. When they found nothing, one of the men grabbed her oldest son, dragged him outside the house, and tied him to the back of one of the horses the insurgents used to ride through their village. The man commanded the animal to run. Jamila's boy fell to the ground. Dust kicked up around his ten-year-old body as he kicked his legs, flipping himself over so his chest faced the sky. The Mujahedeen soldier stopped only to threaten to drag the boy to his death unless Jamila gave them the weapons they were looking for.

Through sobs she screamed. She had no rifles, no handguns. It was impossible for her to give them what they were looking for. Neighbors cracked open front doors and peered out of windows. A few brave witnesses ran toward Jamila's home to shield the young widow's children.

One woman scooped up the baby girl, who had been standing by the home's front door, holding onto what was left of its rickety wooden slabs. Another grabbed the middle boy who stood, in silence, near the home's stone façade. The youngest boy was crying too loudly, flailing too wildly to be moved.

Jamila ran as quickly as she could into her house to retrieve the one weapon she did have, the only thing she thought could stop the insurgents from killing her son. Within the rubble of her once-immaculate home she searched for it, flipping over mattresses strewn in the middle of the floor, picking up clothing that had landed, after the Mujahedeen's destruction, in the middle of what was once her kitchen. She found it peeking out between floorboards that had been broken and piled in a back corner.

The young widow emerged from her home holding a book with worn corners. Her Koran, its edges falling apart, floated high above her head. Frantically, with tears still streaming down her cheeks, she waved it in front of the men's faces, quoting passages about peace. If begging wouldn't free her son, she would shame them, she thought, confronting these men with the religious texts they claimed to so closely and conservatively follow. Her neighbors stood in silence. Women had been killed for doing much less.

The insurgents paused. As she shouted, Jamila grew bolder than she had ever thought herself capable.

But still, the insurgent told the animal to run.

Jamila threw her body on top of her son's, pulling on the rope that kept him tied to the animal. All the while, clutching the holy book.

The men spared her child's life. Perhaps they were finally convinced that if Jamila had weapons, she would have produced them. Maybe the sight of this desperate woman holding the holy book persuaded them that she was telling the truth. But the young mother still didn't feel it was safe for her children to remain anywhere near the family home. She arranged for her kids to live with a family she knew in another village, and she kept in contact with them by delivering messages through trusted neighbors. All her children left except for the youngest boy, who cried so long and hard that it became nearly impossible for him to breathe. This boy, who was so attached to his mother that only she could comfort him, would stay by her side as she began rebuilding her life. They were each other's only constant comfort.

After the raid Jamila and her son spent two weeks sleeping and living in a room off of another woman's kitchen. Her neighbors raised money and spent days using those funds to help rebuild the Abbas family home.

But after her first week back she knew she couldn't stay. The home looked brand new—the pillars had been replaced, the floorboards were a different color and size from the ones she had walked on before, the kitchen had a better stove—but the home held too many memories, ones that stopped her from functioning as she attempted to make her way through life every day. In the morning, when she walked into her kitchen, she could hear dishes crashing to the floor and see her babies screaming. Each time she looked across the yard and toward the hill that sat in the distance, she saw her husband's murder. Closing her eyes didn't stop the memories from coming. Again and again she could see the man dressed in black raise his machete and slice through Amir's neck. She saw them dump his body in the river. She froze midchore, broom handle in the air, overtaken. The psychological damage of that home, she would recall years later, was too great.

On this morning she rose early, as she had every morning since her return, to start chopping wood before she walked the half mile to her local school to teach. Jamila started her day before the sun had brightened the morning sky. Slowly she pulled back the covers to avoid waking her youngest son, who slept beside her. For each load of wood she chopped and delivered, she got paid the equivalent of pennies. But it was money she didn't have before. In the evenings, after she returned home and finished her household duties, she weeded the gardens of families who didn't have time to do it themselves. She also milked cows for extra money and picked up other odd jobs, anything she heard about that she thought she could do, no matter how little it paid. Not only did she need to earn enough money to make up for the salary her husband had once provided, but she also had to save enough money to be reunited with her children and move away from their house filled with memories. Every time she walked out of her home to find work, she was risking her life.

After a month away from three of her children, she was ready to make the first of many major moves away from her home, out of Badaghshan.

A man who had known her husband had a message delivered to Jamila through the widow's closest neighbor. That man would be waiting for her at the Tajikistan border. She was to meet him there in three days. They would cross into Tajikistan as late in the day as possible and settle in a home just on the other side. Once she and the children were settled, the man would cross back over into Afghanistan. How long she stayed and what she did next would be up to her. She was to tell no one about her disappearance—not her other neighbors, not her boss at the school, not fellow teachers. It was hard for them to know who to trust. She had to make it to the border on her own.

She sent her niece to a neighbor, and that neighbor gave the family who was looking after her children one simple message: the time had come for Jamila to be reunited with her kids. She didn't tell them why.

Yet again she was faced with the heart-wrenching task of figuring out what was important enough to take. But this time she wasn't closing a lucrative chapter on a high-end home that she and her husband built together. She wasn't surrendering any perks that came with working for a government she fully believed in. Instead, she was turning her back on tragedy.

Jamila looked forward to starting over in a much more peaceful province with virtually the same name (Gorno-Badaghshan) in Tajikistan. She packed all the money she had saved inside a small bag. In a separate bag she placed a few items of clothing for herself and her youngest child.

As she grabbed her son's hand, she closed the door on her Sheghnan home for the last time. Jamila walked toward the car waiting for her and thought about seeing her three other children again. Her heart filled with joy, she felt the corners of her mouth curl into a smile, and a rush of tears flowed.

THE WOMEN
OF TEAM LIONESS

CHAPTER 3

THE BEGINNING OF
FEMALE ENGAGEMENT

We have to talk about liberating minds
as well as liberating society.

—ANGELA Y. DAVIS

AR RAMADI, IRAQ, APRIL 2004—Army Captain Anastasia Breslow stood with a few Marines on the side of a dusty road, scanning vehicles as they approached a nearby checkpoint.

Cars inched forward, and infantrymen asked drivers to pull off to the side of the road for inspection. Breslow was there in case women needed to be searched.

It was early morning, and the streets, which always reminded the soldier of *Mad Max* after the destruction, were quiet. As the last vehicle pulled off, Breslow glanced up for a brief moment and followed the sight line along the crumbling houses on the adjacent street, searching for the private she called AC. The two women had traveled together to the Marine base where the mission—to root out IEDs, provide protection for the local community, and gather information that could lead to a weapons cache—had begun. They split up just before the convoy took off for downtown Ar Ramadi.

AC was nowhere to be found.

An Iraqi man's voice, booming through a speaker, suddenly filled the downtown streets.

"Allaaahu!"

It was the call to prayer, the second one that morning. As soon as it began, Breslow knew something was wrong. She stood still and listened. Right away she heard the Iraqi man scream his alarming directive.

"Jihad!"

Iraqi insurgents stood up along the roofs of surrounding buildings. They peppered the street with bullets. A Marine fell to the ground after being shot in the leg.

Breslow ran and ducked behind her vehicle. She scanned the streets again for AC and saw the private shielding herself from the firefight behind a nearby building. As bullets flew in Breslow's direction, she ran over to the young soldier to offer her a few words of reassurance.

AC looked up. Her face was pale, her eyes filled with terror. Breslow told her that everything would be okay. That the Marines they were with knew what they were doing. Just follow.

It was the first time either of them had been in the middle of a fire fight.

Even during an attack the foul smell of Ar Ramadi—a mix of burning trash and human feces—was unmissable. The most dangerous city in Iraq contained everything US troops across the Middle East were trying—but failing—to defeat: it was overrun with anti-American militants who dominated neighborhoods where a lack of opportunity left residents desperate enough to follow any group with a strong message, even if that meant rooting against their own interests.

The Ar Ramadi operation was one of the bloodiest battles in Iraq, but it marked an important beginning for the military and the female soldiers who fought in it. Among the women were Breslow, a signals officer; Sergeant Ranie Ruthig, a mechanic; and Specialist Shannon Morgan, a mechanic. They were some of the military's first to participate in female engagement. The combat mission wasn't even supposed to involve gunfire. The women were there to perform searches, bag and tag contraband, and gather information. But the Ar Ramadi

fight showed how insurgent groups in the Middle East had erased traditional frontlines and how women were easily forced into the heart of
conflict. The guerilla-style attack took place on the streets of Al Anbar
Province's capital among the city's women and children. The fighters
had hidden on top of city buildings and taken care to blend in with
the few civilian businessmen who had been milling around the core of
downtown. At least a dozen Marines died during the April 2004 battle,
and about two dozen more were wounded.

Breslow, Ruthig, and Morgan were among twenty-five women stationed at Camp Junction City, the forward operating base (FOB) in Ar
Ramadi that is located about seventy miles west of Baghdad. And Major Kate Guttormsen, a company commander in the 1st Engineer Battalion, was responsible for choosing which of the twenty-five women
to send off the base for combat missions with Marine infantry units
and the Army's 1st Engineers or the 5th Field Artillery. Her choices
depended on the mission and the skill sets each woman had to offer.

Guttormsen, a West Point graduate, later recalled what prompted
her decisions during the PBS documentary *Team Lioness*, which detailed the formation of that first all-female group of fighters in 2003:
Morgan, a farm girl from Arkansas, grew up firing a weapon and was
her best shooter. She brought a sense of grit and determination to
everything she did. Another member of that team, Specialist Rebecca
Nava, was a petite woman with a soft voice who had an affable de-
meanor that immediately put people, Iraqi and American alike, at
ease. That made the supply clerk, Guttormsen said, the perfect soldier
to send on missions to schools, where interaction with area mothers
and children was key. Ruthig was tough, reliable. Breslow was smart,
accomplished, and able to adapt quickly.

Months after the Iraq invasion, field commanders—Lieutenant Colonel Mike Cabrey, commander of the Army's 1st Battalion, 5th Field
Artillery Regiment, and his counterpart in the 1st Engineer Battalion,
Lieutenant Colonel W. D. Brinkley—figured out that patrolling villages without a regular female presence was hurting the overall mission. Attempts by American men to frisk Iraqi women were a cultural
affront. Forcing their will on unwilling populations was turning small
allied communities into enemies.

One night at Camp Junction City, not long before the Ar Ramadi battle, the two men sat in Cabrey's office talking about upcoming missions and brainstorming ways around the gender-based obstacles keeping their men from getting information about insurgents from Iraqi women, who made up more than half of the country's population. Both officers believed in the capabilities of the women of the 1st Engineer Battalion. That night they decided that at least two women would accompany combat soldiers from both units into the field on all missions. They would be responsible for searching Iraqi females and children during raids, talking to the female population during foot patrols, and frisking them at traffic checkpoints. With that decision Cabrey and Brinkley gave women the opportunity to prove themselves in battle. But they also set the tone for the military's most distressing (and last) contradiction in how it used its women—actively assigning them to the most dangerous theaters of combat with little room for advancement, no credit, and no training.

The first group of women took on their new roles with no real understanding of infantry tactics, no knowledge of interrogation techniques, and no experience in searching, frisking, or identifying female suspects. They learned as they went. When male soldiers ran, they ran. When soldiers stopped to frisk Iraqi men, the female soldiers frisked the accompanying Iraqi women and children. Nonetheless, the women became the most useful soldiers in the field. Both the 1st Engineers and the 5th Field Artillery started gaining more intelligence than they ever had before. The handful of women who left Camp Junction City on combat missions built a reputation for being reliable and steady under pressure. The women were the second group of soldiers to enter homes during raids to hunt down insurgents. They participated in knock-and-greets—missions that took soldiers from house to house, looking for weapons. And though the work was voluntary, when asked, the women never said no to taking on a mission and putting their lives in danger. The men on the base soon developed a nickname for this fierce group of fighting females: Team Lioness.

Within nine years of the Ar Ramadi attack, by the time Army Captain Johanna Smoke of Fort Knox, Kentucky, landed in the Zabul Province of Afghanistan, the job of FET leader had become more powerful. In 2013 Smoke developed her own missions and selected not only women but also men from her unit and Special Forces teams who could help carry them out.

INTELLIGENCE PROBLEMS, FET SOLUTIONS

Our intelligence apparatus still finds itself unable to answer fundamental questions about the environment in which we operate and the people we are trying to protect and persuade.

—Major General Michael T. Flynn, US Army;
Captain Matt Pottinger, US Marine Corps;
Paul D. Batchelor, Defense Intelligence Agency

By the time US troops faced insurgents at Ar Ramadi again in 2006, the Marines had adopted the Army's idea of using female troops to reach, frisk, and collect intelligence from local women and created their own version of Team Lioness called the Iraqi Women's Engagement program. And while the female engagement concept was growing, feedback from intelligence officers proved that more programs focusing on relationship building were needed to fix a military strategy that was failing in its efforts to prevent attacks, find weapons, and dismantle insurgent forces. Problems with intelligence collection in both Iraq and Afghanistan that had long plagued the US military were being felt even more acutely by soldiers on the ground. Poor language training among male soldiers made it hard to connect with locals who could potentially provide information about targets; men who tried to develop relationships with male Afghan community leaders sometimes failed because of strained communication between intelligence soldiers and the infantrymen they were attached to as well as between the US Army and area villagers. Intelligence soldiers who developed missions that targeted Taliban fighters bringing bombs into Afghanistan across the Pakistani border were sometimes stymied by commanders who thought the missions were too risky and would yield little in return. In reality Pakistan was and still is a frequent gateway for supplying insurgent forces in Afghanistan. What soldiers were experiencing with an out-of-touch command reflected long-held findings in a 2010 report that criticized an intelligence community that had for too long distanced itself from the Afghans they were tasked to protect. At the beginnings of the wars in Iraq and Afghanistan there was very little effort to find out what members of local communities needed. Currying favor with Afghan elders who could become informative allies would eventually become a key aspect of the FET mission. But during the beginnings of female engagement, not all units thought reaching out to elders was an effective means of taking down insurgent strongholds.

But conversations with locals proved helpful in severing relationships between insurgent fighters and average citizens who didn't want the forces in their communities.

Two intelligence officers and a civilian analyst documented intelligence problems during the wars' beginnings and the slow improvements that groups like the FET helped usher in within their report "Fixing Intel: A Blueprint for Making Intelligence Relevant in Afghanistan." Army Major General Michael T. Flynn, Marine Captain Matt Pottinger, and Paul D. Batchelor of the Defense Intelligence Agency documented failures in intelligence going back to the beginning of the wars and concluded that with more interaction, "the focus shifted to local residents and their perceptions. What do locals think about insurgents? Do they feel safer or less safe with us around? What disputes exist between villages or tribes? As the picture sharpened, the focus honed in on identifying what the battalion called 'anchor points'—local personalities and grievances that, if skillfully exploited, could drive a wedge between insurgents and the greater population. In other words, anchor points represented the enemy's critical vulnerabilities." Finding those anchor points through the collection of atmospherics—day-to-day activities and interactions—is exactly what the FET did well.

But even with some gradual shifts in intelligence collection, dissemination of information was still a problem. Disorganized databases made it impossible to find intelligence that had already been gathered about Taliban targets. Intelligence units throughout Iraq and Afghanistan sometimes had no idea they were following the same targets. Getting permission to use the databases eventually became cumbersome. Leaks by Bradley Manning in 2010 and Edward Snowden three years later made intelligence units suspicious of nearly anyone who wanted access to secret and top-secret data. Requests for access before those nationally publicized breaches sometimes took three to five days, if granted at all. Afterward restrictions put on databases made it nearly impossible for intelligence soldiers to do their jobs. Burning information on CDs while in the field in Afghanistan—a practice at the beginning of the war that allowed soldiers to move information from less secure laptops used during foot patrols and community searches to the more secure computers housed at FOBs—was eventually forbidden, a potentially career-threatening security breach.

The US military's ability to use intelligence to effectively target the Taliban, according to one male noncommissioned officer who spent four stints fighting in Afghanistan, was "not as successful as it needed to be to win during any" time of the war. The staff sergeant, who worked first as a military police officer, decided to become a Pashtu linguist in 2009 after frustrating interrogation sessions paired him with subpar translators who often blocked his ability to elicit information from Taliban operatives. "There were all kinds of issues," he said. "Have we gotten better? Yes. As good as it needs to be? No."

One key advancement in 2006 that helped increase intelligence collection happened as the result of a fundamental shift in the way the military trained and used its engagement teams in Western Iraq. That year Multi-National Forces West released official Marine Corps protocol that required the all-female teams to be combat ready. The guidelines also set out requirements for female staffing among Marine combat units patrolling the area. That one set of rules helped transition the perception of female engagement from a sporadic program to a useful one for Marine battalions throughout Afghanistan.

The directive came at a crucial time.

Ar Ramadi had once again become a target for insurgents. The city's location—a primary entryway into Al Anbar Province and Western Iraq from Baghdad—and the fact that the largest concentration of coalition forces was housed there, made it a crucial win for insurgent forces.

Under the new protocol the women trained in five to ten days at Iraq's Assad Air Base. The sessions quickly filled in the gaps between the basic weapons skills women already had and the intense combat training they had never before seen. They learned how to set up and man entry control points, to fire AK-47s, and to identify and properly search female suspects. The women were briefed on current insurgent threats and learned basic intelligence-gathering techniques.

After fighting had broken out in Ar Ramadi, a group of women who had completed training at the air base were sent to an outpost in Habbaniyah, Iraq, just east of the provincial capital. Along the small city's dusty roads the engagement team set up traffic checkpoints that slowed speeding vehicles heading through Al Anbar Province. The FETs' job was to stop and frisk Iraqi females coming through the entry control points. During the thirty-day mission just five female Marines stopped between ninety and one hundred Iraqis daily, some of them men disguised as women, trying to smuggle weapons, photos of military personnel, and other dangerous materials into Western Iraq.

Still, in 2006, just three years after the Army's Lioness teams pioneered the movement in Iraq, FETs were only slowly starting to trickle to the rest of the country and into Afghanistan. By the end of that year many intelligence collectors still couldn't talk to more than half of the Afghan and Iraqi populations—a limitation that only exacerbated the already frustrating inability to gather, store, and share intelligence. Speaking to women was still, for most combat units that went on foot patrols, an impossibility.

FEMALES IN COMBAT BECOME IMPERATIVE

What started as an idea carried out by a handful of American women under highly improbable, dangerous circumstances in 2003 had, eight years later, become formalized by the International Security Assistance Force (ISAF). In 2011 NATO's ISAF stated that the teams were "battlefield enablers that influence [and] inform." Soon virtually every unit around the world that deployed to Iraq and Afghanistan did so with at least one three- to five-person FET. By the time they formalized the mission, there were 149 teams in Afghanistan from fourteen countries.

The expansion of the FET mission was the beginning of fully integrating women into combat and was arguably one of the most challenging transitions in the military's history—second only to the full racial integration of the armed forces. Women who spearheaded early FET operations caught the brunt of the military's growing pains—which, according to at least one account, included an attempt to break certain females.

In 2010 American women were still fighting against men who didn't want them on the ground. Uniquely American restrictions on female soldiers—like the inability to drive themselves off the base to complete missions and other rules that supported the government's denial that women were in combat—put US FETs significantly behind teams from other countries like Canada, which opened all ground combat roles to women in 1989, and Romania, which did the same in 2002. Women from those countries could freely travel into areas where growing a FET presence helped local women get health care, water, and food for their children. Still, the FET program would spend its entire existence plagued by a struggling dynamic in which its contributions to success in Iraq and Afghanistan were obvious, yet the very institution that needed it often blocked its progress. FET work changed roles for females and improved intelligence collection in the military.

IMPACT IN IRAQ

Team Lioness couldn't have started at a more desperate time for women in Iraq. Elections were being held in 2004, and some women were being used as tokens of progress whereas others were targeted because of their political boldness.

Parliamentary candidate Salama al-Khafaji was an example of the latter. In a push for peace, the candidate headed to Najaf—a city that, for Shiites like her, was considered sacred. To the US military in 2004 it was known as a central location for multiple insurgencies. Skirmishes brought Khafaji to the city. A hand in peace negotiations between Shiite militants and the US military would mean a boost to her campaign. Khafaji was a rare female candidate: she was brave enough to canvas in public despite threats. And her efforts were working. She quickly became the most popular candidate on the ballot, but her gender, in the eyes of insurgents, made her and members of her convoy fair targets. And her son, acting as one of her guards, was in her convoy.

As the line of vehicles left Najaf, heading north to return to Baghdad, a group of militants opened fire. The attack, meant to kill her, killed her son Ahmed instead. He was seventeen. According to Human Rights Watch, Khafaji made the following comment about Najaf during an interview after the incident: "When I was in Najaf, I met many women who had lost their sons, husbands, brothers, and I was very moved by their desire for peace."

By 2008 female journalists and civil rights activists in Basra and Baghdad were being killed; there were dozens of recorded honor killings in those cities, all with no convictions; women were being attacked simply for not wearing headscarves in public—all part of militant quests for power. Multiple wartime elections provided even more motivation for violence.

Iraq's transitional government and the US government sold the years after President Saddam Hussein's ouster as ones of political progress for the country. The provincial elections that started in January 2008 put more than one hundred females on the ballot in Al Anbar Province alone, prompted by a law stating that women needed to fill a quarter of the council member seats in each province and in Parliament. But bubbling under the veneer of progress were the same insurgent forces and acts of terror that necessitated the creation of Team Lioness five years before.

Throughout the country sixteen different terror groups were vying for power. Pascal Warda, a member of Parliament, survived several assassination attempts. A colleague of hers, Aquila al-Hashimi, who was set to become a UN ambassador, died of gunshot wounds after five days of suffering. Fear of violence kept many women—regardless of political ambitions—from leaving their homes.

Despite ongoing violence in Iraq and a female engagement strategy that was making progress, the United States would soon draw down forces and attempt to shift its focus solely to Afghanistan.

CHAPTER 4

THE SURGE
IN AFGHANISTAN

DECEMBER 1, 2009—In front of a class of twelve hundred West Point graduates President Obama outlined his plan for the future of Afghanistan. Between rounds of applause he announced the largest surge in the war's history.

"As commander in chief I have determined that it is in our vital national interest to send an additional thirty thousand US troops to Afghanistan."

"The days of providing a blank check," he later added when emphasizing Afghanistan's need to step up its fight, "are over."

If not a turning point in the war, the strategy the president outlined in his 2009 speech at West Point was a turning point in the country's approach toward and expectations from Afghanistan. His call for the Afghan government to strengthen its security forces included a timetable for US withdrawal that would start in 2011. He was battling growing criticism that the United States was getting bogged down in another Vietnam—a war that lasted too long and for which there was no clear victory or exit strategy.

Obama took office in 2008 with the goal of pulling US forces out by the end of his first term and preached that an additional thirty

thousand troops deployed in early 2010 would provide Afghans' training and stability—through building schools, promoting education, and
building forces—necessary to begin pulling American troops out eighteen months later. By May 2010 the number of troops on the ground in
Afghanistan would, for the first time since both wars started, surpass
the number of troops on the ground at the same time in Iraq, at ninety-
eight thousand.

The fact that it took eight years to build up such forces emphasized
how skewed the US strategy had been, giving much of the military and
political attention to Iraq that, some critics say, should have been going to Afghanistan, where the major Taliban threat had been. Obama
vowed to change that approach.

In Afghanistan drone strikes were failing—sometimes missing targets entirely, but more often killing civilians, taking down occupied
buildings and causing other high levels of collateral damage. Taliban
operatives disguised as Afghan police and security forces were targeting and killing US soldiers, and some Afghan police officers were
involved in corruption and theft. Secretary of State Hillary Clinton
started the hard-hitting approach in November 2009 when she threatened Afghan president Hamid Karzai with cutting off US aid to the
country if political corruption didn't stop.

The Afghan military's tactics to regain control of its southern provinces weren't working, leaving the country in one of its worst political
and social conditions in recent history. In 2009 fraud and intimidation
marred presidential and provincial council elections. Taliban forces
threatened to cut off voters' fingers, causing many to avoid going to
the polls. The Afghan military had been virtually absent when it came
to providing security, and its ranks weren't properly disciplined or
trained.

With a new direction and strong language, Obama was also attempting to provide salve for a war-weary nation—after eight years in
Afghanistan, fewer than a third of Americans thought we should send
more troops—and at the same time pump up forces to expand the
fight to Pakistan, a place quickly becoming a safe haven for the Taliban
and elements of al-Qaeda.

His goal, he said, was to reverse course in a country where the Taliban, in the eight years since the United States pushed them out of Kabul, "has gained momentum."

Obama's call for the Afghan government to strengthen its fight for human rights in the war on terror reflected the importance of the female engagement teams that formed after a new ISAF mission and hit the ground in 2010. They were the main tool international forces used to combat the Taliban's continued aggression against women and children across the country.

"We will support efforts by the Afghan government to open the door to those Taliban who abandon violence," Obama said, "and respect the human rights of their fellow citizens."

EROSION OF AFGHAN WOMEN'S RIGHTS

The Taliban—and before them the militant Mujahedeen—had ensured that generations of women and girls received little education and rarely saw the light of day.

The other side of the war in Afghanistan—the one most people outside that nation would never see—was the oppression of the country's youngest and most vulnerable. And it had started long before the United States decided to fight. The seeds of that war had been planted during clashes more than forty years before.

Western values—including rights and education for women—that Afghans strongly espoused in the 1960s and that continued under the Daoud government were obliterated during conflicts led first by the Soviet communist takeover of the country in the 1970s, then during an attempted coup by the insurgent Mujahedeen (which was, in part, funded by the United States) in the 1980s, and finally by Taliban rule, which started in 1996, waned slightly in the country's capital in 2001, but was still going strong in the Pashtun areas of Afghanistan during US surges between 2007 and 2010.

Rights for girls to get an education and for women to make a living and provide basic needs for their families like food and shelter diminished more with each conflict. As late as 1977 women got college educations, voted, and had careers. Most Muslim women throughout the country didn't wear burqas except in a few rural, highly conservative villages in the south.

Young girls forced to stay home in 2010 would have been in a classroom in 1970.

By 1992 the Mujahedeen had fought their way to controlling nearly all of Afghanistan's thirty-four provinces. Mujahedeen fighters instilled intimidation and fear among Afghans by driving through city streets in vehicles overflowing with armed militants wearing highly conservative Muslim garb—long beards, kaftans, and turbans. They jumped out of vehicles, randomly chasing and threatening prosperous and poor alike. Another control tactic was the rape, kidnapping, and forced prostitution of girls and women. The militant organization made it difficult for women to work. Controlling the female population—pushing households that had two incomes down to one and forcing desperate men to take any job they could find, even if it supported the terrorist regime—made it easier for militants to control entire families, communities, districts, and, ultimately, the country.

The Mujahedeen instituted a law that forced females to wear burqas in public. That edict objectified and simultaneously empowered women, according to Floortje Klijn, an Oxfam researcher who worked in Afghanistan off and on from 2000 to 2013. Originally from the Netherlands, Klijn lived in the country while it was under Taliban rule. She experienced firsthand the subservient lifestyle imposed on women and girls. But as a human rights worker, she also knew that life had started diminishing for women long before the Taliban controlled the country.

Soon after the Mujahedeen took over, if a female above the age of twelve simply walked down the street in Western garb, she was committing a crime. Mobs of men, Klijn said, would surround women who wore pants and dresses and, sometimes in public, beat and gang rape them.

Many women, Klijn explained, felt that if they were covered up—if their bodies were made virtually invisible—their chances of being raped would fall. The burqas were a reminder for anyone who saw women throughout Afghanistan that the misogynistic Mujahedeen controlled the country. But, in the twisted world of terror politics, that simple layer of cloth also gave women a sense of safety—and limited power over their bodies—from the very men who used the garment as a tool of oppression. The invisibility meant to subjugate women became a source—though limited—of strength.

"A lot of women told me that they felt safer in the burqa," Klijn said when she spoke to me during a 2015 interview, three years after she conducted research on the state of women in Afghanistan. "I certainly felt safer. I felt like I would be left alone."

When the Taliban overthrew the Mujahedeen in 1996, they limited women's rights even further, making it illegal for a woman to leave her home without the accompaniment of a male family member, even if that family member was her preadolescent son.

It wasn't just rape that women and girls needed protection from; kidnappings and some accounts of prostitution, even among police-women, increased as the Taliban came to power and continued long after the militant group was pushed out of the nation's capital.

In 2012 Klijn interviewed female police officers across the country for a report that she coauthored in 2013 on efforts to build forces. Klijn and her research partner sat down with female officers (in some provinces that meant just one or two women, in others up to fifteen) for group discussions about their treatment, their duties, and their transitions onto the force. Klijn also visited and lived with families all over the country.

The report's findings were sobering. Rumors about the prostitution of Afghan female officers have stopped many women who may have been interested in a policing career from joining the force. Anecdotally, sexual harassment from within the force and rape, kidnappings, and assassinations from militant groups and other men in the community had been happening almost daily in the early 2000s, during the original postoccupation efforts to rebuild a female police force.

And more than a decade after NATO forces declared victory over the insurgency, women and girls in rural areas where the Taliban established strongholds after being pushed out of Kabul in 2001 still suffer. Zabul Province police chief Mirwais Khan Noorzai admitted in 2015 that there was a problem and that women's lives remain in danger. The province, nearly 200 miles south of Kabul, is still dealing with infighting between insurgent groups grappling for territory, including the Taliban. The province also happens to have one of the highest rates of illiteracy among girls and the least number of schools in all of Afghanistan.

In the Pashtun area of Southern Afghanistan two teenage girls stood on the roof of their home—a two-room mud dwelling that was the largest on their compound and that they shared with their seven siblings, father, mother, and their father's other wife. The roof's flat, rough surface was the closest the girls, who were twelve and fourteen years old, had gotten to the outside world since they were very young children. And Klijn was the first adult the girls had met aside from those who lived in their home or immediate neighborhood.

In 2011 Klijn lived with the family while working on a water project, one that would establish wells within the community for women to retrieve water for their households. The goal was to give the women a shorter and, consequently, safer trip to meet their household needs. On the roof that morning the aid worker realized just how isolated girls like the ones she lived with in Southern Afghanistan were.

As Klijn stood in the middle of the roof measuring the distance between that home and the nearest water source, a group of birds sat near the edge of the building. They stared at the two girls who had followed Klijn to the roof. The young women stared back. As the birds flew away, the girls ran after them as far as the roof would allow, then watched the animals cut a path through the sky until they disappeared. They asked Klijn questions that she had a hard time answering: "Why do birds fly away? Where do they go? Why don't they come back?"

Poor infrastructure under the Taliban made it impossible for families in rural areas to leave their neighborhoods. Destitute families had to rely on wealthier ones like the family Klijn was living with—who still struggled—in order to get the basics like food and transportation.

"It was an economy of survival under the Taliban" for everyone, Klijn said, even men. And male struggles often led to weightier struggles for women.

Destroyed roads and poor transportation made it difficult for men to find and keep work, and some men took the pressure of those failures out on their women. Men could rape, beat, or kill female relatives with little or no consequence. Fathers pushed their teen and preteen daughters, some as young as twelve, into marriages with men twenty years their senior.

The Taliban's fight against women and girls wasn't restricted to roadside bombs on random city streets or three-day gun battles that pushed insurgents out of town centers.

CHAPTER 5

ALWAYS WANTED TO BE A COMBAT FIGHTER

We are determined to foment a rebellion and will not hold ourselves bound by any laws in which we have no voice or representation.

—ABIGAIL ADAMS

CAMP PENDLETON, CALIFORNIA, JULY 2010—Sergeant Sheena Adams stood, laptop in hand, at the front of the helicopter hangar. Her boots straddled the line where the hangar's concrete floor ended and the outdoor tarmac began, giving her the perfect position to watch the mechanics' daily routine before moving to work on the choppers lined up behind her on the adjoining lot.

Marines maneuvered around choppers that needed repair; their boots clomped across the mechanic shop's hard surface. Ladders tapped lightly against the choppers' sides as mechanics climbed to the top. The glow from industrial lamps that hung between the ceiling's aging white slats mixed with the late-morning sun pouring into the hangar through the generous opening where Adams stood. The mix of light in the room cast bright yellow over the tops of the choppers' dull-colored blades. Inside the hangar, mechanics did complex work. They pulled engines apart and removed transmissions.

But Adams was headed to the line—that part of the tarmac where choppers, perfectly spaced, waited for smaller, routine fixes and final inspections. She approached the first helicopter. The wiry outline of her frame became even more pronounced the closer she got to its massive metal-and-glass front. She looked down the line at the five other machines—Hueys and Cobras—prepped to fly out, some for deployment to Iraq and Afghanistan.

Her job was vital. If choppers fly out unprepared or repairs aren't done properly, botched mechanical work could turn what would under normal circumstances be a routine flight into a deadly task. The burden of getting it right—the idea that these deceptively simple vehicle checks could have even the smallest impact on the future of anyone who entered the chopper—was heavy.

In the short time she had performed her job as a mechanic she never managed to enjoy it. But she stayed in the position—the Marines were short on mechanics and needed as many bodies as they could convince to take on the role. Adams knew that and made the sacrifice. Detailed inspection forms had only gotten more burdensome over the eight months she'd been doing the job.

Inspecting all the choppers on the line can take hours each day. And each day the job is only a slight variation of the same routine: Adams shakes the thick metal ladder slightly to ensure its position against the side of the chopper is sturdy before she makes her way to the top. She opens a small set of tools and pulls out a flashlight to begin her inspection. She has to be familiar with each component of the Huey in order to identify what could potentially be wrong with the machine. She shines a small flashlight on the battery and runs her fingertips over the engine, picking apart the individual components in her mind. An irregularity prompts her to pull out a small notebook and pencil from her front pocket. She jots down the problem and heads back to the hangar to look up the fix in a shop manual. Her Toughbook—that military-style laptop with the hard outer casing that can be dropped on rough surfaces without breaking—is one of the few items that Adams can bring back with her on the line. In it she makes a record of her work, then slowly walks around the gray chopper. She squints, looks up briefly at a set of blades, then works her way down the line, making sure to check every moving part that corresponds to her assignment list. Her superiors will review her work when it's done. The choppers that pass inspection will fly out, some the following morning. As part of the 1st Marine Expeditionary Force, Adams has completed the same routine for months.

But this morning, as she removed the black flashlight from her tool kit, her hands shook. Her sweaty palms left faint outlines on the sides of the Huey helicopters. It was the second day of negotiating what she hoped would be a journey to Afghanistan.

The day before, her shop commander had told her that there was an opening—one opening—for a female willing to travel with a FET that would be attached to a frontline infantry unit. The team would support the 1st Battalion, 8th Marines. As soon as she heard the news Adams was on a mission to convince her command to let her go.

She was a good Marine, but she wished she'd had a stronger history of military commitment. This wasn't her first enlistment; she'd served once before but left after four years. She thought she could do more than her job at the time allowed. In the years after her separation she regretted that she hadn't tried to re-enlist in a different specialty or put in more time that would have shown she wanted a military career, not a minimum enlistment. Now, early into her Marine Corps service, she was asking to leave the mechanic shop where she was one of only two women and a dozen or so Marines responsible for the upkeep of Cobra and Huey helicopters.

Despite speeches from Washington to the American public stating that the conflicts in Iraq and Afghanistan were strategically sound, actions on the ground indicated that the opposite was true. By 2010 the United States had spent more than $3 trillion on combat in Iraq, and that year the Islamic Army in Iraq (a Sunni insurgency that formed in response to the 2003 invasion of the country) claimed responsibility for attacks on US military vehicles. The 2007 surge, during which President George W. Bush sent more than thirty thousand American troops to Iraq, managed to control some militant groups, but violence returned after the operation was deemed a success and troops began to withdraw. In 2010 insurgents were regaining strength by exploiting growing dissent against the al-Maliki government, creating the basis for a return to insurgent power through ISIS. October of 2010 also saw the release of more than three hundred thousand secret documents and field reports that revealed ugly truths about the actions of American forces—the revelation that members of the military had indiscriminately killed Iraqi civilians and destroyed trust between American troops and the local population. And trust was key to gathering intelligence. Rebuilding it was one of the most important aspects of the FET mission—and one of the hardest.

For coalition forces in Afghanistan 2010 was the war's deadliest year.

By September 520 coalition service members had been killed—nearly matching the total number of coalition deaths for the previous year. Nine Americans died in one chopper crash in Southern Afghanistan's Zabul Province in September, killing more Americans at once than any other crash. In all, 711 coalition service members—499 of whom were American—lost their lives in Afghanistan in 2010. That year's battles brought the total number of deaths since the war's beginning to more than 2,000.

But even if Adams had known how deadly 2010 would be, her determination to jump into the heart of the conflict wouldn't have faded.

Adams had always wanted to be an infantry Marine.

When she was running around her hometown in Hawaii at the age of five she dreamed of wearing combat gear, envisioned herself maneuvering through fields and escaping enemy fire. She had tried hard to internalize the feelings of pride she knew Marines must have experienced after taking down enemy forces. And even when she grew old enough to understand that for females the word *Marine* didn't mean combat, that it couldn't, she held onto the possibility that for her, somehow, one day it could.

As much as Adams tried to put thoughts of combat out of her mind, even during her first tour in the Marines, her desire to be on the ground with infantry troops grew stronger. Training in other military professions felt like a distraction. The work she was doing several months into 2010—combing through mechanics' manuals, making notes on flight inspection sheets—had never been a part of her plan.

When her commander called her into his office and told her there was an opening on a FET that would be landing in Afghanistan in a few months, Adams fought to keep her feet planted firmly on the floor. Her first instinct was to jump up and shout. She had heard about the all-female teams months ago. They had a unique job—to fight the Taliban through frisking and building relationships with Afghanistan's women. Filling that slot was the closest she'd get to infantry.

The women who eagerly filled the ranks of the FETs pushed the program beyond the military's initial expectations. They started connecting with Afghan women, often through the common bond of motherhood. During scouting missions and on patrols American women would talk to Afghan moms who revealed how difficult it was for them to keep their children from getting ear infections and how hard it was to get food and blankets for their babies. American women expanded the FET mission to include classes on hygiene and baby care and medical exams for kids. The face of FET members became one of trust. Afghan women began to invite FET members into their homes when their husbands were at work—and sometimes their conversations centered on Taliban activity. At home, unable to work or leave their villages because of Taliban restrictions, mothers witnessed terror networks' daily efforts at recruitment. They watched teenage boys who were old enough to fight disappear from their compounds, presumably forced into a local cell of the insurgency. Other Afghan women talked about needing work—some were married to men who had other wives and children and could financially support none of them; others were widows who were starving because of Taliban laws that kept them from leaving their homes and getting a job. The mission of the FET grew to include economic empowerment for the poorest of Afghan women, and that fed the military's nation-building objectives. The FETs helped Afghan women start small businesses and make money to support their families. That assistance helped strengthen poorer villages' economies, making them less vulnerable to the promises of financial stability that insurgent groups offered. Stronger villages became less of a target for Taliban recruiting.

Adams also knew how challenging the job was: some FET members faced resistance within combat units from infantrymen who didn't think women belonged there. And as much as the military needed women on the ground to successfully push the Taliban out of Iraq and Afghanistan, it wasn't fully prepared to support the effort. Combat units didn't allow women to drive off forward operating bases, making the completion of FET missions difficult. Women had to rely on men to drive them to the villages in need of FET support, but many combat units didn't have enough vehicles for multiple missions. If FET support was required in a village that was close by, walking there was a possibility. But even marching off the base was difficult. To leave the wire, at least eight people were needed. At times it was impossible to round that many up. The work of infantrymen always took first priority.

As she listened to her commander talk about the FET opening, an inkling of doubt about whether she would make it from Camp Pendleton to Afghanistan entered Adams's mind. Perhaps if her job was less critical or if the opportunity had come up at a time that was less hectic, she thought, her chances of making it would have been better.

The Marines were in the process of replacing outdated helicopters. Choppers that had been in service since Vietnam were gradually being retired. The rush of helicopters flowing into her mechanic's bay wasn't going to stop simply because Adams wanted a coveted FET position.

Then the words she feared came out of her commander's mouth: "I told them you weren't interested," he said. "You've only been here for a few months." It didn't seem, he continued to explain, like the right time for her to leave.

She stared at him for a few seconds, at first not knowing how to respond. She wasn't even sure she had heard him clearly. His words, like a delayed echo, finally resonated. An argument for her deployment eventually came to her.

She would make a much more significant contribution to the war by working with the FET program than she could from a mechanic's bay, she explained. In a day, the time it takes to inspect four or five choppers, she could have helped save an entire Afghan family or gathered a significant amount of intelligence that could aid in the capture of key figures in the Taliban.

Her commander's answer did not change.

Before turning to leave his office Adams, who had never been low on courage, did something rare. She requested a meeting with the next officer in her chain of command in an attempt to overturn the decision. Her commander made an appointment for her for the next day.

As she walked into the shop that morning and stood at the opening of the helicopter hangar watching Marines climb to the tops of Hueys and listening to the constant clank, clank, clanking of boots on ladders, she knew that that day could change the course of the rest of her life. Her shaking hands were the least of her worries.

Even if she were able to convince her commanders that she deserved the chance to serve in the FET, there was no guarantee she would get the spot. She would be competing for it against fifty-four other women.

Adams walked into her battalion commander's office feeling slightly intimidated. She looked to her right and was surprised to see her shop commander also waiting for her.

The sergeant reminded herself why she wanted to be a member of the FET. The possibility of being an infantry Marine—or the closest thing to it that the military had for females—motivated her. But giving hope to women and girls half a world away also felt like a calling. In Afghanistan girls lose their childhoods quickly. They are pushed into a world of little education and limited possibilities. Adams had long ago been told that her childhood desire to be an infantry Marine was never going to happen, that it didn't fit societal expectations. But she never gave up on it. The wives, mothers, and young girls of Afghanistan were losing much more basic dreams. Afghanistan's girls simply wanted permission and protection to go to school. Women wanted to walk in public without a male family member present to watch their every move. Soldiers had witnessed girls as young as twelve being forced into marriages. Adams wanted to be an example for the five-year-old Afghan girl who, like her, wanted more than society would allow. At the very least, the sight of Adams walking through villages side by side with men—holding the same weapons, wearing the same gear—would show girls that the female body didn't need to be a prison sentence and that women's lives could be full of possibilities.

The officers listened, sitting only a few feet away, as Adams made her case. Unlike her company commander, her battalion commander didn't say no. Instead, his answer left her future in limbo. If she could be spared, she was told, she would be.

Adams spent the next few weeks walking the line, pulling out her flashlight, jotting down notes about engines, blades, and transmissions. Between inspections she met with various members of her command and talked about one subject, the FET, more than she'd ever talked about any subject before. She answered questions—often the same ones coming from different people—about why she wanted to leave her job to fight in Afghanistan.

One morning, four weeks after her company commander called her into his office to tell her about the opening, Adams walked toward the choppers waiting for her on the line. She heard her name echo through the large metal structure she had just left behind.

"Adams! Where's Adams? Adams!"

She entered her company commander's office and stood in front of his desk. Her heart wasn't racing with anticipation. Her palms weren't sweaty with nerves or excitement. She'd had so many of these meetings that the questions she had to answer had become routine:

"Why do you feel like you deserve to go?"

"What do you hope to accomplish?"

"What do you think your chances are of making it if we put your name on the list?"

And although she hadn't given up hope, the thought that she would be on the next deployment to Afghanistan had become more remote.

But this time her commander said the words she had longed to hear for weeks:

"You're going to Afghanistan."

CHAPTER 6

THE LONG MARCH

HELMAND PROVINCE, AFGHANISTAN, NOVEMBER 2010—Sheena Adams felt the blast.

She felt the truck fly through the air and hit the ground, bouncing several times like a bucking horse as the engine fell to the ground. The butt of her weapon slammed against the center of her forehead as her head quickly jerked forward, then back. The mine-resistant ambush protected vehicle (MRAP) stopped moving.

Her head grew heavy as it dropped to her right side and she lost consciousness. After a few minutes, she wasn't sure how long, the sergeant slowly opened her eyes and felt an intense pain pounding the back of her head.

A supply bag—the one she had placed on the floor of the MRAP before she and her FET started their journey to the rural outskirts of Salaam Bazaar near Musa Qal'ah in Helmand Province—was swinging from a busted rod.

As she turned her head she heard her Kevlar helmet scrape against her rifle. Thick smoke that had compromised her vision was dissipating. She saw, through the MRAP's front window, fellow Marines from other vehicles in the convoy scrambling outside her truck. Slowly, outside voices, which had initially sounded like they were floating through water, grew louder, clearer. She heard her name. She heard someone in the distance calling in the vehicle's destruction.

The hilltops breaking the flat desert told her that the convoy was still on the one pathway that led out of and into the town's center. She saw a tire from the MRAP a few hundred feet down the road.

She tried to move her legs, but ammunition cans had landed on her thighs and shins, weighing down her lower body, pinning her in place. A sharp pain resonated through her lower back, the first sensation she'd felt below her waist. She pushed the ammo cans off her body so she could move her torso, then bent forward and moved the cans away from her shins. She was finally able to kick her legs free.

It didn't take long for her to join the commotion inside the vehicle. The Marine to her left slowly sat up as he regained consciousness. Adams worked to free the gunner—a duty that posts Marines partially outside the vehicle and that can be the most vulnerable to attack. His legs, which had been firmly planted between Adams's seat and another during their ride to the bazaar, were now slightly slack. The Marines in the vehicle had been calling out to one another to make sure everyone was okay. Aside from a few groans, the gunner had been unresponsive.

Adams reached for one of the quick release straps that helped keep the gunner in place and pulled. The sling he had been sitting in loosened, and he slowly fell back inside the vehicle. The four Marines worked to catch and stabilize his body.

Adams saw a lump on the gunner's neck. His collarbone was broken. His breathing was labored.

She yelled for a medic.

The gunner had grown more responsive but was still barely audible. "I can't move," he mumbled. "I can't breathe."

ONLY A COUPLE HUNDRED members of a once-strong Taliban force remained in this most remote area of Helmand Province. In 2007 more than two thousand Taliban had ruled neighboring Musa Qal'ah and Naw Zad districts and their villages, suburbs, and farms, including Salaam Bazaar. Poppy fields in the countryside were vital for the insurgent group's opium trade, its primary source of money. That year some four thousand troops—including American service members and International Security Assistance Forces (ISAF)—led by the British, battled for three days, killing members of the Taliban and pushing some from the district center to the mountains. Other insurgents were pushed to even more remote areas like Naw Zad's Salaam Bazaar, an extremely rural town centered around a low-scale, run-down market-place, considered illegal, where the Taliban dominated. When Marines traveled to and from Musa Qal'ah, it wasn't at all unusual for insurgents from the Salaam Bazaar area to attack. The insurgents left behind in Musa Qal'ah continued to wage small skirmishes in an attempt to retake the district center. The three-day battle, waged from December 7 to 10, 2007, was one of the most significant in Helmand Province because it helped to stabilize the region.

By March 2010 control of the region had been transferred from British to American forces, and the US was working to keep the Taliban insurgency from rebuilding a powerful stronghold. American troops waged small battles throughout 2010 that kept Taliban forces weakened and on the district's outskirts, including a thirty-six-hour skirmish in Karamanda—a northern Musa Qal'ah suburb. Regular US patrols also built on the progress made by British forces.

By September 2010, when Adams showed up, the main threats from the Taliban were occasional shootings at district bazaars and the use of IEDs, employed mainly in rural areas where US forces were most vulnerable.

At the time of that 2007 battle of Musa Qal'ah, IEDs usually killed—or severely maimed—troops who encountered them during patrols either on foot or in convoys led by lightweight military vehicles such as Humvees that weren't designed to stand up to increasingly powerful roadside bombs.

That year the Department of Defense—prompted by media coverage that exposed inept Pentagon protections for troops in the field—began to send significant numbers of MRAPs to the front. The rollout was slow, and by the end of 2013 roadside bombs had killed three thousand US troops and injured thirty-three thousand, according to a *USA TODAY* report.

MRAPs, like the one Adams had been riding in, did save lives.

While roadside bombs nearly always ripped through the light undercarriages and thinly built doors and windows of the Humvees that had been standard issue in the desert, the fortified outer casing of

MRAPs provided levels of protection that troops desperately needed. Before MRAPs, service members had to fend for themselves and cobble together makeshift protections, keeping death tolls high. Troops nailed plywood to the bottoms of their vehicles and affixed sandbags to the floors of lighter trucks in hopes of making them less prone to being ripped apart. They reinforced the outer carriage of Humvees with heavier steel and metal scraps scrounged from the wreckage of obliterated Iraqi tanks. Several Army units refused to carry out certain operations in Iraq because their equipment was insufficient, calling the orders "suicide missions," according to a 2004 *60 Minutes* report.

In three hundred attacks on Marine MRAPs in Iraq in 2006, not one service member died, according to a *USA TODAY* report.

But MRAPs came with devastating problems. Their top-heavy build made them vulnerable to tipping and rolling over. Troops were significantly more protected from death, but some injuries, especially internal ones like spinal injuries and traumatic brain injury, shot up. And the new vehicles weren't immune to some of the same issues that plagued Humvees. Though it happened less frequently, MRAPs sustained tire explosions or rips in the front carriage. In the worst cases explosions could shatter the vehicles in two.

Some of the few remaining Taliban, who hid in the mountains and rural villages of the Musa Qal'ah and Salaam Bazaar areas, appeared to have been waiting for Adams, her crew, and the infantry team to drive through. Her team left the FOB regularly to interview women in surrounding villages, collect intelligence, and distribute medical and hygiene supplies, food, and other items many young village mothers needed.

Two months before that morning trip the sergeant had met the gunner and other members of the 1st Battalion, 8th Marines for the first time. Adams walked onto the FOB carrying not just the responsibility of leading an entire team of women but also the satisfaction that comes with fulfilling a lifelong dream that so many had said was impossible: she was a woman in combat.

Musa Qal'ah's main forward operating base was dotted with one-story dorms that had walls of hardened stucco. A series of long, light brown tents ran in two different directions down the middle. With the addition of women in the war zone, one tent would soon have a large plywood sign outside, propped up on green sandbags with black lettering: "Females in the shower."

On one of her first missions she left that FOB and headed toward Shir Ghazay, a small base (about five tents and two outhouses) that took most who entered it a bit longer to get used to. Along the way her team stopped overnight at Patrol Base Talibjan, their first time in that section of Musa Qal'ah District. Adams and the two women she worked with took on FET missions for an entire battalion of 260 men. Their seven-month stint meant a tireless rotation of combat missions throughout Helmand Province.

In Talibjan, Adams recalled much later, a group of Marines invited the FET to join them on a patrol that she believes was designed to break them.

Before the march began she pulled the women aside and gave them a terse but encouraging pep talk. Adams wanted to lead mainly by example, but she had the feeling that the patrol ahead would be a test.

"Whatever happens," she said, "keep up with them. Don't complain. And don't you dare start crying."

Adams stepped off the base wearing full gear—a forty-pound rucksack and body armor—and carrying her M4 rifle. The two women on her FET followed. The combat Marines she followed took a sharp left just beyond the perimeter of the base, passing tall fencing topped with barbed wire surrounding the installation, and moved twice as fast as any Marine march Adams had ever seen or participated in. The women kept up with them step for step.

The FET didn't know it, but the patrol was on its way to a few small villages just outside of Patrol Base Talibjan. It was a journey that normally took squads about thirty minutes to march. But the FET's journey of two hours had just begun.

Outside the base Adams saw a set of trees a few hundred feet to her right. Directly in front of the group, a few miles ahead, she saw the upper ridges of low-lying hills. They headed toward the hills.

Adams saw the right foot of the man in front of her sink into the river that separated her group from the ridges ahead. She stepped in behind him and felt tepid water soak through her boots. When the water reached knee level, she raised her weapon above her waist to protect it, unaware of just how deep the river would get. On the other side she glanced behind her to make sure her team was there. They were still marching strong.

Thirty minutes later they had reached the edge of the first and lowest hillside. By that time it was midday. Her pants had dried and so had her socks. Each was covered with a thin layer of mud that she felt cracking with every step as she climbed. The hottest part of the day was approaching, and she was beginning to feel dehydrated. She tried as much as she could to step directly in the boot prints made by the man before her, as all desert troops had been trained to do in order to avoid potential IEDs. She reached into her right pocket, pulled out her canteen, and took several gulps of water, keeping her eyes on the pathway ahead as she walked. Her T-shirt was soaked through with sweat.

By the time she reached the backroads near the village center she was breathing heavily. She hoisted her rucksack, which felt more like it was one hundred pounds instead of forty, higher onto her back. She wanted to slow down. She didn't. She thought about the FET members behind her and repeated to herself the same words she had imparted to them at the start of their journey: *Whatever happens, keep up. Don't complain. Don't cry.* She ignored the pain in her right side and pushed forward.

Tall barriers on either side of the backroads formed a narrow path for the patrol to walk along. As the barriers ran out, the first small village came into Adams's view.

The dusty road they were on continued toward a very small bazaar: a few rundown structures in dull browns and grays. They walked by a mosque where boys sat outside studying the Koran. Their voices and that of an elder reciting religious text filled the air surrounding the shops. Out of the corner of her eye Adams saw one of the members of her team slow down. The leader fell back to walk beside the Marine who was lagging.

"Whatever you do," she told the FET member again, "just make sure to keep up. You can do this."

She would give different versions of that pep talk often during her seven-month run in Afghanistan, and the women would thank her for keeping them strong.

A photo displayed on *Time* magazine's website captured it well. In pink, yellow, and blue chalk on the dark, cave-like walls of Adams's dormitory was written, "Dear Sergeant Adams, We're glad to be on your team! You motivate me. Kristi."

Makeshift awnings—torn pieces of cloth propped up with sticks—provided shade for a few market fronts in the village bazaar just outside of Talibjan.

The street was nearly empty.

Using the little bit of basic Pashtu they had learned during FET training, the women tried to reach out to two civilian males. In addition to talking to Afghan women, FETs also spoke to men—business owners, husbands, brothers, and fathers. Sometimes they had to speak to the men first to get access to their women. Frequently men would share more information with engagement teams than they would with male troops. Afghans, men and women, tended to find American females less threatening.

But on this trip their usual inquiries—*How long have you been living and working in this area? Has the bazaar been busy lately?*—were met with lukewarm replies. The men of the 1st Battalion, 8th Marines knew that the village was a resistant one. According to a Public Radio International report, it took more than two months after Adams and her FET team arrived in the country for a villager to even come onto Patrol Base Talibjan—a great accomplishment. The male combat troops had already been in the country at that point for nearly five months.

After patrolling the second village the Marines headed back toward the hillsides that had started their two-hour journey toward the village.

The squad leader didn't spare the women on the return trip. As he cut through side streets, Adams and her team kept pace. They went back through the same rough terrain they had traversed to get to the downtown bazaars. The pace was still faster, Adams knew, than a march was generally intended to be. The distance, she would find out later, was multiple times longer than needed.

The women never fell behind.

Adams and her FET followed the men back onto Talibjan. The patrol leader removed his Kevlar helmet and revealed smudges of sand caked into the faint wrinkles on his forehead. Streaks of sweat left pale paths in the thin layer of dirt between his eyes. His hair, close shaven but usually a bit spiked on the top, was flat against his head. Adams could see slight creases in his hair from the webbing inside his headgear.

She lowered her head slightly, grabbed the hard brim of her helmet, and removed it. Her hair, which had been smoothed into a tight bun that gathered at the nape of her neck just above her collar, was smudged along her hairline. The usually neat part was muddled. When she looked up, Adams locked eyes with the Marine who led the march. He nodded—the first sign of approval she'd gotten from the men of the 1st Battalion, 8th Marines.

The next day, after they arrived at FOB Shir Ghazay, located on the southern border of Musa Qal'ah District, Adams and her FET began knocking on doors—part of a larger mission to collect data on families throughout the country. Periodically the military conducted a census to get updates on how families were progressing in troubled districts: How many people were in each home? Were they working? How many military aged males lived there?

Sending FETs to collect answers to census questions helped the military in multiple ways. It was another chance for teams to build relationships by putting a friendly, nonthreatening face on the military. The more American women did that, the more Afghan women—and men—shared information. Positive answers to some questions signaled progress. More Afghan women and men at work meant less Taliban control over a village.

On FOB Shir Ghazay Adams heard one of the commanders warn the males that FET women would be on the base for the next few days and that the combat Marines weren't to talk to them, hit on them, or to do or say anything inappropriate. She could feel tension as her team trekked off the base with a group of men who appeared reluctant to have the women accompany them. It was as if, she said much later, "they had pulled the short straw."

The homes surrounding the base were minimal, built of mud and set inside compounds with hilly land and open courtyards. The doors were constructed of scrap metal found on the street. Some FET leaders described walking through neighborhoods in remote districts of Afghanistan as going back to biblical times—unadorned dwellings, unpaved streets, some folks still using animals as their main mode of transport. Donkeys and other livestock roamed freely.

At the first house a male combat Marine stepped in front of the FET and knocked on the door. The Marine wasn't heavy on the pleasantries. Very quickly he jumped into the survey questions. The man who answered the door retreated into his home without saying a word.

The same thing happened at the next house. And at the third.

Adams finally stepped in. She knocked on the door of the fourth house, smiled, and started the conversation not with a question but by introducing herself and the members of her FET. She told the man who answered the door a bit about herself. He smiled in return. She explained that they were just trying to get to know the community. She asked if he was willing to answer a few questions. He stepped a bit further outside his door, open to the prospect of speaking with her. He answered everything required for the census. She ended the conversation by asking if there was anything the man needed, anything he was concerned about.

At that moment the male Marines took a backseat to Adams's FET. The women knocked on twenty-five doors the first day and gathered good information from the families in each home.

When they returned to the base, members of the 1st Battalion, 8th Marines reported to command that they got more information with the FET than they had ever gotten before. They gave the same positive report over the next two days the teams worked together.

On the fourth day, as the women were leaving, the Marines asked when the team was coming back.

For Adams, military progress was seen not in data but in the smiles and invitations from the Afghans she interacted with every day. When moms opened up their homes without waiting for a knock on the door, she knew that FET objectives were getting met.

That happened often near Musa Qal'ah District headquarters, where Adams helped a family start a small clothing business. The woman of the household needed a sewing machine. She was making colorful dresses for her children by hand, and her neighbors and friends loved them. Adams suggested that the woman increase production to make money for her family who desperately needed it. Weeks after Adams helped her get a machine, the woman had made enough clothing for her husband to sell at the local bazaar. A month later relatives of that family asked Adams to meet their newborn baby. The Marine, who says such an invitation was a rarity in Afghanistan, was honored to sit in their home with her FET. She held the baby, and the mother gave her an update on the relative's family business. Adams, who would soon become a mother herself, learned to swaddle her son by watching the young woman do the same.

In Shir Ghazay, a few weeks after her first visit, the FET leader returned to the home of another woman she had helped once before. The woman's toddler watched the Marine sergeant and her interpreter kneel down on the bright red rug. As soon as Adams pulled out her notebook, the little girl ran into the only other room in the small, dark home. There was no furniture aside from a rug on the floor of the back room and rugs that overlapped on the floor of the front room where the mother had been most of the morning. There was an old stove in the far corner.

On a previous visit the Marine sergeant had given medicine to the daughter, who had been suffering from a cold. This time, as before, she and her translator had tea with the young mother before the conversation got too involved. The woman slowly rose to her feet as soon as she saw Adams walk through the door. As the woman approached the stove she asked Adams, through the translator, how she had been. She thanked her for taking a look at her daughter the last time she was there and updated her on the young girl's progress: she was running around the house again, giggling. Adams took notes on the girl's improved condition.

The woman balanced a cup and saucer in each hand as she lowered herself to the floor and crossed her legs comfortably for a chat.

Adams took a sip and savored it, one of the few moments in her day when she got to taste real Afghan tea, which she had come to enjoy. The woman mentioned that she had seen a few teenage boys hanging around on her street instead of spending the day in school, a change she had only recently noticed. The Afghan woman confirmed Adams's suspicions that the behavior among these boys was new. She also told Adams about the teen boy who lived next door but went missing recently. Her husband, she added, had been having a hard time finding a job.

Adams didn't write those facts down right away; instead, she looked directly into the eyes of the woman who was speaking. She smiled when her translator imparted something funny. She nodded without judgment when the stories were more stark than she had expected. She rarely took notes unless mothers were passing along medical complaints about their children. During the course of casual conversation Adams wanted to engage. More important, she wanted the Afghan women to feel comfortable, as if they could say anything to her. If the women thought Adams was reporting on their every move, natural interaction would have been lost.

But when she returned to her dorm she wrote a summary of the information and her analysis in a report: the Taliban appeared to be recruiting.

THE MORNING OF the IED blast Adams had been the last one to step into the MRAP. She pushed the bulging tan bag—which was filled with blankets, toothpaste, and medical supplies—into a small space between the last seat on the left and the back of the vehicle, one of four trucks in the infantry convoy.

The sergeant, her FET of three, a translator, and thirteen combat Marines were headed to the remote Salaam Bazaar area. The town was so secluded that the families who lived there had no access to medical care, no running water, and no indoor plumbing. Each FET member loaded into the back of a different vehicle, insurance that if something happened to one of the vehicles—if one of the women died or was pulled out of the country because of a serious injury—the

FET's mission, for however long they remained in Afghanistan, could continue. The infantry unit wanted to find out how much progress had been made in this most remote village after attempts to push out the Taliban. The FET would find out what the people needed and how well they had been coping economically as well as attempt to strengthen the connection between the Marines and members of the village. Adams and her team would also interview the women, collect information, provide basic medical needs for the children, and hand out blankets.

But about an hour after they arrived the team realized that something in the village was wrong.

As Adams walked through the bazaar she noticed that the buildings and shops along the dusty streets were completely empty. There were no children outside playing, no men or women selling goods. It was oddly void of life.

The team stumbled upon one woman walking through the bazaar and attempted to start a conversation.

Adams introduced herself and asked the woman her name. The woman was hesitant to respond, looking back and forth between Adams and the FET translator. Unlike the welcome responses they'd gotten while patrolling downtown Musa Qal'ah, the few responses she got in Salaam Bazaar were either icy or timid.

Adams asked why downtown was so quiet.

No response.

She tried to find out whether it was normally this quiet.

Still not much of an answer.

The woman sped off, and the unit kept marching.

The deeper they got into the village, the eerier the village felt—carts that were normally full of merchandise were turned over, some were falling apart. The few people who walked by did so in a hurry and avoided eye contact. The unit was slated to march through the entire downtown area, but the mission's leader signaled for the Marines to stop. The feeling that someone was watching them, targeting them grew too strong. Each squad headed back to their vehicle, and the convoy drove out of the district along the same road they had used to drive in.

As soon as Adams heard the IED blast, the windshield and side windows of the MRAP went completely black. She felt a series of jolts. She heard a downpour of small rocks and sand hit the roof of the vehicle. She saw the ammo cans fall onto her legs. When she came to, she unpinned herself. Then, as quickly as she could, she tugged on the straps that pulled the gunner to safety.

The Marines outside were scanning the area to ensure that no other IEDs had been planted—a must before rescuing those trapped inside the busted MRAP. After Adams yelled for a medic and realized that one wasn't coming, she looked up and saw, through the front windshield, that people outside the vehicle were slowly backing away. One Marine stood still, a look of terror on his face.

A small piece of metal pushed up through the sand just inches from his feet. It set off the compact detector used to spot potential explosives in the field. The Marine had to determine whether the IED was real. Adams watched the man slowly lower himself to the ground. Carefully he straightened his right leg behind him, then his left. Without disturbing the sand in front of his face, he scooted himself back on his stomach until his body was fully stretched and his hands could comfortably reach the area surrounding the metal.

With short, precise strokes, and without touching the suspected explosive, he brushed light puffs of sand into the air. He needed to reveal more of the disturbed area around the object to inspect it.

Fffit.

Fffit.

Fffit.

Everything, to Adams, felt as if it was happening incredibly slowly. The area had fallen relatively silent. Commotion among the Marines outside the vehicle had, for the moment, stopped. The flat piece of metal finally came into view.

False alarm.

Adams raised her right leg, still throbbing from the impact of the blast, and used her foot to pound on the side door. Another Marine yanked on it from the outside. Everyone else in the vehicle did the same until the doors, stuck from the blast, finally opened.

Several Marines clutched the gunner and helped pull him to safety.

He was too injured to walk. Adams watched as several men carried him to a different MRAP.

Three of the four vehicles in the convoy sat in a perfect row, one several feet behind another, along the side of the roadway. The one Adams had been riding in was in pieces. Its engine was on the ground in front of what was left of the vehicle's body. A tire sat just up the roadway. The sun was beginning to go down, and Adams, her head still throbbing, could hear an infantry Marine, in the first vehicle, trying to get assistance after he had called in the attack:

"Our convoy has been hit by an IED! One man is injured."

Before he got a response Adams heard gunfire.

She ran behind the second vehicle parked along the roadway and laid on her stomach, hiding part of her body behind one of the tires. She left just enough of her shoulders and head exposed to see her target. Resting her elbows on the ground, she looked through her weapon's scope and saw an insurgent stand up on the roof of a building a few hundred feet away. He raised his rifle in her direction. She remained steady, took a deep breath, fired, and watched him drop.

She could hear gunfire raining down on the convoy from the opposite direction. Her fellow Marines were rapidly returning shots.

Another insurgent stood up on the roof of an adjacent building. Adams and the infantry Marine crouched beside her both fired in the insurgent's direction. He quickly fell.

Two other Taliban operatives stood in rapid succession. Adams fired several rounds but missed.

She reloaded her weapon, quickly pulled the scope up to her right eye, took a deep breath, and fired several more rounds. She watched the man furthest away fall. The Marine to her right continued firing, and the insurgent closest to them dropped out of sight.

Silence. Adams scanned right. Nothing. She scanned the horizon to her left. Still nothing. She lowered the scope and looked to her immediate right to make sure her fellow Marine was okay. Before she had the chance to speak, enemy fire resumed, this time from a different direction.

The seventeen Marines scrambled to change their formation.

Eight of them shot at the insurgents still popping up in the distance as Adams ran and then dropped to the ground to join a staggered line of fellow fighters to her right. She dug her elbows into the sand to prop up her weapon, then fired several shots in rapid succession to provide cover for other Marines as they moved forward to form another line several feet ahead. Out of the corner of her eye she saw a FET member join her line and start shooting. The team of seventeen held their ground for another thirty minutes.

As darkness fell and the evening call to prayer began, the insurgents retreated.

After the nearly hour-long skirmish the rescue squad they called for still hadn't shown.

One of the squad leaders placed another call.

The response came: all other companies in the area were on missions. There was no tow vehicle available. Adams's team would have to wait.

She grabbed a packaged meal and sat in the back of the second MRAP in the convoy. She opened the packet of French toast, heated it up, and ate quickly, knowing that her shift to stand on night watch was coming up in two hours—not much time to sleep. The adrenaline rush from the firefight was fading, and her pounding headache slowly returned. She could feel all the bruises on her legs and arms from the ammo cans that fell on her during the crash. She was sore. She ate in silence, then rested near the back of the vehicle. She felt someone tap her shoulder. She grabbed her weapon and changed places with the Marine who had been standing guard outside the vehicle. Adams took every fourth shift for the rest of the night.

As the sun rose the next morning the rapid pops returned.

Taliban insurgents had surrounded them again, slightly closer this time.

Adams ran to the side of the vehicle where she had been standing guard. She knelt by the rear gate to get a better look at her target. As she prepared to fire, a bullet hurtled toward the Marine to her right. It skimmed the dirt between them and hit the back of the vehicle only inches from Adams's face. Together the two rapidly returned fire.

There were fewer Taliban fighters, and their closer proximity made them more vulnerable to gunfire. Not feeling as safe as they had the night before, they quickly retreated.

A squad leader called again that afternoon to see whether another rescue team had been sent.

The team had been on its way but had to retreat after getting hit by an IED. They would send another team as soon as one was available. They didn't know when that would be.

At midnight a rescue team finally showed.

As the vehicles pulled up, one of the FET Marines warned them to move quickly. "We're surrounded by the Taliban," she said.

The group wasted no time hooking the wrecked vehicle onto the tow truck.

Adams and the infantry unit formed a 360-degree perimeter around the vehicles, prepared to return fire. Taliban insurgents popped up on rooftops again, firing as rapidly as they could, trying hard to take one of the Marines out before the group left. The FET leader climbed into the back of the last MRAP, and the convoy, now with six vehicles, sped out of the area.

The team followed the one road out of the town center and back to the FOB. The hum of the vehicle's tires exacerbated the pounding in Adams's head. She lifted her hands to the sides of her face and rubbed her throbbing temples—the first signs of a traumatic brain injury that would follow her from Afghanistan all the way to the halls of Congress.

MARIA RODRIGUEZ
2011-2012

CHAPTER 7

INVISIBLE

The most hateful aristocracy ever established on the
face of the globe . . . which ordains all men sovereigns [and]
all women subjects, carries dissension, discord and rebellion
into every home of the nation.

−SUSAN B. ANTHONY

ZABUL PROVINCE, AFGHANISTAN, JUNE 2011—The Afghan provincial assistant walked into the governor's office carrying a silver tray overflowing with appetizers: small plates of breads, dates, and nuts as well as bowls of fruit and yogurt. Maria Rodriguez was waiting for the first of several Sunday morning meetings with the provincial governor to begin. She watched as the assistant maneuvered around the velvet sofa she sat on to serve the men in the room first.

The ornate carvings at the tray's center peeked out between the round bottoms of a teapot and delicate glass cups. And the pleasant smell of bread baking in a small factory up the road wafted into the room, mixing with the musty smells of Afghanistan that Rodriguez had gradually grown to accept.

The assistant's uniform made an almost imperceptible swishing sound as he sped by.

Between the wooden floors layered with plush rugs and the thick golden curtains flanking the large windows behind the provincial governor's desk, the office looked more like a banquet hall than a place for the heads of US and Afghan military units to hash out strategies in a war zone. But Rodriguez saw, through the room's vast windows, the reminders of conflict. Outside, directly in front of the concrete building, sat the opening of a sandbag-and-barbed-wire fence that encircled the entire military compound. Along the dusty roads between the fence and the building American and Afghan military vehicles sped past, kicking dirt onto a maze of muddy sidewalks.

Rodriguez was anxious to talk about the treatment and progress of the Afghan women who were hired to serve as police officers. She had heard rumors that there were six to twelve Afghan women being kept somewhere on the compound—not working and not being well looked after either—and she intended to find out where they were and what they needed. But she knew better than to push her commanding officer to jump into business conversation right away. She also knew that it would have been considered a cultural affront for her, the only woman in the room, to speak before the men. When the compound commander, Lieutenant Colonel Tony Thacker, introduced her to the governor, the politician declined to shake her hand; instead, he raised his head, nodded to acknowledge her existence, and then looked past her to his Afghan National Army soldiers and the colonel. Rodriguez kept her hands tucked behind her back and turned toward Thacker, allowing the insult from the governor to pass.

The major had worked hard to become an officer, and she didn't get there by being the meek woman in the background. Her dedication to the military had meant personal sacrifice—time away from her children, who were always on her mind. Long hours and frequent deployments led, in part, to two divorces by the time she hit the ground in Afghanistan. She resented the fact that she was expected to accept the absences and moves and late nights that both of her husbands (also soldiers, the first an aviation warrant officer and the second an infantry staff sargeant) brought to the relationship. Pressure for men to be as understanding of the schedules of military wives wasn't nearly as high.

As the provost marshall (the military equivalent of a police chief) for the 1st Stryker Brigade, Rodriguez was in charge of one of the most powerful military police units in the Middle East. She wasn't accustomed to holding her tongue—or condoning overtly sexist treatment. Every moment she had to do that in Afghanistan was a strain.

Progress for women in Afghanistan, Rodriguez had grown to understand, often meant setting ego aside, swallowing pride, and making compromises.

Of the dozens of FET units serving in Afghanistan from all over the world, women in the American military units frequently had the hardest time adjusting. In addition to the lack of logistical and strategic support from the military, which women from other countries didn't struggle with to the same degree, the approach from Afghan male soldiers who worked with American women sometimes included sexual harassment and intimidation. At least one American woman had become a target. And one Afghan man became an example of the lengths this latest provincial governor would go to in order to build trust with the American military.

About a week after Rodriguez arrived at FOB Lagman in Zabul she was able to piece together parts of the story.

An Afghan guard had been kicked out of the provincial governor's service and dismissed from the military for sexually harassing an American military female. The details were unclear, but Rodriguez did know that the woman had been seen talking to the man alone—something that American women were instructed not to do—and walking with the man, who was married, from the provincial governor's office to other places on the base, including the cafeteria. These are moves the woman likely thought were safe and that she had probably done with American military men on bases all over the world; however, the Afghan officer read her actions as less than innocent. After his requests for dates were rejected, he became aggressive. He started cornering her in the building where she worked, demanding to know why she had rejected his advances. She threatened to report him to the provincial governor, but her threats simply fueled his aggression. He found her walking home alone one night from the provincial governor's office. From what Rodriguez understands, the man pushed the woman against a wall late at night in an unlit area of the compound, pinned her shoulders back so she couldn't move, and began to force himself on her. The woman managed to break free and run. She reported the assault to her commander, who spoke to the provincial governor. The man was immediately dismissed.

Rodriguez was happy to learn that the provincial governor's approach to dealing with Afghan men started from a place of respect for American women. Although he didn't think of women as equal, he always followed through on his zero-tolerance policy for actions deemed offensive by the American military—even offenses that, culturally, Afghan men didn't necessarily acknowledge or understand.

But the biggest lesson Rodriguez learned from the experiences of an American woman she had never met was how, as a female officer, to navigate the world of Afghan male diplomacy. That skill would be an essential part of proving that Afghan female police—who their male colleagues frequently wrote off—were a vital tool in pushing the Taliban and other insurgents out of the country. To some Afghan men, friendliness, beyond what was deemed by their society as professional, could be seen as an overture, and confidence was viewed a threat, Rodriguez said. Part of negotiating as a woman among Afghan men was learning how to blend into the background with just the right amount of energy: participate enough not to be forgotten; be harmless enough not to be met with aggression. The tactic of being the mute woman who spoke through American men—though often hard for Rodriguez—opened the doors of progress.

She used those tactics during that first meeting with Zabul's provincial governor.

As Rodriguez walked into the building that Sunday she removed the cap of her uniform and placed it in the right pocket of her cargo pants. She hurriedly fished for the headscarf from her left pocket so she could cover her jet-black hair, which was neatly pulled back in a sleek bun, comfortably sitting above her uniform's collar. The scarf was modest, monochromatic, acceptable. The week before, she scrambled to replace the bright-colored, jeweled scarf she had originally bought when she first landed at the Kandahar Airfield. She knew that in the country she would need to wear a headscarf and thought the ornate scarf was pretty. But a few days later an Afghan she had met on the base gently pulled her aside and told her just the opposite. The jewels on the end of the scarf were considered flashy, not something a proper Afghan woman would wear.

When she walked into the governor's office she saw a large wooden desk flanked by plush, high-backed chairs. Following Thacker, Rodriguez walked by four large sofas in order to sit on the first one, close to the governor's desk. To her left was the colonel and, across from her, officers of the Afghan National Army, men whose missions were, in part, wrapped up in solving educational and tactical problems among their soldiers—problems the American military had resolved decades ago. And they were hoping that men like Thacker could help them fix the multitude of roadblocks preventing their soldiers from pushing out the Taliban.

Despite the surge of US troops in 2010, there had been little to no progress in building Afghan security forces that could have helped stabilize local governments in provinces like Zabul in Southern Afghanistan, one of the most economically, politically, and socially challenged sections of the country. That year the Taliban killed three candidates who were running for Parliament. "Everyone affiliated with this election is our target," said a Taliban spokesman, according to a report by Human Rights Watch. "Candidates, security forces, campaigners, election workers, voters are all our targets." Political leaders in many villages in Southern Afghanistan rarely made public appearances and left key positions in local governments unfilled. In other areas throughout the country the only faces of government were those of the Afghan military, which was struggling to train and educate its soldiers. Where a woman like Rodriguez fit into fixing those problems, the provincial governor hadn't even considered.

The morning of that first meeting Thacker sat down in the first open spot on the sofa to the provincial governor's right. To the governor's left were two of his assistants. Rodriguez slowly lowered herself onto the sofa beside Thacker. But almost immediately a third provincial assistant motioned for her to stand. He whispered something to her in broken English that she didn't completely understand, escorted her to the far end of the last sofa in the room, and motioned for her to sit. Although his English may not have been completely clear, the universal language of segregation and isolation certainly was. As the only woman in the meeting, Rodriguez was relegated to the most subservient, distanced spot in the room. She was seated so far from the provincial governor, his assistants, and the rest of the meeting's officers that she was prevented from easily communicating with any of them, including Thacker.

After she settled into her far corner of the room, she watched the Afghan provincial assistant walk past her to serve the men—the governor, then Thacker, and then members of the Afghan military—first. He carefully handed each a delicate glass cup filled with tea, steam swirling just above the rim. She heard her translator deliver in English the customary small talk that began most business meetings in Afghanistan. The chitchat could last for thirty minutes or more, a practice that regularly tested Rodriguez's patience—a by-product of her fast-paced New York upbringing that sometimes made the much slower environment of Afghanistan hard for her to take. Finally, the assistant who had painstakingly walked around her minutes earlier returned with a cup of tea in hand.

As the men began to talk, Rodriguez pulled out her notebook. The pristine white paper waiting to be filled reminded her of the notebooks she used as a Catholic schoolgirl learning to write cursive. She warmed up her wrist, just as she remembered the nuns instructing, by drawing consecutive circles for several seconds on the first sheet of paper in the notebook. She flipped to the second page and started at the top of the alphabet: "A, a, a, A. b, B, B, b. c, c, C, C . . ." Once in a while her ears perked up when she heard one of the Afghan military officers bring up an issue that she thought her FET could address. The curves and links of her meticulous doodles were interspersed with the much straighter lines of hastily written notes: "Illiteracy rates high among Afghan military men," she wrote. She looked up at the Afghan officer and listened attentively as her translator made clear that more than 50 percent of men within Afghan military units couldn't read. "FET units could host literacy sessions. Teach men to read," she added to her notes. She flipped to the next page and jotted down a message for Thacker. "When are we going to talk about the FETs? Can you ask the governor about the Afghan policewomen on the compound? Where are they? What do they need?" She ripped the page from her notebook, folded it, and, while crouching, slowly walked over to Thacker. She handed him the note and moved quickly back to her designated, distanced spot. Though frustrating, Thacker was her only means of communicating, and notes were the only way she could convey her thoughts.

Thacker glanced down at the message, refolded it, and placed it in his pocket. He turned slightly to make eye contact with Rodriguez and slowly shook his head. Rodriguez sat further back on the sofa. She would get no more information.

She looked up at a chandelier that hung high above her head, its crystals catching her eye. The ornate governor's office sat in stark contrast to the office one floor above—one that at that point was still a mystery to Rodriguez. But the isolation felt by the women inside each was very much the same.

THE SECOND-FLOOR OFFICE was empty save for a battered, metal desk and a few simple wooden chairs. As the morning meetings kicked off downstairs, the routine on the second floor was much slower, the actions of its occupants much more tentative. In that space an Afghan female police officer known as Bibi was in charge.

Bibi stared at the paperwork that sat on the metal desk's modest surface through the small holes in her dark burqa. With her right hand, which was also covered, she reached for a pen; with her left she flipped through empty time schedules, occasionally writing down a woman's name, with nothing else to place beside it. The thought of her daughter's face—round, innocent, topped with wild, curly black hair—made her smile, and then brought tears to her eyes. Bibi thought of her daughter frequently, along with the other child she left behind to become a police officer in Zabul Province. Members of the Taliban had beheaded two of her brothers, and she thought that joining the police force would give her life order. But the nightmare of Taliban activity followed her. The terrorists threatened her life because she was an officer; they called in bomb scares and made assassination attempts. Every woman in the room had a similar story. But looking down at that paperwork every day was a reminder that she and the rest of her team were isolated from her fellow police officers. They rarely heard from the police chief and had no police-related duties. Their days were spent hidden away in this small room. Their sacrifices had, up to that point, been for nothing. She was powerless.

The other women, also fully covered, found busywork wiping the room's bare white walls. They scrubbed the floors with the same multipurpose mixture, and the smell of cleanser permeated the small space. They dusted the chairs and rearranged small lamps that, aside from the fluorescent ceiling light, brought the only bit of brightness into the otherwise gray space, with its cold, stone floors and thick, iron bars outside of its only window. Heavy black curtains blocked the gaze of any men or women who may happen by and be tempted to look up and wonder about the plight of the women inside. Those Afghan female officers who hadn't run from the grips of the Taliban had run from equally dangerous male family members who threatened to kill them if they joined the police force.

Yet these women still fled their homes, and each found a way into the heart of Zabul Province's capital of Qalat City.

AFTER THEIR SECOND MEETING Rodriguez closely followed Thacker out of Provincial Governor Mohammad Ashraf Naseri's office. As they exited the building she quickly rummaged through her right-side cargo pants pocket for her uniform cap. She removed her headscarf and asked again about talking to the provincial governor about the Afghan women hidden somewhere on the base. Is that something, she asked, that could come up during the next meeting?

Thacker began walking along the dirt path that led from the governor's office building to his. Rodriguez kept in step, and he listened again as the major emphasized the importance of working with members of the Afghan female police. They need to be prepared to take over after the FETs leave, she said. They need to continue searching female suspects. They would be economically empowered. And once the police unit was successful, other women may hear about it, leave their villages, and join the force. The more the Afghan female police force expanded, she continued, the better position they would be in to take on insurgents.

Thacker stopped walking just before he reached the gate surrounding his office building. He turned to Rodriguez and told her the most important lesson that she would learn during her entire stay in Afghanistan: without patience in this country, there are no victories. Things move slowly, he explained. For every one thing that you want, Rodriguez remembered him saying, "I've been trying for years to accomplish three more." He punched the keypad to get through the gate. He paused on his way in, turned to look at her, and asked, "Okay, exactly what do you want?"

"Just a meeting with the women. Just an initial meeting."

"I'll try to bring it up the next time."

During Rodriguez's third meeting with the political and security force leaders she knew exactly what to do. She followed Thacker through the double doors of the first-floor office. She sat on the far end of the last sofa in the room. As the men settled in, hot tea, breads, and cheeses were passed around to all, and she reached into her right cargo pocket, pulled out her notebook, and began the waiting game. A, a, a. B, B, B, b. C, C, c, c. She interspersed her doodles with notes: marksmanship skills were poor; leadership training was needed.

She wondered when her turn would come.

Thacker sat on the sofa beside the governor, crossed his right leg over his left, and sat his hands in his lap. He nodded as he listened to Naseri speak, waiting for a pause in the conversation. After about an hour he found an opening. The colonel glanced at Rodriguez and then turned back to the governor. "We understand that there are women on the base," Thacker said, "who are members of the new female team of the Afghan police. Are they working? Rodriguez would like to meet them. There may be an opportunity for training," Thacker explained, "and ultimately for improving the Afghan National Police."

The governor stared at Rodriguez for several seconds. She returned his gaze. He nodded toward one of his guards and motioned for him to take the major upstairs.

Rodriguez and her translator followed the third assistant.

He was a tall, slender man who walked with a smooth stride as he climbed toward the second floor. At the top, near the end of the hallway, was a narrow door with scratches and indents. The provincial assistant pulled out his baton and used it to knock. Rodriguez looked down and noticed the dull-colored knob. It started to slowly turn; the major looked up.

The escort moved aside, signaling for Rodriguez to enter. But she did not. Instead, she paused and looked directly at Bibi, whose head was peeking out from the other side. She had opened the door only a few inches. It took a minute or two for Rodriguez to distinguish between the burqa and the darkness of the dimly lit room. As Bibi's figure became clear to Rodriguez, the first thing the major noticed was a set of intense brown eyes. She saw in them a fear and hesitation that told her to approach gingerly.

The soldier smiled to say hello and slowly walked into the room, closing the battered wooden door behind her.

CHAPTER 8

POLICE IN NAME ONLY

The Afghan women had not expected to hear a knock at the door. No one ever came to see them.

Bibi quickly looked up, shifting her gaze from the dull surface of the desk she had been staring at all morning to see the other women, who had been milling about the small space for hours, frozen. They looked back at her with a similar mixture of fear, surprise, and concern. It was midmorning, and the sound of the wooden baton rapping loudly on the thick oak door echoed against the walls of the virtually empty room and cut sharply through the quiet.

The woman in charge of the group, the one known simply as Bibi, placed her pencil on the desk and glanced several times from the door to her fellow Afghan female police officers. The blank papers on her desk, the ones that should have been filled with time schedules and assignments, rustled in the small puff of air generated by her hijab.

They all stood still, listening for another sound from the front of the room, assurance that the first three raps at the door weren't a mistake.

Pap, pap, pap! Pap, pap, pap!

Bibi paused just before reaching for the knob and took a deep breath.

She dipped her head to adjust her hijab so she could see more clearly through the eye holes in the cloth that covered her face. The sun was shining brightly through the windows in the hallway, creating a halo effect above the head of the woman with the olive skin whose face Bibi could hardly see. It took her eyes a few moments to adjust from the darkness of her room with the covered window.

The guard who knocked on the door moved slightly to Bibi's left, and the dark brown eyes of the woman in front of her slowly came into focus. So did the scarf that covered the woman's head. It was plain, not offensive. Its loose fit revealed that it had been tied in a hurry. The knot wasn't centered, causing the front of the scarf to slant and the sides to reveal a good amount of the woman's dark hair. The dark material was slack under the soldier's chin. The entire, hasty contraption barely touched the collar of this mysterious woman's uniform. Bibi noticed the small black insignia near the top of the woman's garb—a dull oak leaf at the center of her chest where the two sides of her uniform's jacket met.

Bibi stepped back, instinctively hiding herself behind the door. She had seen a uniform like that only once before, and it was worn by men, not a woman. The memories she associated with that camouflage and its attached insignia made her limbs feel weak, her body defenseless. Taliban insurgents had shot at several men in her village and beheaded her two older brothers. Large tires attached to American military Humvees and MRAPs barreled down her street. Military men inside beige vehicles yelled at one another before some jumped out, others continued driving, and all had their weapons drawn. Some fired shots. The day after that raid she decided to leave her husband and children behind and make her way to Zabul headquarters to become a police officer. As she stared at the soldier standing in front of her now, she tried to calm her nerves.

Bibi noticed the guard looking straight at her. Impatient, he pushed the door open, and Bibi stumbled back. Rodriguez hesitated before entering, as if she were waiting for a signal. She made eye contact with Bibi, smiled, and then moved slowly over the threshold and sat in one of several small chairs placed around the room.

The Afghan women watched the stranger.

Rodriguez shifted in her seat, and the chair's legs scraped against the floor, uncomfortably cutting into the silence. Rodriguez's translator, an Afghan female, sat down. The major looked around the room, taking in the black curtains and small lamps on either side of the window.

Then she looked straight at Bibi—who felt the stares of the other Afghan women behind her—and the officer smiled. The soldier couldn't tell, but the Afghan women were not smiling back.

Bibi watched the woman's smile fade. Then she saw her lips move and heard words come out that she couldn't understand. The Afghan woman sitting next to the soldier, the one who was dressed in the same protective gear as the major, translated:

"Hi. My name is Major Maria Rodriguez."

She waited for a response from Bibi. When she heard nothing, she continued: "I'm an American soldier, a police officer, and I'm here to help you. I would like to help you in any way I can."

Still nothing. She looked at each female in the room for some sign that they understood why she was there. Three women sitting to the left of Bibi shook their heads in affirmation. Rodriguez pressed on.

"What is it that you need? What do you feel is lacking?"

More silence. Rodriguez looked again to the woman who appeared to be in charge of the group.

After a few moments she heard a shaky but determined voice. Bibi's arms, which had been crossed over her chest, quickly flew into the air as she spoke.

A translation of the terse message followed: "Nothing. We don't need anything from you."

The soldier's smile faded. Her mouth tensed as it closed.

"So you are happy with the way things are? Do you feel like you are able to do your jobs as members of the Afghan police?"

No response.

Unsure of what she was missing, the soldier remained silent.

Bibi watched Rodriguez wring her hands. Her palms were beginning to turn red.

The provincial governor and security force officials had paid little attention to the Afghan women since they had been stowed away in the room above his office. They had not worked. They had not been properly trained to do anything. Though a much larger group of women had finished about two months of police academy training to become officers, the standards hadn't amounted to much. Some of the women were based in a different police unit that worked with females in the community and was geared toward investigating incidents of sexual assault, abuse, and harassment. But by the time Rodriguez showed up, about 90 percent of the thirty who participated in the classes had abandoned police life, unable to take the threats lobbed at them from the Zabul community. As soon as the Afghan women showed up, men began calling police headquarters with threats to kill, bomb, and behead the women if they continued to work. A woman working in any capacity was a violation of Taliban law, but to be a police officer, a position of authority and power, was even more deserving of torture and punishment. The female officers were called sluts. They had no uniforms. No weapons. No place to sleep. There were rumors spilling through the community that the female police officers were prostitutes and that male officers were sexually abusing them. Still, Zabul police headquarters was the safest place for the few women left to escape massive poverty and Taliban threats and fighting. The last thing her group needed, Bibi thought, was to be labeled needy women complaining to an American woman who might report them to the governor. They had made too many sacrifices, run too far.

Another officer named Bibi had deceived her husband in order to work. When he found out she was a police officer he divorced her. She told him that she quit, even though she continued to do the job. Satisfied that she was no longer an officer, her husband decided to remarry her. If she was found out, the consequences for her could be dire. Working was important enough for her to continue without her husband's approval, trusting that her fellow female officers would maintain her secret.

Concealing jobs from their husbands wasn't easy. She likely hid the money she made and gave creative explanations for her absences when she had to be gone for extended periods of time. Although most women slept at homes in town, women who worked in secret took the extra risk of returning home as often as possible so they didn't arouse their husband's suspicions.

After nearly an hour—during which eight women, in a very small, nearly empty room in the middle of Afghanistan, sat and said very little to one another—Rodriguez rose to leave.

Her Afghan companions stood, and as the soldier walked toward the door Bibi sped ahead of her to open it. Rodriguez extended her hand and said thank you.

Bibi slowly drew her hand from behind her burqa. As her hand touched Rodriguez's, she felt what she could only think of as relief to see the major go.

After she locked the door Bibi returned to her desk to once again shuffle through blank paperwork. One woman began rearranging chairs; another scrubbed down the walls and wiped scuff marks off the floor. Another woman followed with a broom to sweep up the dust that had fallen from the bottoms of Rodriguez's boots. They fell back into the routine of anonymity—one that was previously disconcerting but now seemed, somehow, comfortingly familiar.

Rodriguez knew that Thacker would be ending his meeting with the governor soon, so instead of walking into the governor's office, she waited outside the closed double doors. She kept running through that first meeting with the Afghan female police in her mind. She thought about how uncomfortable she felt sitting in that cold chair. She wondered why the women were so hesitant to answer her questions or to pose ones of their own. And she reveled in the fact that, despite the poor communication, just getting the meeting—with women who were erroneously thought of as incapable—was a win.

As Thacker exited the building, Rodriguez followed, walking beside him along the path back to his office. The colonel stopped in front of the little white box that hovered at eye level and punched in the key code. The gate opened. Rodriguez waited for the right moment to announce her plan to meet again with the six women hidden in the upstairs office of the provincial governor's building. As she closed the gate behind her, she asked for permission to bring the entire FET.

CHAPTER 9

WAITING

The major stood with her back against the white barricade, one of many tall concrete structures near the military police kennels on the base, waiting for the Stryker vehicle that was supposed to take her into a local village—her first chance as a FET leader to connect with poorer residents in lesser-served areas like Naw Bahar and Shinkay.

She spent Sundays trying to cajole the provincial governor into letting her train Afghan female police and weekdays trying to connect with as many women surrounding her FOB (a short ride from the governor's office) as possible.

She lifted her hand to the brim of her cap to shield her eyes from the brightness of the desert sun. It was just beginning to beat down on her neck, causing beads of sweat to slowly run down her shoulders to the small of her back.

It was 9 A.M. on FOB Lagman.

Leaning against the front of the barricade, her rucksack on the ground by her feet, Rodriguez could hear the military police dogs barking inside the kennels, some of them straining at their leashes, longing to run free. Each of the K9s had a service member handler who worked with the dog every day, slept beside the dog every night, and ran with the dog each morning. Some chose to leash their dog during down time; others didn't. But all the dogs knew that their place was beside their handlers. Their world, when they weren't working, was the series of tents that sat on the sand- and gravel-filled pits that covered nearly a third of the base. Green Army-issue sleep cots lined the left side of the smallest sleep tents, and behind each cot sat a duffle bag with the name of the soldier who slept there. Near the space's center, attached to each cot, was a leash that kept the K9s in place during the night. On the right side of the small sleep tents, lined up in a neat row, were green lockers. On the front of each was a different dog's name stenciled in faded black letters. Each animal had its own set of equipment stored inside—an extensive food supply, brushes for grooming, muzzles, and extra leashes. The floors of the tents were hosed down every morning and washed out each afternoon, but that didn't stop the smell of kennel—wet dog mixed with a faint hint of waste—from baking in the desert sun and wafting past Rodriguez as she waited for the day's convoy to come through.

When the K9s were working, their world was much more dangerous. They sniffed out IEDs and crawled into caves that were too small for soldiers to fit through. Their goal was always to protect their handlers, to make sure that bombs hadn't been planted in small crawl spaces or that insurgents weren't lying in wait to blow up themselves and the Americans who surrounded them. And, as the provost marshal, it was Rodriguez's job to make sure that the dogs and the service members who cared for them, trained them, and whose lives depended on them were well protected on the FOB. When she wasn't working a FET mission, she, like all the women on her team, still had regular jobs to do. And the security of soldiers and detainees constantly traded places with her work with Afghan women as her primary wartime concern.

Rodriguez looked down at her watch. She had been waiting for nearly two hours. She bent over at the waist and touched the tops of her boots to stretch her back. The arches of her feet felt tight. Her heels began to throb. She lowered herself to the ground and leaned back against the barricade. In the distance, through the scrim that covered the tall metal fence surrounding the entire perimeter of the FOB, she saw several military vehicles speed past. She watched as village men wearing intricately woven turbans and sand-colored tunics walked by in one direction. Soldiers in desert uniforms passed them walking in the other. They were just close enough to the FOB for Rodriguez to see the faint outlines of their bodies. They navigated journeys beyond the sandbags piled high around the gate and the military vehicles that further separated the base from the outside world. There were no women to be seen. The relative absence of females on so many Afghan streets was still unsettling to her, even after being in the country for several months now.

Rodriguez's eyes wandered to the observation tower that sat just behind the fence on the inside of the compound. The tall metal structure was one of six that dotted the perimeter. She could see the sun's rays peeking through the metal rods that crossed and recrossed between the legs of the structure. Her eyes followed the base to the glass control room at the tower's top, which hovered several hundred feet above anything else for miles. She saw a soldier sitting in the booth—one of twenty military police under Rodriguez's direction. They manned the tower twenty-four hours a day, ready to shoot at, detain, or investigate anyone who approached or posed a threat to the FOB.

That control room, the military police officer who occupied it, and the fence topped with barbed wire were the only things separating the base from surrounding insurgent groups. The Taliban were constantly attacking, patrolling, and planting bombs in surrounding villages. Their goal was not just to control villagers for the moment but to recruit enough young men so that their forces would remain strong for decades.

Stepping off the FOB was always a risk, and women weren't allowed to do so without a male soldier accompanying them—no matter her rank, no matter how competent she was at her job, no matter how much she outshined the average man in her unit when it came to performing combat duties like firing a weapon.

Rodriguez successfully oversaw and implemented strategies that shielded the base from insurgent attacks. She was the officer in charge of securing and transporting detainees. But even she had to wait every morning for a male to make space for her on his convoy so she could get off the base. Some combat soldiers were generous; others were not. Her ability to follow through on noncombat FET missions, like the information collection she was trying to do this morning, was limited. But at least the Sunday beforehand she had finally met members of the Afghan female police—a hard-fought victory.

The major glanced at her watch again.

II A.M.

She wiped sweat off the back of her neck with a brown handkerchief. She could feel heat emanating from the barrier behind her. As she repositioned her body against the concrete, Rodriguez looked to her left and saw the sandpits soldiers used for recreation. It wasn't unusual on a Saturday afternoon for soldiers to play touch football in one of them at the center of the base. And Rodriguez knew that as long as she could hear those sounds in the middle of Afghanistan, she must have been doing something right in her efforts to keep the FOB safe.

Rodriguez thought about the woman she had searched during an earlier mission. She wondered what had happened, if anything, to her. As provost marshal, she was also in charge of the facility, which had three cells, where her unit held detainees. She would inspect it later that day.

The fact that she couldn't drive herself off the base, she thought, was preposterous. She was surrounded by testaments to her success as an officer. The mammoth sand-colored containers that stared back at her across the road from the barricades had been her idea. She wanted them placed there to house larger supplies vital to force protection. The concrete barricade that surrounded the base's K9 unit and lined the main entryway onto the FOB stood there because of her strategic thinking. The dogs who, when bored, reacted to the least bit of light and sound, needed extra protection to stay focused and remain combat ready.

The irony of the morning wait, a routine that would become a cornerstone of Rodriguez's life at Lagman, was not lost on her. Looking back on her days at the FOB, Rodriguez admitted that in many ways there were parallels between the military practice that kept her trapped on the FOB and the Taliban law that kept Afghan women—the very ones Rodriguez was assigned to protect—trapped in their homes. The Army stipulated that no American military female was allowed to leave the base without a male combat soldier. Taliban law stated that no Afghan woman was allowed to leave her home without being overseen by a male family member at all times. And although the Army practice was intended to protect and ensure safety, it hindered FET independence.

Rodriguez stood again to wake up her right leg, which had started to fall asleep. She stretched her small frame, her fingertips just clearing the top of the barricade behind her. The Army major hoped the armored vehicle she heard approaching was part of the convoy that was expected to have arrived more than an hour prior. She walked toward the gate and peeked out of the FOB through the holes in the black mesh that wrapped around the fence's narrow metal wiring. In the distance, just beyond the sandbags and the small motor pool of vehicles, Rodriguez saw the large tires of three Stryker vehicles slowly moving closer to the front gate. But instead of the military vehicles turning right and moving through the FOB's front entrance to navigate the main road and park near the kennels, the vehicles continued down the road. Rodriguez heard the engines crescendo and then begin to fade. She listened until she could no longer hear tires grinding against the roadway or the familiar ting and churn of the motors as the vehicles lurched forward.

She returned to the spot she had occupied all morning, sat down beside her rucksack, and continued to wait. There was still time for a different convoy to pass through the area and enter the base so that its soldiers could pick up personal supplies from the makeshift PX—a small series of connected trailers that was a scaled down, minimal version of the military shopping centers found on bases throughout the United States. Many units drove through the Qalat City area on their way to other FOBs. Just because one unit kept driving didn't mean the next unit wouldn't stop. She would give it another hour before giving up.

The job of at least one of the female soldiers on Rodriguez's FET was, in fact, driving. But the military, Rodriguez said, made it impossible for her women to get the training needed to drive in Afghanistan. It took Rodriguez a few weeks just to get permission to wait for a convoy. She had developed a strategy to get around the maze of rules that showed that the military wanted FETs but wasn't ready to fully support them.

The night before, Rodriguez sat in the creaky wooden chair in front of her desk, one of several lined up against the wall of her shared, first-floor office. She stared at the ceiling in an attempt to gather her thoughts before the meeting with her brigade commander to brief him on mission progress, something she had done every night since she had arrived in Afghanistan.

The daily report, delivered at 7 P.M., was always the same: status and location of all working dogs, status of all force protection equipment assigned to the brigade, number and status of detainees, conditions of the FOB, and the status of evidence collected to use for prosecution.

And by 7:45 she was working in a few words about her FET's needs with an eye toward finding out when the women, who were just as ready as she was to interview the few females they'd seen on the streets of a nearby village, would be able to get regular rides.

And every night, she recalled, her efforts to move the FET mission forward were stalled. The conversations had become all too routine.

"How's it going with the FET goals?"

"Not great, sir. My team needs equipment. We need permission to leave the base. I need permission to leave the base to go out into the local villages and find out what the women need, what the women are going through."

"What equipment do you need?"

"We need vehicles. We need training."

"Not possible. Those vehicles are needed by the men in the field, the combat soldiers."

Silence.

"Can I at least get permission to leave with one of the convoys in the morning? One of the convoys that comes through to gather supplies?"

"Not yet, Rodriguez. We'll need you for other work in the morning. Let's just wait and play it by ear."

"Sir, it's impossible for me to use the women on my FET effectively if we can't get off the base whenever we need to, not just to go on missions with the men when they need us. We have our own separate missions, some of which you have already approved and are asking us to fulfill. How are we supposed to do that?"

The brigade commander ended each briefing by saying, "I'm on your side, Rodriguez. These things take time."

Women couldn't take vehicles, her commander explained, away from the men who needed them. Rodriguez's interpretation of the commander's message: the military couldn't be bothered with treating women like real combat soldiers, although it gave women real combat responsibilities.

Despite the obstacles, Rodriguez knew the commander was among the good guys. He was trying, but regulations beyond his control left him with few options. It was impossible for her to make the case that the women on her FET deserved more equipment and more time to complete missions. Supplies were limited. And her FET members were combat soldiers in every respect except the one that mattered most—name.

Rodriguez could hear the commander's words—women don't have a real combat directive, supplies are limited, you can't take items needed by men—all day, every day. She began to dread the nightly briefings.

So she developed a plan: she would check every morning to see what time trucks were expected to arrive at the base the next day and work the rest of her schedule around the convoy schedule. That way, whenever she briefed the brigade commander, her workday conveniently left openings when convoys were expected. The plan was well thought out. But it wasn't foolproof. There were plenty of days when convoys either weren't expected or failed to come through.

After the 2010 ISAF directive Rodriguez was among the first FET leaders to try to formalize the Army's female engagement team mission and create a standard operating procedure that could guide women across the United States who were preparing for deployment. FET missions always included female searches during raids. But whether a FET could fulfill other aspects of the mission, including key outreach programs, varied depending on the whims of the men commanding the combat units to which these women were attached. If the commander believed in the FET, then he helped facilitate missions; if he didn't, the women had to fight for the opportunity to perform operations not related to direct combat missions. Around the time Rodriguez was pushing for a formal standard operating procedure (SOP), female soldiers were expected to complete FET missions between their official military duties. Being a part of the FET was considered an additional job. That standard, for Rodriguez, was another hindrance to FET mission completion. Sometimes the major was unable to pull together a FET because company commanders were unwilling to let female soldiers in their charge drop other duties. Rodriguez had to make sure all women who deployed were FET capable.

The Army and Marine Corps would eventually deploy women to Afghanistan solely to work on FET missions for seven- and nine-month rotations. More commanders began to recognize that the work FETs were doing was changing the course of the war and, in response, eventually made vehicles and helicopters more readily available for mission fulfillment.

By the time Smoke landed on the ground in 2013, the year after Rodriguez left, FET leaders would ask for permission to complete missions with the full confidence that if the mission was sound, it would get support.

But not yet.

Rodriguez and other women like her were heading FETs at a time when the struggle for legitimacy was difficult.

Her brigade commander understood the important role female soldiers played in winning the war. Yet he remained reluctant to allow Rodriguez to jump on a convoy that didn't involve the men in her own unit.

Until that final conversation on that final night before Rodriguez's first morning wait.

The brigade commander began the conversation as he had so many others. Her report that night, just like it had every night before, detailed the progress the military police were making on and off the FOB: a detainee had been brought into custody that day, and the investigation was ongoing; one of the Taliban suspects had been transferred for further interrogation.

When he asked about the FET she gave him the same arguments she had before, pushing, respectfully but persistently, for her soldiers' needs. He listened, as always. But this time, reluctantly, he met her halfway. She and she alone could take the next convoy that came through. Just her. Just a scouting mission. "Keep it short," she was told, "and remain with the men in the unit at all times."

"Thank you, sir." She sat back and smiled. Finally, another small victory.

Rodriguez measured progress for the group in small victories. Just getting the FET program to Afghanistan had been an uphill battle.

RODRIGUEZ HAD STARTED this last phase of her military career in a cushy office in Fresno, a reprieve from her deployment to Iraq. The office, on the seventh floor of a government building that sat across from an open-air shopping center, gave her the perfect perch to watch stay-at-home moms wheeling strollers into bookstores and women sitting through long business lunches. And even she occasionally stopped at the outdoor café only steps away from her building. As cushy as the desk assignment was, and as much as she loved the expansive windows that lined her office walls, she knew it would go by quickly. Her time was coming up soon for another deployment. She began to call the personnel office every day to see what units had openings and to make a bid for assignment to Alaska. She had gone to college in Alaska. She had met her first husband in Alaska. It was a state that held happy memories and in which she was very comfortable. She also knew that the 1st Stryker Brigade Combat Team, located on Fort Wainwright, was slated to deploy to Afghanistan soon. She was torn. She didn't want to leave her children again. Her son was only five, her daughter seven. But she knew that she would have to, and this time she wanted control over what unit she left with and where her children stayed during her deployment.

She was set to arrive in Alaska in September 2010.

The hardest part of that duty change was explaining to her kids that they wouldn't be able to come with her. She often struggled with her love for the Army and her undying love for and devotion to her children. Her daughter needed special care—she was legally blind, had scoliosis, chronic lung disease, ADHD, and a moderate developmental disability. The specialty doctors her daughter needed were in Anchorage. Fort Wainwright, where she would be stationed, was in Fairbanks, which was eight hours away.

As soon as her orders came, she and Chris—her ex-husband and the father of her children—sat down with the kids in their California home to explain that mommy would be gone for a year. It was the longest stretch of time she had ever spent away from her kids. Her work had taken her on overnight trips to Monterey or other California cities that weren't too far away. Her deployment to Iraq had lasted only six months. And whenever she was gone, even for one night, Rodriguez would talk to her kids several times via Skype—once when she arrived, at night before bedtime, and the next day before she returned.

As the sun flooded the living room of their home, her kids looked up at her, waiting for whatever news they had gathered to hear. Even though her daughter was seven, she comprehended and reacted to information like a child who was much younger. She smiled wide, her chubby cheeks forming deep dimples. Even her eyes, through her thick, dark-rimmed glasses, managed to look bright with anticipation. Her son looked toward Chris, waiting for either of his parents to speak.

"Mommy's going to Alaska for the Army," Rodriguez started the conversation. She wanted to say everything fast before she choked up. "I'm going to be gone for a year. But don't worry. We'll get to talk every day."

"Like when you're in Monterey?" her son asked.

"Exactly. We'll talk on Skype every day."

"You're going?" her daughter was trying to understand. "But when will you be back?"

Chris jumped in to explain things again. "It will be a year," he explained. "But you'll see Mommy every day, and you'll stay here with me in our home."

She was plagued with doubt about whether her kids were understanding why she was leaving them. Did they think she was going away because she didn't love them? She wondered if she was doing the right thing. Feelings of guilt, for Rodriguez, were constant.

"I knew that when I accepted motherhood this was a possibility," she said years later as she reflected on that departure during an interview with me. "As a commander I had sent brand-new mothers with one-year-olds on deployments. I knew I would have to do that." But knowing she'd have to leave her kids, she admitted, never took the sting out of doing it.

As hard as the conversation was, she didn't dream of leaving the Army or trying to avoid deployments. Getting out of the military would have meant resigning her commission as an officer, and she'd worked too hard to even entertain the idea. She was comforted in the knowledge that Chris would take care of their children.

Rodriguez's ambition and strength, which benefited her as a soldier, sometimes made her life as a wife and mother difficult.

Chris was her second divorce.

The first time she married, Rodriguez was incredibly young. She was twenty-four, her husband was nearly fifteen years her senior, and she thought it would last forever. While his career was headed toward retirement, hers was just starting. She loved the challenge the Army brought to her life. Many of her uncles had been soldiers and Vietnam veterans. A couple dozen male cousins were soldiers. She wanted the chance to prove herself as a soldier just as others in her family had. Her first husband had climbed through the officer ranks before he retired, and she had expected him to understand her desire to do the same.

In 2001 she spent several months in Kosovo just after the armed conflict ended. After she returned, her husband was unexpectedly hospitalized. He was tired, sick, and months from retirement. He had created a good, comfortable life for them. And he didn't understand why she preferred to work instead of enjoying the benefits of his accomplishments.

They tried counseling, which simply added to her frustration. Neither Rodriguez nor her husband could back down. As a couple, they weren't inching toward compromise. She realized that in order to fulfill her military ambitions—leading a police unit was one of them—she couldn't stay married, at least not to him.

Her second marriage, to Chris, lasted for eight years before his deployments as a military contractor caused too much strain for them both. While she had entered her first marriage with a twenty-four-year-old's naiveté, she entered her second knowing that military separations meant twice as much work when couples reunited. There were no unrealistic expectations. She had married her best friend. And she needed him to get through some of the most difficult times she would encounter.

Their daughter's early life was complicated by hospital visits and surgeries. And during one visit doctors weren't sure the little girl was going to make it. Rodriguez stood in her daughter's hospital room flanked by her husband and mother, waiting for the doctors to return. Her mother began to cry. Rodriguez excused herself and walked slowly out of the room. Her heart was breaking, but standing next to others, the soldier felt stifled. She couldn't express her emotions.

She walked down the hall from her daughter's room and turned the corner. On the wall next to a set of double doors was a small sign: PRAYER ROOM.

Instead of pews, there were rows of small folding chairs. There was a podium near the front, and behind that a large cross. Rodriguez lowered herself to the floor and began to pray. Kneeling in front of the first row of folding chairs, her chin tucked toward her chest, her eyes closed, she asked God to save her child. And in the silence, in the isolation, the tears began to flow. After doctors arrived, Chris found Rodriguez and brought her back to their daughter's room. She leaned on him the entire way.

Chris had served several tours during peacekeeping missions before he left the Army. He tried to stay at home with their daughter while

Rodriguez went back to work. But the stress of being a househusband was, for him, worse than the pressures of being in combat. He felt lost, so he went back to what he knew—serving on the ground with the military. He became a civilian contractor and left Rodriguez with the baby. When he returned to the United States, communication with Rodriguez was strained. She resented his absence, and he didn't know how to explain why he needed to go. Instead of figuring out how to stay, he kept accepting contracts to Iraq. And each time he managed to stay away a bit longer. The last time he came back Rodriguez essentially gave him an ultimatum. She was pregnant with their second child, and she couldn't do it all alone. She also loved him enough to let him go. She wanted him to feel happy, but she was beginning to resent him more for leaving. He decided, for her and his children, to leave contracting behind.

But two days after their son was born, Chris's wanderlust returned. He deployed again, and she filed for divorce. He didn't want to sign the papers, but he did. He signed for her. Because he knew it would make her happy. She could stop feeling angry—and feeling guilty for feeling angry—and he could be in Iraq but still be a part of his kids' lives. They managed to make their unconventional relationship work.

TWO MONTHS AFTER she arrived at Fort Wainwright her commander informed her that she would head the FET program in Afghanistan and that she needed to develop an SOP for female engagement.

By 2010 she had heard of the FET program but had never seen an SOP. She knew that the groups of women had been used to navigate the strict gender roles in Iraq and Afghanistan, but she wasn't sure how to work the other missions she had heard about—economic empowerment for Afghan women, building schools and educational programs for young girls, hygiene and health care for mothers—into the training.

She scribbled three things on a notepad:

- Search and seizure
- Intelligence collection
- Education and economic empowerment

She knew she could train any potential FET volunteers in the basic military police skills.

Intelligence collection, however, was not her area of expertise. The FET women would also need to learn basic Pashtu and Dari to ask simple yet pointed questions and to build trust. After spending time in Kosovo she knew that speaking the local language—or at least making an effort to—showed a level of cultural appreciation that goes a long way. FETs would need to know what types of questions to ask and how to interpret the answers, especially the more complex responses that often come through the filter of an interpreter. What information would be considered an intelligence breakthrough that was worth passing along? What information should be saved and used to inform future missions?

As a military police officer, she was familiar with questioning suspects. But in a region where intelligence collection was vital and failing to report even the smallest bit of information could cost lives, Rodriguez needed help training FET members on observing social changes in Afghan villages and figuring out what those changes could mean and how and when to report them. The FET women also needed to know how to broach Afghan women, talk to them in their homes, build trust, and find out what the women needed and how FETs could provide it for them. All those things went a long way toward getting Afghan women to talk not just about their needs but about what was happening to their sons and the sons of their neighbors, which could be the key to finding out where the Taliban had and hadn't been and the towns and villages where young men were being recruited.

Rodriguez stared at the short list, scrutinizing it for what may have been missing. She thought about who the right people were to provide the language and intelligence training the women of the 1st Stryker Brigade would need to create a stable and effective FET.

Standing next to her window, she felt the crisp Alaska air and missed the warmth that used to spread across her bare arms when she stood close to the windows of her Fresno office. Rodriguez walked the carpet's well-worn path back to her desk, picked up the phone, and dialed the number for a female intelligence officer she knew in a building across the base. The goal, she explained to the intelligence officer who had served in the Gulf War, was to formalize an SOP, to create a concrete set of procedures that any woman, no matter where she was stationed in the United States or headed to in the Middle East, could use. It needed to be thorough enough to lay out every single aspect of the FET mission but open enough for flexibility so that women could adjust procedures based on the needs of local females. Ten minutes later the intelligence officer and Rodriguez were sitting across from one another in the major's office, brainstorming how they would write what turned out to be a one-hundred-page document they hoped would set the standard for American FET unit training.

Rodriguez would concentrate on the first section of the SOP. She would describe, in detail, how to search a suspect, lay out instructions on bagging and tagging evidence, and include a list of equipment that military police officers and, therefore, FET members had to carry with them at all times—including plastic gloves and metal and plastic handcuffs—in case they encountered a suspect during a routine patrol or a scouting mission in a new village—moments when they may unexpectedly come in contact with Taliban members, cells, or families. She would also write a list of basic questions that women should ask each suspect they encountered and ways to explain to Afghan women that their children also had to be searched. Approaching a child the wrong way or without first informing their mothers of what was about to happen could cause tensions that might hinder relationship building, harm future intelligence collection missions, and hamper a subsequent FET's ability to get to know these Afghan women well enough to find out about the violence in their homes and their villages—a critical tool in rooting out possible insurgent targets and locations.

It would be up to the intelligence officer to write the second part of the SOP, which would cover intelligence collection—how to recognize atmospherics worth noting, how to approach women in their homes, how to talk to men in area villages without offending them and in ways that could lead to more information. They would both work on finding someone for the third part—a primer in Pashtu and Dari phrases and other very rudimentary aspects of the language such as the alphabet and the ability to recognize and read street signs.

The intelligence officer also decided that her section should include detailed instructions on how to speak to Afghan women—but for different purposes. American FETs needed to gain a basic understanding of what normal life was like in each village so they could learn to recognize significant changes and figure out what those changes may mean. For example, if women were seen selling goods in local markets or opening and owning stalls in village stores after having been forced to stay in their homes for years, that could be a sign that the Taliban's grip in that community was waning or that the American military had successfully forced insurgents out. In the villages where shops owned by women were disappearing, the opposite could be happening.

The FET members also had to learn how to talk to Afghan women in a way that was culturally sensitive so they would feel comfortable opening up about the work opportunities for the older male children, how frequently and where their husbands worked, and which children in the village had gone missing and how old they were. They had to learn to write reports that included the most vital information that should be passed along to the head of their intelligence units so they could be included in and analyzed with larger intelligence reports.

FET members also wanted to provide Afghan women with a means of making a living, something that many, depending on their age, had never thought possible. It was illegal in some villages for a woman to step out of her home, let alone develop the skills needed to hold down a job. Rodriguez recounted stories of widows begging on the street for money to buy food, unable to work after their husbands had died and only able to leave their homes with their youngest sons by their side. They decided to include illustrations and sample documents in the manual where they would be most helpful. The intelligence officer knew of an Army linguist who was a teaching assistant at the Defense

Language Institute. They would call on her to develop the last portion of the SOP. The women had two weeks to pull the training manual together.

A month later, just before California desert training—a must before deployment to Afghanistan—Rodriguez found herself speaking in front of a room full of female soldiers. The women had been called to the auditorium for a mandatory meeting near the end of their workdays.

As Rodriguez walked the dark corridor that led to the hundred-seat multipurpose room, the hum of conversations grew louder, and she tried to guess how many women had shown up for the FET meeting. Each woman on the base had received an email about the effort and was encouraged by her command to attend. Every woman on the base needed to be familiar with the FET program and be prepared to serve. The small teams usually consisted of three to four volunteers, but Rodriguez's plan was to train as many women as she could and then narrow the core team down to the ones who picked up the skills the fastest.

The major approached the front of the hall, and pockets of conversations began to fade between calls of "shush" echoing from the audience. She stood beside a small folding table she had set up the day before that was covered with pamphlets detailing the FET responsibilities she hoped women in the room would be eager to learn.

"Hello, everyone," Rodriguez began. The few remaining conversations in the room faded.

"I'm Major Rodriguez. How many of you have heard of the FET? Please raise your hands."

A good number of women raised their hands, but some of the nearly one hundred women who filled the space looked around with blank stares.

"Not everyone will be leaving on deployment in April, but we'll need some volunteers to be a part of the female engagement team that's needed to accompany the men on combat missions."

The din that had quieted down so quickly began again. Knowing that some of the women had just come back from deployments,

Sergeant Alice Dunne, a Marine Lioness, heads to Camp Korean Village, Iraq, from Al Asad for a thirty-day rotation on the team that was created to circumvent cultural barriers and work with Iraqi women. The Army originated female engagement through its Lioness teams in 2003. Before then the military either didn't search Iraqi and Afghan women or used men, which risked turning some villages against the US military. (Department of Defense; photo by Staff Sergeant Raymie Cruz)

The original Lioness teams went without combat training on frontline missions with infantry units. Eventually training was incorporated into preparation for placement on a Lioness team. Here Marine Corporal Samantha Garza trains with Sergeant Nicholas Meche during instruction on various weapons, including the M240G medium machine gun and an AK-47. (US Marine Corps; photo by Corporal Jessica Aranda)

Lioness members, from right, Marine Corporal Rachelle J. Fernandez, Lance Corporal Holly M. Burd, and Sergeant Leticia L. Eslinger during a civil affairs mission in Rutbah, Iraq, in 2009. Six years after female engagement began in Iraq, the goals and tactics remained the same: accompany men on raids, conduct searches, and learn more about insurgents by talking to the female population. (Department of Defense; photo by Corporal Melissa Attlee)

Marine Corporal Nicole K. Estrada was in Rutbah, Iraq, supporting India Battery, 3rd Battalion, 11th Marine Regiment. When she searched women she looked for weapons, large amounts of money, or suicide vests. (US Marine Corps; photo by Corporal Cindy Alejandrez)

Marine Sergeant Sheena Adams led a female engagement team throughout Helmand Province in Afghanistan in 2010. Part of her team's role, like
many FETs in the Middle East, was to patrol bazaars with combat units.
(Photo by Paula Bronstein/Getty Images)

From left, Adams, FET leader, and her team, Lance Corporal Kristi Baker
and Hospital Corpsman Shannon Crowley, were attached to the 1st Battalion, 8th Marines. Adams sometimes allowed the women on her team to
lead missions, prompting one, Adams said, to leave a message on Adams's
wall: "Dear Sgt. Adams, We're glad to be on your team! You motivate me.
Kristi." (Photo by Paula Bronstein/Getty Images)

Adams found working with children in Afghanistan to be one of the most fulfilling parts of the FET mission. Here she greets a group of children outside the FOB in Helmand Province. This photo was one of many illustrating the work of engagement teams that hung in the home of former vice president Joe and former second lady Jill Biden. (Photo by Paula Bronstein/Getty Images)

Abdul and Adams connected almost immediately. She often joked with his father, an elder in a village near FOB Shir Ghazay, that she wanted to adopt him. (Courtesy Sheena Adams)

In Musa Qal'ah, Afghanistan, Adams stops to draw a happy face inside a boy's hand. He had his eye on her gum and reached inside her pouch to grab it. (Photo by Paula Bronstein/Getty Images)

Adams tries to show a few young girls how to write Pashtu as she hands out school supplies in a village near FOB Shir Ghazay in Helmand Province. The girls were sitting just outside a compound owned by the village elder. Girls in rural villages in Afghanistan were sometimes punished if they attended school. (Photo by Rita Leistner/Basetrack/courtesy of Stephen Bulger Gallery)

Army Major Maria Rodriguez, third from left, trained Afghan women in Zabul Province who were among the first members of the Afghan Female Police. When Rodriguez, who was also a military police officer in charge of force protection for the 1st Stryker Brigade Combat Team, arrived in Afghanistan, there were only about six women left on the force. The majority had quit after death threats from the surrounding community and insurgent forces. In 2011 in Zabul Province women were prohibited from working. (Department of Defense; photo by Private First Class Andreka Johnson)

ABOVE: By the time Army Captain Johanna Smoke, center, and her translator, Edna Sahdo, left, arrived in Zabul Province in 2013, they had to redo some of the work that earlier FET leaders such as Rodriguez had accomplished. Smoke had to train a new set of Afghan Female Police. She worked to rebuild a local women's center, which was supposed to be funded by the government. She also participated in government meetings. Smoke was assigned to the 3rd Brigade Combat Team, 1st Infantry Division. (Courtesy Johanna Smoke)

A member of Smoke's FET holds a baby before the child's medical examination. Some mothers outlined their children's eyes with a combination of soot and oil, thinking it would protect the children from evil spirits. (Courtesy Johanna Smoke)

ABOVE: Army Major Shayna Thompson works with another member of Smoke's FET to prepare a baby in Tarnak Wa Jaldak District for an examination. (Courtesy Johanna Smoke)

OPPOSITE: Thompson treats a little girl during a shura, or meeting, in the Tarnak Wa Jaldak District of Zabul Province in Afghanistan. During one women's shura, Smoke tried to accomplish multiple missions—medical treatment for women and children, voter registration, and intelligence gathering. Thompson was part of Smoke's medical team. (Courtesy Johanna Smoke)

Smoke listens to see if a baby is still alive. Some mothers sedate their children with opium to keep them quiet. Others use opium because they have too many children to keep up with—the drug becomes a babysitter, Smoke said. This baby's breathing was incredibly shallow. (Courtesy Johanna Smoke)

This young girl attended a shura in the rural outskirts of Zabul Province with her mother. She reminded Smoke of the age when innocence is lost for many young girls in rural areas of Afghanistan. Smoke thought the girl was around twelve years old, an age at which many girls in Afghanistan's southern provinces are married and begin having children. (Courtesy Johanna Smoke)

ABOVE: Sometimes the most important thing a FET leader can do when Afghan women are registering to vote—a dangerous pursuit that can attract Taliban attention—is keep the children occupied. Smoke found creative ways to do that, including a game of duck, duck, goose. (Courtesy Johanna Smoke)

BELOW RIGHT: Smoke hands out food and supplies to women and children in Zabul Province. She served as a FET leader for nearly a year in some of the poorest and most desolate areas of Afghanistan. One of the toughest parts of her job, she said, was keeping the members of her team motivated on tough days. (Courtesy Johanna Smoke)

LEFT: The FETs often held female-only shuras, during which women could flip back their burqas—as long as there were no men present, Afghan women didn't have to worry about being fully covered. Here an older woman gets an exam from Thompson. (Courtesy Johanna Smoke)

ABOVE: Women gather at a center in Qalat City with their children. The women's center not only was a hub for classes and meetings but also helped women escape abusive and neglectful relationships and helped girls escape child marriages. The word spread quickly among women about the center's ability to help. It took men longer to figure out what its feminist leader was doing, and the Taliban even longer. (Courtesy Johanna Smoke)

BELOW: Zabul Province's women's center, funded by the government, held classes in sewing, gardening, and literacy, shown here. Jamila Abbas ran the center, and Smoke helped her rebuild it after terrorists bombed it. (Courtesy Johanna Smoke)

ABOVE: Two women proudly show that they registered to vote during a shura in Tarnak Wa Jaldak. (Courtesy Johanna Smoke)

A member of Smoke's team on guard during a mission in Tarnak Wa Jaldak, one of the poorer areas of Zabul Province, Afghanistan. (Courtesy Johanna Smoke)

Smoke directs her FET members and two members of the Afghan Female Police just before a shura in Tarnak Wa Jaldak. (Courtesy Johanna Smoke)

A helicopter takes off after dropping Smoke off for a combat mission in the Arghandab District of Kandahar Province. (Courtesy Johanna Smoke)

Smoke and a member of her FET have a bit of fun as they ride through the streets of Qalat City in Zabul Province, Afghanistan, where they worked on repairing the Bibi Khala School for girls. (Courtesy Johanna Smoke)

One of Smoke's "guardian angels." Smoke often set aside her weapon and gear when around large groups of Afghan women. Her goal was to show the women that they were safe. Smoke's "guardian angels" were always armed and stood guard beside the soldier, stopping anyone who looked suspicious. (Courtesy Johanna Smoke)

A moment of reflection in Tarnak Wa Jaldak. (Courtesy Johanna Smoke)

Members of Smoke's FET return to the FOB after a combat mission. (Courtesy Johanna Smoke)

During a mission in the remote area of Kandahar Province's Arghandab District, Army captain and FET leader Smoke snapped this photo showing one of the infantrymen in her unit. Smoke conducted female shuras with her FET but was often the only female present during all-male shuras. The Army used Smoke to show Afghan men that their wives, sisters, and daughters could serve equally well on security forces. (Courtesy Johanna Smoke)

Smoke needed the help of male soldiers to complete some missions. At left a group of unit engineers helps Smoke's FET make repairs to a local girls' school, Bibi Khala, in Qalat City. The school, built in 2009, was once touted as the most advanced in the region. By the time Smoke arrived in 2013 it had fallen into disrepair—the electricity only worked three hours a day, the computers were outdated, and the students had no paper. (Courtesy Johanna Smoke)

LEFT: Army Staff Sergeant Starla Hawkins provided protection for Smoke during many missions. Here Hawkins holds her weapon as the team rides through Tarnak Wa Jaldak, where FET members provided medical services and helped a local feminist to register women to vote, in defiance of Taliban threats. (Courtesy Johanna Smoke)

The bracelets, Marine Sergeant Sheena Adams explained, were her way of telling close friends that they could make it through anything they encountered in Afghanistan, just as she had. They were woven from the same cords found in parachutes. Passing them along was a tradition that Adams's commander had handed down to her. After Adams returned to Camp Pendleton from combat and started training women to be FET members, she continued the tradition. The Marines aren't to remove the bracelets until they make it home from combat. (Department of Defense; photo by Corporal Joshua Young)

In May 2012 Adams was named the Marine of the Year at the USO's annual Women of the Year Luncheon. To Adams's right during the medal ceremony, which took place in New York, was Army General Ann E. Dunwoody, the first female four-star general in the US armed forces. Dunwoody retired three months after this picture was taken. (Stuart Ramson, USO)

Army Captain Johanna Smoke, who led a FET while assigned to the 3rd Brigade Combat Team, 1st Infantry Division, receives a medal for her service in Zabul Province, Afghanistan, during a ceremony on FOB Apache. (Courtesy Johanna Smoke)

Rodriguez had expected the FET mission to be a hard sell. She was also aware that she was asking women to do work above and beyond their normal jobs. Women who were cooks, for example, would still need to be cooks in addition to putting their lives in danger during raids in ways they never had before.

"Wait," Rodriguez recalled one woman saying, "I just got back from Afghanistan less than a year ago with another unit. You're asking me to go again?"

Other women spoke up from the crowd with similar concerns: "I can't leave my kids again for something that's volunteer" and "What exactly would we be doing?"

"I know. I know," Rodriguez cut in, raising her hands to quiet the room. "I know that some of you have just come back from deployments, that volunteering is a lot to ask many of you who have children. But this mission is a chance to do something incredibly meaningful for the women of Afghanistan and to have a direct impact on the work that intelligence and combat units are doing."

"How long would we be gone for?" another woman asked.

"How much danger is involved?" Rodriguez heard from someone else.

"The mission would last for the entire deployment," Rodriguez explained. "You would be searching Afghan women because the men can't do that job. You may also be tasked with collecting intelligence information from women and observing villages. You'll also be participating in infantry maneuvers, so there will be, as in any combat situation, a certain amount of danger."

The room fell silent.

"Does anyone, based on what they know now, want to volunteer?"

Rodriguez saw only a few hands slowly rise.

"If more don't volunteer, people will be selected. Training begins for everyone tomorrow. Please pick up a pamphlet that details FET duties and responsibilities on your way out."

Rodriguez selected three women to be a part of the brigade FET (which she would lead) after the two-week training session. Twenty-one other female soldies were selected to be FETs in their respective battalions. The other women who deployed also had basic FET skills and would be used as alternates.

STANDING IN THE desert sun on FOB Lagman, Rodriguez again looked at her watch.

11:45 A.M.

The convoy still hadn't shown. She would give it another fifteen minutes. At noon she had to inspect the kennels. She also had to walk over to the holding cells to check on some of the suspects who had been brought in several days ago. The heart of her day had to begin.

The sun beating down on her reminded her of the heat she experienced during combat training in the Mojave Desert—nearly a month of work for the 1st Stryker Brigade Combat Team, intended to make them mission ready just before deployment to Afghanistan. She should have known that completing the FET task on FOB Lagman would be tough. Her team had been completely ignored during training in California.

The 1st Stryker Brigade's officers had been on the base—which looked in every respect like the streets of Afghanistan, complete with dirt roads, underdeveloped downtown markets, and cave-like dwellings inside compounds—for about a month when Rodriguez's FET women arrived in May 2011. The officers landed early to oversee the setup of communications tents, offices, living quarters, and planning and strategy. Rodriguez was ready to incorporate FET training into the combat simulation. She wanted the women on her team to train with real combat soldiers—a step beyond the rudimentary drills she had put them through in Alaska—before they were confronted in combat with real Taliban suspects.

In an early-morning planning meeting for the unit's first simulated mission, officers discussed the training scenario: the invasion of a suspected Taliban stronghold. They had decided to put up small concrete blockades along the road to recreate difficult desert drives and unpredictable Afghan terrain. They mapped out how the soldiers would approach and surround the building and who would enter first. As provost marshal, Rodriguez decided that her military police would use three K9s on the mission. All the officers in the climate-controlled tent collectively agreed to remind soldiers that communication—silent effective communication—was a must.

"And what about the FET?" Rodriguez asked. "Where do they fit into all of this?"

The tent fell silent. Rodriguez looked around the room. No one had considered that FET members needed the same level of training as the male soldiers they would be assisting.

She was told that women weren't serving in primary combat roles. "We'll get to the needs of your FET females later," one of the officers in charge of mission training stated. As much as Rodriguez pushed, later never came. Her FET entered Afghanistan with nothing close to real-world training.

Waiting for that convoy, Rodriguez was again waging a battle against her military superiors. It was, in many ways, more nefarious than the one she was waging against groups outside of the FOB. She was confronting a world that appeared to be working toward female equality but was instead setting up logistical roadblocks. Greater vehicle support alone would not be enough to bring Rodriguez and other FET women the recognition they deserved. Battlefield equality would only be achieved with the erasure of the military's male-dominated culture. It was a culture that had, in its early years, denied women the opportunity to work as radio operators, intelligence collectors, and mechanical engineers. It had delayed weapons training for women who went to Vietnam and denied certain promotions until President Lyndon Johnson signed a law requiring opportunities for advancement in 1967. It is a culture in which sexual trauma is one of the leading causes of PTSD for women. It's a culture that in 2010 prevented, through intimidation, 86 percent of females who were assaulted from reporting the crime. And it is a culture that denied Rodriguez some of the support she needed for her FET to follow through on its full mission in Afghanistan.

Giving Rodriguez more support would have given her team more freedom to talk to Afghan mothers and girls. And more than that, it would have given her FET members greater input in military strategy.

At every turn Rodriguez has been reminded of just how difficult change was.

She looked down at her watch again.

Noon.

She glanced through the fence one last time.

No convoy.

She would begin the routine again the next day. And the next morning, like so many others to come, Rodriguez would stand for hours, waiting for a Stryker that never showed.

CHAPTER 10

BREAKTHROUGH

ZABUL PROVINCE, AFGHANISTAN, AUGUST 2011—Maria Rodriguez's smartphone beeped and then vibrated. The soldier to her right turned her head sharply and looked down at the major's cargo pocket. The phone did it again: *Ping! Buzzz! Bzzz! Buzzzzzz!* The major's cell phone was the only thing that had made a sound in the room for the fifteen minutes since the four FET women had taken a seat.

The female members of the Afghan Police Force were on the other side of the room in their burqas—some colorful, others black—sitting in two neat rows of three each, waiting for something to be said.

A FET member cleared her throat, turned to the translator, and instructed her to ask, "Are you happy with the work you are doing? Would you be open to more training?"

Rodriguez leaned slightly forward in her seat.

The entire FET turned from the translator to look at Bibi, who was sitting in the middle of the first row.

The American soldiers had been introduced to Bibi and the other five women who worked in the small office. Rodriguez tried asking the first questions of the day:

"How are you?"

"How has your week been?"

"How has the police work been going?"

She spoke before anyone sat down, thinking the innocent inquiries could, unlike the last visit, help the women open up. They didn't. It was hard to find safe questions to ask of women who lived in a world that teetered between war and shattered hopes for progress—to be able to work without threat, walk down the street without being watched, and vote without fear.

The women had already brought small changes to their eight-by-ten world. For some, the space was a safe haven from abuse. Others had outsmarted their husbands to escape their villages despite declining infrastructures, which had worsened under the Taliban and made it nearly impossible for men to leave communities and find and keep work. The major was trying hard not to rock the comparatively safe domain the women had created for themselves.

Rodriguez could have guessed the answers to her questions. They had likely done no police work that week. In fact, they hadn't done much of any since they had come to Zabul. She knew this because she had inquired with the provincial governor about the duties and responsibilities of the Afghan female police.

If Rodriguez had visited police stations in Afghanistan just two generations earlier, she would have likely encountered very different women—ones who were more independent, who were being treated as equals, and who had been given proper training and full police responsibilities.

The first woman to become a police officer in Afghanistan joined the force in 1967. And women continued to openly serve on police forces until the 1980s, when political conflicts had changed not just the ruling party in Afghanistan but also the treatment of women in urban areas where they held down jobs and had dressed, voted, and lived very much like their Western female counterparts.

Today poor training isn't isolated just to policewomen. Until 2010 men on the Afghan National Police (ANP) force also received little to no training, according to a 2013 Oxfam report. A large percentage of male officers were recruited and assigned to a police station with the promise that training would come later. Unfortunately, later for a good deal of these men never came.

But lack of police knowledge didn't keep male officers off the streets. The general "recruit, assign, train later" approach, used not just by the Afghan government but also by international forces working with them, led to gruff relationships between communities and the officers who were supposed to protect them. In 2010, 2,777 civilians were killed in Afghanistan. That number surpassed the civilian death toll of any year since the war had started. And 10 percent of those deaths were at the hands of Afghan security forces.

In some villages police used their status to intimidate and control the local population and were described as "another gang." Men who were considered members of Taliban extremist groups one day became members of the Afghan Local Police (ALP), a subset of the ANP, the next, giving legitimacy to extremism, terror, and control. Local police factions sometimes recruited and then abused children from their communities.

By 2005 US forces took the lead in training Afghan policemen—and had provided billions to the Afghan Security Forces Fund. The goal was to prepare Afghan forces to take over once American troops withdrew. And although strategic and tactical training improved by 2010, the year that training became mandatory, skills needed to develop community policing largely hadn't. The majority of the eight-week officer training course for the ANP was devoted to weapons training and other combat aspects of security; very little time was spent teaching productive ways of communicating with the public. The training course for the ALP was even shorter.

But when it comes to getting and holding down jobs, any jobs, in Afghanistan, men are given priority over women. And as difficult as it's been for the country to get male police officers properly trained, the difficulty in getting female police officers trained and recruited has been even greater—and institutional discrimination has been one of the tools used to keep women out. Low literacy rates, for example, are a problem throughout Afghanistan—only about 31 percent of adults can read. That rate is even lower for women, with an average of about 17 percent. Yet literacy requirements are more stringent for female police recruits than for males. And while *rumors* of sexual misconduct forced women on the Zabul police force who trained with Bibi to quit, assault at the hands of male police officers in other provinces throughout Afghanistan went beyond rumor and became all too real. Anecdotes of women being sexually abused were present in many northern provinces when the female police force was initially revamped in the early 2000s, according to Oxfam worker Klijn's report "Women and the Afghan Police: Why a Law Enforcement Agency That Respects and Protects Females Is Crucial for Progress."

And the mechanism for reporting sexual misconduct in some provinces at that time was nonexistent. In other provinces it simply failed. Women can only make complaints to other women. So in provinces such as Panj Sher and Nuristan, where there were no female police officers two years after Bibi had been recruited in Zabul, women in abusive relationships or who had been raped had no recourse or concept that laws existed that could have helped save their lives.

The American military was making great efforts to improve the skills of male police recruits, but it was women like Rodriguez who took it upon themselves to ensure that their American FETs were making equal efforts to train Afghan women. Those women would be needed to continue the vital work that female soldiers provided to push back the Taliban. Female police officers would be needed for night raids, to inspect other Afghan women in suspected Taliban safe houses who may have held evidence of future terror attacks, and for ensuring that male insurgents, who often tried to disguise themselves as women in an effort to avoid being inspected at checkpoints, were caught.

Rodriguez knew the history of female police in Afghanistan.

Each time she walked into that room their struggles fueled her determination to return female forces to the accomplished units they once were.

This time, when she was greeted by the stiff grip of Bibi's handshake, the Afghan woman turned to the translator and threw out a few words: "You ask how it's been. It's been normal. The same way it's always been."

Now seated, the American soldiers and Afghan female police officers faced one another as if on opposite sides of a scrum.

Rodriguez stared intensely at Bibi. The soldier leaned forward slightly in her chair, extremely anxious to find out the woman's answer to whether her group would be open to more training.

Bibi stared back and said nothing.

A buzz and din from Rodriguez's right cargo pocket echoed again through the room.

The soldier to Rodriguez's right scooted her chair forward and shifted her body weight to give her right hip a break.

A few minutes later the translator crossed and uncrossed her legs.

They all sat in uncomfortable silence.

Rodriguez glanced toward the covered window and asked, "Do you ever open the curtains?"

"No."

Rodriguez glanced at her watch and saw that nearly an hour had gone by since they had entered the room.

She turned to her team of women, pointed at her watch, and nodded toward the door.

Rodriguez stood, and her team followed.

The FET walked down the long stairwell from the second floor to the first in silence. They exited the building and quickly switched their head coverings for the Army-issue caps required outdoors.

After several minutes of standing on the dirt-covered walkway, one of Rodriguez's soldiers broke the silence. She wondered out loud about the purpose of the meetings and whether the women actually wanted to be helped. She wondered if the FET's time on Sundays wouldn't be better spent helping other women in Afghanistan whose circumstances were much worse.

Despite the barrage of questions that followed from her team, Rodriguez never doubted her plan.

She remembered when she stood just a few feet away and had a similar conversation with Thacker—only the roles were reversed. That day, as she followed the commander on the dirt path to his office building, Thacker took on the role of patient listener. Rodriguez pressed him about bringing up the condition of Afghan female police officers with the provincial governor and Afghan security force leaders. She had sat through several meetings with Thacker and the provincial leader but still had no idea where the women were and what they needed. He gave her the best advice she would ever receive in Afghanistan.

"Change," he said, "takes time." The best weapon in winning the political and cultural war, she remembered him explaining, would be patience.

The lieutenant colonel's words echoed through her mind as she told her team to hang in there. She reassured them that the Afghan women would eventually open up. She told them that the two groups would find a way to connect. "Things take time," she heard herself saying.

"The key here," she added, "is patience."

As darkness fell over the desert horizon Rodriguez returned to the FOB. The sun had almost completely faded when she looked over her shoulder and saw, in the distance, near the edge of the FOB, beyond the makeshift playing fields and beside one of the watchtowers, the sand's orange reflection. Looking at it every night gave her some sense of stability. No matter what may have happened on any given day, that glow was always there.

Later that night she reached into her pocket and took out a photo of her kids—torn along the edges, slightly creased in the middle. That photo had been with her through multiple deployments. Her daughter will always look to her the way she did in that picture: five years old, with wild, tossed black curls and a wide smile. Her little boy was three, his straight hair sticking to his forehead.

As she emptied her pockets she wondered what she and her FET would talk about the following Sunday with the Afghan women. The hours of silence in that office—small, hot, sticky—may soon take a toll on her team's confidence, morale, and desire to help build the police force.

Before she went to sleep Rodriguez pulled a thin blanket up to her waist and tried, as she did every night, to put the worst parts of the day behind her. Learn from each day's struggles and begin anew. The next morning she would rise early to try again. But for right now it was lights out.

THE AFGHAN WOMEN had grown used to American military women coming to see them. Bibi had helped the five other women on her team arrange the few chairs in the room. They lined them as neatly as possible—not to encourage conversation, but not to discourage it.

So she sat, just as she had during the last three Sunday meetings, in a wooden chair at the center of the first row. Her arms were crossed in her lap. She sat in front of the woman she had been told to call Rodriguez.

Bibi watched the major look around the room. To the major's right, the soldier who had asked a question the last time was saying something to the translator. The Afghan translator turned to her fellow countrywomen and asked, "Do you have children?"

This seemed to be the first question that sparked a genuine interest in Bibi. She quickly looked up and shifted her gaze between Rodriguez and her colleagues. The major saw, for the first time in Bibi's eyes, what she could only interpret as a smile. The very tops of her cheeks appeared to plump, forcing her lids to close slightly. She stood, reached under her burqa and into her pocket: *"Yes! I have two. A boy and a girl."*

She pulled out a photo of her kids—smiling, standing side by side, each in bright blue, red, and gold outfits. They squinted as they looked up at the camera, standing in front of what looked like a small, brown cave. The photo's edges were fraying, its center slightly creased. The girl looked as if she was six, the boy four.

"I do too! I have a boy too. And a girl," Rodriguez said as she reached into her right cargo pocket.

She felt the tattered edges of her photo slip through her right fingertips as she handed it to Bibi, who looked down at the small photograph and chuckled. She pointed out how similar their children were in age and size and appearance. Rodriguez thought the same as she felt the crease of Bibi's photo and its soft edges. Other women on both sides reached into their pockets for pictures of their sons and daughters. Soon they had abandoned their cold chairs for what had become shared neutral territory in the office's empty center.

She could tell that some of the Afghan women, just like herself, had been away from their kids for some time. Each small rip in the photographs told a story of regret—of the times when decisions to fight or run meant tracing the outlines of smiles on paper instead of touching flesh and bone. They were brought together not just by the fact that they had children but because they knew the pain caused by not being around them.

They talked about morning routines that used to be filled with cooking breakfast for their kids and evening routines of cooking their mothers' dinner recipes for their families.

After a pause in the chatter Rodriguez shared a traditional Spanish recipe.

The rice, she said—looking at her translator—should be cooked just under done. It should be yellow rice. Then you add meat—Rodriguez cupped her hands in front of her, moving them from left to right as if placing chicken and sausage into a frying pan.

Bibi listened and soaked in every step, motioning with Rodriguez. She shook her head in understanding as the interpreter described adding the peas and corn. Bibi's eyes grew with a tinge of familiarity. She clapped her hands in recognition.

The dish was very similar to one many considered the national dish of Afghanistan, Bibi explained. It was called *Kabuli pilau*, she continued, which included rice, lamb, and vegetables, all in one pot.

All the women smiled, and Rodriguez felt comfortable enough to circle back to one of the first questions she ever asked.

"What is it that your group of women wants? What do you need?"

Bibi, who had just stopped talking, looked at Rodriguez. *"We want to work,"* Bibi said through the translator. *"We are here. We've risked our lives to be here. We've left our children. We want to be able to be police officers. We need uniforms."*

Rodriguez reached out to Bibi and gently touched her forearm.

"We'll do the best we can to help you," Rodriguez said, just before she rose to leave.

Bibi, now filled with hope, sped ahead of the major to open the door for her and her team. This time she was the first to extend her hand. She looked Rodriguez straight in the eye and said, in broken English, "Thank you."

On this day Bibi was not happy to see the FET women go. She feared that her tight-knit team of women, who had already started restoring the small wooden chairs to the far corners of the room to sweep and mop the floors, would go back to being ignored, hidden. Bibi locked the door behind Rodriguez and walked back to her desk, where she began shuffling through paperwork.

FOB LAGMAN, I A.M.—Rodriguez sat at her desk and flipped on her computer.

She waited a few minutes for her children and ex-husband to pick up the Skype call in California, where it was 1:30 P.M.

The internet access on the FOB was unreliable. Her children waved and yelled, "Hiii!" Their voices sounded slightly tinny, like they were in a tunnel. Their small hands moved in stops and starts, the bad connection slowing down the image, as they moved them in midair.

Her daughter spoke first.

"When are you coming home? What are you doing?"

She could feel how much her daughter missed her, and she wanted to hug her.

Tears rolled down her face when she answered her daughter's questions. Her son waited for his turn to speak, looking at his sister attentively, knowing he had to be patient. He was young and learning about patience. His sister was, in her own way, teaching him quickly.

He decided to help his sister's line of interrogation: "Are you in Monterey?"

He looked up at the world map that covered nearly an entire wall in the den, just above the computer. He pointed to the thumbtack that marked California and the other that marked Afghanistan.

"Mommy, they aren't that far apart," he declared, unable to calculate miles or conceive that distances beyond what he could see with his eyes actually existed.

She reached out and touched the screen as he devised a plan to get in the car and drive to her. Chris sat in the background, his image a bit smaller than theirs.

"Well, I'm a little bit further than Monterey," she said.

Chris spoke softly, breaking the awkward silence, telling her it's okay. And he reassured the kids as they looked back, asking what was wrong.

"Everything is okay," he said once again. His voice was soothing. He saw his job as one of sounding board and encourager. He was there to nudge when needed, which was often.

The children started getting antsy. Her son was grabbing his feet. Her daughter allowed her mind to wander. She looked away from the screen to a picture on the wall behind her. They were done. They waved good-bye and ran off to play. It was only 1:45 P.M. in California.

She watched their little bodies leave the room. As soon as they were out of earshot, Rodriguez's tears really started to flow: uncontrollable sobs that made it hard for her to speak or breathe.

Chris moved closer to the screen. He waited for her to speak, wanting to do his best to prop up her wartime efforts. He'd been through three tours in Iraq. He knew what it felt like at the end of the day to want to cry. He didn't. Rodriguez communicated better. She shared her fears and concerns and ugly cries freely with him—the one person around whom she could be completely herself. He admired her ability to be strong and soft at the same time.

The week had been an especially tough one.

Two Special Forces soldiers tried to force their way into her detention facility, Rodriguez explained. As she spoke to Chris, her chest was still heaving, but she could just manage to get the words out through her tears.

They threatened her and the noncommissioned officer (NCO) on her team—the woman in charge of running the day-to-day operations of Lagman's detention facility, which had three small cells, each holding one detainee, and a small front office.

When the women weren't performing FET duties, protecting detainees was one of their main concerns. And after prisoner abuse and torture of detainees at Abu Ghraib, detention facilities all over the world were under extra scrutiny. If a detainee had a scratch that wasn't documented and treated immediately, Rodriguez had to answer for it.

No one could interrogate anyone in their facility without the proper paperwork, which the Special Forces soldiers did not have.

The two men, both over six feet tall and a couple hundred pounds, had towered over Rodriguez's five-foot frame, she explained to Chris. After their divorce he was still her best friend. Remembering the incident, the tears were still flowing.

They threatened to kick down the gate and grab the detainees if the women didn't unlock the facility. Rodriguez glanced at the M9 pistols on their hips and felt for hers for reassurance. Without blinking she stood her ground against the two men, all the while not feeling nearly as confident as she was projecting. She was terrified. *They could break me*, she thought as she barked back at them, *like a twig*. She sent her NCO to get the brigade executive officer.

"If you try to break into the facility, we have the authority to shoot," she told the men. "No one is authorized to walk into this facility and do anything to these detainees without the proper paperwork."

"Do you think you're going to stop me?" one of the men said as he walked closer to Rodriguez. "You're not going to stop me."

The brigade officer turned the corner and walked toward the facility. The men left almost immediately.

She stood strong and never let tears show during her workday. Do that, and the military will eat you alive. But at the end of her day Chris was her comfort.

"Stop," Chris said. "Dry your tears."

She wiped her face.

"You are the tallest five-foot-tall woman I know," he said. "I'm scared of you. Everything you're doing, you're doing right. Don't let them change you. You're one of the strongest women I know. I would follow you into war any day."

She smiled. The tears began to subside.

Chris's smile slowly faded. "You really are great," he added. "The kids are lucky to have you as a mother. The Army is lucky to have you as a leader. I was lucky to have you as my wife."

She took a deep breath. He always said exactly what she needed to hear.

CHAPTER 11

THE AFGHANS, THE ROMANIANS, AND THE AMERICANS

The three groups of women stood in front of the provincial governor's headquarters watching Rodriguez. The major's boots wore a light path in the slightly ruddy sand as she paced the small portion of grounds they occupied. She walked slowly to ensure that each woman could clearly see what she was doing.

Burqas fluttered to the major's left as the six members of the Afghan Female Police (AFP) tried to keep up with the demonstration—a lesson on FET tactics. Although they were anxious to learn, many of these women had no formal education; others had left school when they were eleven or twelve to get married and hadn't been in a classroom in years. Rodriguez kept that in mind, thought quickly as she spoke, and tailored the lesson accordingly, closely watching the reactions of Bibi and the others on the AFP team. Although there were two other groups of women there and the major considered the session a joint training exercise, it was the AFP that Rodriguez had to be sure she reached.

As she walked to her right, Rodriguez passed the American FET and approached the Romanians, women who were members of a much more progressive military than the US Army had ever been, one that, as far as she could tell, viewed females as combat soldiers equal to their male counterparts. The joint training exercise was the first the major had conducted. She kept her FET in the middle of the two groups; she wanted them to be ready to jump in and help whichever side needed it the most.

Rodriguez rummaged through one of her cargo pockets as she explained: "Before searching any individual, including children, properly fitted gloves are vital." The latex glove made a snapping sound as she pulled it over the palm of her hand. "Make sure," she continued, "to pull each glove over your wrist and onto the outside of your uniform. Don't tuck the glove inside your uniform." She called a member of her FET out of the group. The woman stood in front of Rodriguez and held her arms straight out to the side. Rodriguez quickly demonstrated the proper way to pat down an adult woman. She told the women to ensure that they felt along the waist, under bra straps at the collar bone, and down each leg. "Make sure to explain each step of the process before you begin," Rodriguez said. "These things sound simple, but doing them incorrectly could ruin relationships with the very women we're trying to save."

The trainees partnered up, practicing the tactical strategy on one another, each woman pulling out a pair of gloves as she explained the pat-down procedure to her partner.

Rodriguez stood and watched, her back to the provincial governor's headquarters.

It also wasn't lost on Rodriguez that as she was training the Romanians—a group of women who had full combat equality—she was probably showing them a lot of what they already knew. But Rodriguez regularly consulted with and for the soldiers, who were also stationed at FOB Lagman. That was reason enough for the Romanian unit to participate: they were examples for Afghan women of how far progress for their gender could go as well as inspiration for American women that combat equality was possible. The first time she met them, she was impressed, to say the least.

About a month into her mission she walked into their section of the FOB and found a group of women who regularly left the base without the aid of men. They quickly set and carried out their own missions.

Their male counterparts fully respected and appreciated the women's military work.

For this first of several training sessions the Romanians sent only a handful of FET members, their least experienced, which seemed appropriate.

As Rodriguez turned slightly to the right to walk by the group of AFP women and toward the American FET, she caught a glimpse of Bibi, the woman she had grown closest to of the six Afghan female officers. Rodriguez stopped to observe her, compliment her quick ability to pick up the training, and give her a few pointers. "Always pat in circles," she said. "Take your time. Remember that sometimes you're trying to feel for something as small as a cell phone memory card."

The women didn't even have uniforms or weapons yet, but they were eager to train, especially Bibi, who made up for the timidity of some of the others on her team with her sense of determination. In the face of bomb threats and calls from men who promised to kill women who stayed on the force—incidents that prompted several members of the AFP to quit—Bibi remained unfazed. Perhaps that's because she had already experienced some of the worst of what the Taliban had to offer. The insurgent group had beheaded two of her brothers. Being a police woman was the only thing that brought a sense of stability to her once-overwhelming life. And as she was training to fight back against the Taliban, it was working to rebuild itself across the country.

BY 2010 THE Taliban had made Zabul Province one of the most dangerous in Afghanistan.

"This region and neighboring [provinces] are the cradle for nurturing of and killings [by] the Taliban," said Marwais Noorzai, who took over as police chief in Zabul province in 2015. "Bin Laden is not dead. He [through others] is working to make this region insecure."

Noorzai's bin Laden metaphor is a powerful one. As ringleaders of terror like Bin Laden (who was killed by US Navy SEALs in 2011 after he was found hiding on a compound in Pakistan) die, their political and social destruction lives on. Poverty, unemployment, and other disadvantages breed future generations vulnerable to the apparent power and comparative wealth that terror groups like the Taliban offer. Desperate and life-threatening circumstances make joining insurgencies a viable option.

"People have no source of secure income, nothing to do," Noorzai continued. "These terrorist groups come and give them money, train them, and use them as their forces."

In 2011 Zabul was ripe with those ills—especially in the province's Khak Afghan region, known as one of the most dangerous in the entire country. It was notorious for kidnappings, murders, and rapes. In some ways the country has gotten worse since the United States pushed the Taliban out of Kabul, Noorzai said during a phone interview from Zabul police headquarters. Although the Taliban's power and numbers have dwindled—due, in part, to the efforts of women like Rodriguez and Bibi—other factions like the Islamic State (ISIS) have seen the Taliban's shrinking numbers as a weakness, an opening for them to begin to take over territory. Fighting between ISIS and the Taliban would come to define areas like Khak Afghan and others on the outskirts of the province and would soon force women like Bibi to work only in Zabul's district centers.

"Khak Afghan"—which translates to the "soil of Afghans"—"is the center of terrorists in the region," Noorzai explained. "We've always had insecurities here due to all of these things. We can't have a lot of [police]women. The situation is too bad for women to work. Women are not really capable of fighting against these . . . fighting against this strong threat." But none of Zabul's officers—not just the women—have been fully capable of cutting off the strong terrorist threat.

By 2015 Zabul still had one of the smallest police forces in the country, with only four thousand officers. Just fourteen of them were women. Helmand Province had ten thousand officers, around forty of whom were women. But greater numbers in other provinces haven't given policewomen a greater ability to protect themselves against threats from inside or outside departments. In 2013 the two highest ranking women on Helmand's police force were assassinated. One of the women, according to a report in the UK's *Telegraph* newspaper, had received death threats from her brother who, on three separate occasions, tried to kill her. The most damaging mark left by the Taliban's once-powerful hold across the entire nation is not just its laws instituted to keep women at home and uneducated but the idea that a man—any man—could justifiably use whatever level of violence he deemed necessary, up to and including death, to keep women from working. A large number of men still saw any grab for work by women, no matter how noble, as a grab for power and, by extension, a threat.

"Where we have people we need to have police," Noorzai said. "[Most] people think of women police as something positive and something good. Still, problems exist because of very low levels of education in the area, especially in the outskirts. We have barely an educational system working there. What we have to do is work on people's mentality. We have to provide education and make them understand. Lack of education is the root of all of the problems we are having here."

Female officers in Zabul still didn't have their own sleeping quarters in 2015. Police officers in Afghanistan traditionally sleep and live in barracks near police headquarters during the week, even if they are married and have families who live elsewhere. On the weekends they travel home, spending a little over two days with their spouses and children before making the trip back to work. The fourteen women on Zabul's police force were squeezed into two rooms during the week— one at security forces headquarters and another a few miles away at a center that investigates drug use and trafficking issues. They had no separate bathroom facilities.

And the lack of power on the part of female officers in Zabul was felt even more during the sputtering restart of all-female police forces in the early 2000s. Stories of sexual assault were rampant among more remote forces in the north and in southern Afghanistan. Noorzai's response was that "such things do not exist." But the report by Klijn, the Oxfam worker, proved that those things did exist.

Noorzai's denial—and the denial of other police chiefs throughout Afghanistan—that sexual assault existed is part of what allowed male police officers to get away with the crime for so long. Women who wanted to report misconduct had nowhere to turn. And there was no formal protocol within police departments to press charges against a male officer. Female police officers who complained to their police chiefs were often told to stop making trouble. If those same women tried to lean on the police force's women's issues department and use the same route available to civilian women, the reports sat on desks for months at a time with no investigation. Men did not take complaints seriously, and women were too scared to push for investigations to be moved forward.

By the time Rodriguez left Afghanistan in 2012 female police at least had a protocol for reporting abuse. But, still, not much was done. Some of the women who left the department did so because of rumors that men on the force were raping and sexually abusing women. The number of those that turned out to be true in Zabul is hard to know. But in more northern provinces the anecdotal evidence Klijn collected was irrefutable. Women on police forces were raped and harassed.

DESPITE THE DIFFICULTIES, Rodriguez remained determined to train her women.

And trying to get women into uniforms in a city where most of the men who lived there were working against the advancement of the province's female police force was much harder than Rodriguez had expected.

Her first job was convincing the man who controlled the province, Naseri, that policewomen were vital to fight the Taliban and that they couldn't do it without uniforms. And in order to do that, she had to again play the waiting game, at which she had become very adept.

The following Sunday, the week after the Afghan women spent a long training session absorbing FET strategy, Rodriguez sat, as she had nearly every Sunday morning since her arrival in the province, far from the provincial governor.

The provincial assistant walked around her, as he always did, to serve the men in the room first. The aroma of Afghan chai hit her nose as she followed the assistant's quick pace and looked around a room that, no matter how many times she sat in it, still carried an opulence.

She thought of Bibi and the women in the stark office above her, hidden from view.

During a lull in the conversation Rodriguez scooched to her left and stretched her body as far as she could, managing to reach Thacker.

She dropped the small piece of paper, which she had hastily ripped from her notebook, into his hand. On it was written one simple word, which she had, with very little effort, managed to turn into a challenging question. Thacker unfolded the piece of paper to find the familiar inquiry: *Uniforms?*

She had asked about them several times before, after the first meeting she'd had with her AFP recruits. *All in good time* and *patience* were the mantras she kept repeating to herself—familiar phrases from Thacker that had allowed her to get through these meetings without resenting the lack of progress. But now that the women were training, surely it was time. Surely they had waited long enough.

Thacker glanced back at Rodriguez. This time she refused to give in to patience and time. Her unit would be leaving Zabul in about a month, and the last thing she wanted was to leave the women with one of their primary goals—one of the first priorities they openly shared with the FET—unfulfilled. She met Thacker's look with an equally long glance and smiled.

The colonel turned back to Naseri, and Rodriguez waited for her moment to speak.

Five minutes later she stood directly in front of the provincial governor making her case.

She repeated a line she found herself saying often: "The women are ready, sir."

Naseri clasped his palms together and sat them on his desk.

"They want to look like police officers. They've started training."

Naseri leaned forward and asked about the extent of their training: "How were they doing? What had they learned?"

She explained the search techniques the women had been taught and that they would be taught to make a proper arrest and perform all the duties that the American FET now conducts. The thought of women being trained to take over when the American military finally left the country for good seemed promising to Naseri.

A few days later they arrived—dark blue, black-buttoned uniforms in neatly folded piles on a wooden table in the conference room just to the right of Naseri's office. Black headscarves were softly folded on top of each pile. Large, dark sunglasses were nestled to their right. Those glasses, though the smallest piece of the uniform, were the most important. They would help cover the women's faces, taking the place of burqas. But, more important, they would help to hide the officers' identities, protecting them, their husbands, and children from threats.

The female police had been invited to join the provincial governor in the conference room, something that had never happened before. When the time came they took their time walking down the stairs, cautious about what such an invitation could possibly mean. Rodriguez stood, a large smile across her face, in front of the table, waiting for the women to arrive.

When they entered they looked first to Rodriguez. She nodded at the uniforms.

Each picked up her uniform and headed to the bathroom to change. Moments later the women returned to the conference room, eyes beaming. The pants, cut for men twice as tall, swallowed any sign of a feminine shape and sagged around the ankles where they were tucked as far as they could go into black boots. The folds of their standard black headscarves billowed around their necks where the women had pushed them underneath collars that were a bit too wide. For the first time the six officers stood with their backs straight and tall, their hands by their sides.

A few days later Rodriguez stood on the ruddy sidewalk that encircled the provincial governor's office supervising another training session. The major smiled, reveling in the progress and in the uniforms, which crinkled at the waist underneath the pressure of the thick black belts that were the only things keeping the pants in place. There were moments when she doubted that the six Afghan women, who were now learning things like the proper way to use handcuffs, would make it out of that small room. The progress was limited, but Rodriguez felt, in those small moments, like she and the Afghan women on those grounds with her had moved mountains.

It was a fitting end to one of her last weeks in Zabul Province. Her unit was packing up and moving further south. Rodriguez had made progress on the training and uniform front, but getting civilian women to leave their homes and travel to district centers over the next month in a new province would prove a much harder task. Taliban control over southern provinces was still strong, and women still lived in fear.

By the time the major left Zabul the AFP were patrolling with the men in their units and conducting full-body searches. The women had found purpose, and Rodriguez had accomplished the broader goals she set for herself even before that first meeting with the provincial governor. She had been silenced, isolated from her colleagues. But her FET had, at least for the moment, circumvented the structures that so frequently diminished ambition among two very different groups of women in Afghanistan.

CHAPTER 12

BUSINESSES MORE IMPORTANT
THAN BOMBS

PANJWAI, AFGHANISTAN, JANUARY 2012—On her first day there the man leading her military unit's briefing—an Army officer who had been living and fighting in that district for nearly his entire tour—told Rodriguez that her FET plan to bring women from the village outskirts to the district center would never work. The women, he said, would never show.

In Panjwai District, once the epicenter of Taliban recruitment and the cradle of the insurgency's birth in Afghanistan, women never left their homes. Taliban law forbade it.

Rodriguez had just left Zabul, a province where so many of the women had been strong enough to endure death threats and brave enough to leave their homes and work with her to build a police force that slowly gave them the power to jail men. In some cases those men were the very operatives threatening to kill them. Villages teeming with Taliban in Zabul taught Rodriguez how to make the impossible possible. Afghan women, she knew, were stronger than most American military men understood. But now, in Kandahar, the challenges were greater.

During one of her first FET missions in Panjwai—one that sent her through a local village—Rodriguez paused along the dusty district road on which she and her team had been walking to talk to a village elder.

The major tried, as often as cooperation allowed, to gain the support of tribal elders—traditional village leaders who were a large part of conflict resolution and often set the tone for local progress more than elected officials. Engagement from elders—even if negative—allowed her to measure the possibility of and, in some cases, ensure success during certain kinds of FET missions.

Much of her team's achievements in districts like Panjwai—where their goal was to reach local women—was based on the reactions women saw among their village elders. Leaders who were outspoken and talked about building a more progressive village and Afghanistan were the most willing to risk their lives to make progress happen and, by extension, to work with the American military. Women in those villages often felt safer attending FET meetings and classes at district centers. They were willing to learn how to build small businesses and followed through on using grant money that allowed them to make and sell handmade goods in district shopping centers. They felt that it was their right to push back against Taliban laws restricting their lives.

The major also learned that, at times, elder support could backfire. In villages where women didn't trust leadership or had witnessed behavior that made elder motivations questionable, walking up to a village female with an elder credential actually made women turn away or stop speaking entirely. It was hard to know ahead of time which response she was cultivating when she stopped to chat with these men who had very little outward political power but wielded great force in the social advancement and day-to-day operations of the villages the Army major was trying to penetrate.

Rodriguez took a chance during that first patrol on the man with the gray beard whose back was hunched as he sat cross-legged and invited the soldier to converse.

The major slowly lowered herself onto the rug and crossed her legs as she sat across from him. She asked her translator to explain that she wanted to invite women in his village to a series of classes. She would offer the Saturday workshops at Panjwai's district center, which was only ten minutes from the American military's FOB. He attentively watched the major as she spoke. "The goal would be to enable women to make an economic contribution to your village," Rodriguez said, "and to sustain their households. How receptive," she asked, "do you think village women would be?"

Slowly the man leaned forward and explained that there were already women in the village who were anxious to work. He agreed that education was key to improving their lives.

The elder's support reaffirmed what Rodriguez already knew—that women in Panjwai, like women throughout Afghanistan, longed for a strategy to fight back. Rodriguez thanked him and prepared to rise. The old man reached out to her, "Before you leave," the elder said, raising his right hand and pointing a crooked forefinger down the dirt road, "I want you to go to that house."

His direction led her to another dirt road that looked like so many of the rest.

The major nervously walked up to the small mud home that sat at the center of the neighboring compound. She hadn't been in the district for long, and approaching an unknown location was always a risk. But she could hear the din of feminine laughter echo through the open doorway and into the alley between the house and the wall that separated the compound from the outside world.

The women inside were sitting on rugs strategically spread across the floor. They invited Rodriguez and her team to sit and have tea. Rodriguez asked the women if they knew the village elder and told them that he had recommended she talk to them. The mothers, who had introduced themselves and their children between sips of tea, sat in a circle, with Rodriguez, her interpreter, and her FET closing the loop.

The American military wants to offer courses, the major explained, to help women find work, learn how to turn hobbies into livable wages, and to boost the village's economic empowerment.

Silence.

Rodriguez looked at the woman directly in front of her for some sign of interest or understanding. She shifted her gaze to the woman on her right. Then her left. She was reminded of the resistance she experienced during her first meetings with the Afghan Female Police in Zabul. An internal dialogue kicked in that told her to hang on. Find another way in.

"What do you like to do? Do you like to sew? Grow vegetables?"

The woman directly in front of Rodriguez finally spoke up. She sews, she said. She makes small products and sells them through a man she knows in the local market. It would be better, she said, if she had more material. She wants to be able to make and sell more.

The few days Rodriguez had been in the province hadn't produced much useful information for her. Her team's encounters with women had been infrequent. She feared that her branch of the FET program might be scrapped.

But her FET report that evening would be full of information that could benefit American intelligence. She surmised that the area was gaining stability. Women were selling goods at the local market, and there was at least one vendor who supported female economic development. The Taliban is around, but this village, she concluded, seems less afraid of the insurgency.

The intelligence Rodriguez gathered that day was a predictor. The patterns of behavior found among those women supported what happened a year later when villagers throughout Panjwai joined American and Afghan forces to push the Taliban out of the district for good. The series of 2013 uprisings were the most significant of the war not simply because they resulted in a Taliban defeat but also because they proved how internal shifts in power could help defeat the insurgency. The victory, led in part by Panjwai's own citizens, is also a symbol of American strategic success. Tactics used during the uprisings were dictated as much by internal Afghan forces as they were by outside US and NATO leaders. Average folks from a district in the conservative south were able to return an area that birthed Afghanistan's most dangerous killers back to its pre-Taliban roots.

Rodriguez pinned up a sign, one of many she was posting all over local villages, announcing what the FET's Saturday courses, workshops, and gatherings would include: information about grant programs for small businesses, instructions on hygiene and child care, opportunities to work on and develop sewing projects.

Then she waited.

Rodriguez and her FET sat inside the gates of the district center most of the first Saturday after her classes were announced, waiting for a woman, any woman to show. No one did. The following week yielded only ten, and the words of the officer who conducted her in-brief began to echo through her mind. Her evening reports were nearly void of information on female engagement.

Just before the third weekend of Rodriguez's push to bring classes and opportunity to women in Afghanistan's Panjwai District, its governor, Sayed Fazuldin Agha, who was known for working out peace strategies between insurgent fighters, made an announcement on the local radio station. Women, he said during a program that resonated throughout all villages across the district, should take advantage of the classes offered at the district center. Economic empowerment for women brings them one step closer to freedom.

After the announcement a suicide bomber crashed a vehicle, which was laced with explosives, into a moving car that carried Agha, his two sons, and two guards. All six men were killed; ten others were injured. Agha was working too closely with the American military, the Taliban said, according to a report by the *Long War Journal*.

Two days later fifteen women walked up to the gate at Panjwai's district center, ready to follow through on the governor's last rallying cry. Rodriguez had hoped for more. Frustrated, she walked from the front gates, down the alleyway, and into the building in which classes would soon start, leaving it up to her FET to search those women and any others who might trickle in.

Five minutes later a member of her team radioed for assistance.

"Major Rodriguez," she heard a voice coming through on the receiver attached to her belt, "we need you."

She made the trek back down the alleyway. As she turned into the open space of the courtyard just beyond the dark, narrow walk, a sea of blue met her eyes. The small crowd of fifteen women had turned into fifty.

Quickly Rodriguez joined the few women on her FET detail at the gate trying to search as many women as possible before allowing them into the space. She had only secured one translator for the event. She had no one to watch the women's children, whose high energy and curious laughter began to dominate.

Soon fifty women turned into more than one hundred.

AN ATTEMPT TO TRANSFER CONTROL

Two months after Rodriguez landed in Kandahar the vicious acts of an American soldier in an Afghan village shocked the world and gave the Taliban an excuse to pull out of negotiations.

On March 11, 2012, after a night of drinking, Sergeant Robert Bales walked a mile from his FOB to Panjwai, a district in the southern province that was a former Taliban stronghold. He was alone, off duty, and armed. In the pitch black he walked from home to home, knocking on random doors. When families didn't answer, he forced his way in, backed innocent civilian men, women, and children into corners, and executed them, many with just a single shot to the forehead. He killed sixteen people that night, covering some with blankets and setting their bodies on fire.

In the days that followed, Afghans dragged the charred blankets to Kandahar Province's Camp Belambay to protest the soldier's actions.

That incident had followed another, during which NATO and American forces set one hundred Korans on fire at Bagram Air Base.

Not only did the Taliban use the slaughter in Panjwai and the act of religious aggression by a few US troops as opportunities to step away from a possible end to conflict, but Afghanistan's President Hamid Karzai also responded by limiting the reach of US forces. He ordered all troops pulled from outposts and requested that Americans remain on bases.

The peace agreement, had it happened, would have come near the end of Rodriguez's deployment and could have given the women she was working with a possible foothold into equality. Similar chances for negotiations would be tossed aside twice more in the next two years.

Karzai pulled out of 2013 negotiations because the location posed a threat to Afghanistan. The Taliban opened offices in Doha, Qatar, for the June 19 talks, calling the location the "Islamic Emirates of Afghanistan"—the same thing terrorists called the country when they controlled its capital—and flying the Taliban flag out front.

On the table were three demands from the United States: that the Taliban end its insurgency in Afghanistan, that it publicly disavow al-Qaeda, and that it recognize the rights of women.

Although the Taliban had slowly been losing military and political power in the country's major cities, the terrorist threat to women throughout most of Afghanistan was still strong. And by the end of 2013, the FETs and community activists were pushing voting in the April elections as the best way for women to exercise power and eventually regain lost rights.

Lack of safety was one of the main issues keeping women from registering across the country and keeping both men and women from going to the polls in the most rural areas.

A delegation from the National Democratic Institute (which included US Ambassador Karl Indurfurth) released a report to the Afghan people in December 2013 assessing the country's preparation for the 2014 presidential and provincial elections. According to the report, registration for women in those areas was especially low because of poor education and the security concerns that prevented female elections officials from conducting registration drives. Just one-third of the 3.2 million voters registered since May of 2013 had been women.

The registration process was complicated even further by the fact that Afghanistan had no national list of registered voters, making it easy for precincts to issue multiple voter registration cards to the same person. And those multicard mistakes paved the way for voters and elections officials to manipulate outcomes. In rural areas, where voter turnout was especially low and candidates could win with as little as 1 percent of the vote, it would take only a few residents who were double or triple registered to determine the makeup of the next provincial council. Efforts by the Independent Election Commission (better known as the IEC) to create a national list that would link eligible voters to specific polling stations were stymied.

During the 2009 national elections the Taliban killed at least one candidate and threatened to kill residents who dared walk out of their homes to go to the polls. And by early 2014 it was clear that Afghan military and police forces had not significantly improved. According to Afghan generals on the ground, the country's forces weren't ready to secure the nation from terrorist threats without help from US and NATO forces, which had already begun turning security leadership over to Afghanistan.

In January 2014, just three months before the election, Karzai re-fused to sign the Bilateral Security Agreement, which stated that US forces would stay in the country beyond 2014 if the Taliban didn't come to the negotiating table and that the president invited the United States to leave after 2014 if negotiations didn't happen.

The head of Afghan forces, Lieutenant General Murad Ali Murad, publicly disagreed with Karzai's suggestion that the country could survive Taliban retaliation without American troops. "We will have challenges and problems when it comes to the equipping and training of the Afghan national army," Murad said in a BBC report. "We don't share the view that Afghanistan will slip back into civil war, but we need more support and resources so we can deal with the threat posed by the insurgents especially during elections."

In the run-up to national and local elections the US posture in Af-ghanistan had certainly suffered major setbacks. Taliban forces had not returned to the negotiating table. Defense Secretary Leon Panetta had announced that the country's combat mission would be coming to an end. Troops, instead, would be tasked with providing security for a country that had lost trust in the US military and whose leader called for American forces to limit their activity to forward operating bases.

As citizens prepared to go to the polls—against a backdrop of con-tinued Taliban aggression and calls for an end to fraudulent election practices—an Afghan woman named Jamila was waging her own revolution. And a once-reluctant FET leader became her second in command.

JOHANNA SMOKE
2012-2014

CHAPTER 13

VERY OLD CONCEPT, VERY NEW MISSION

> Women who stepped up were measured as citizens of the nation, not as women. .... This was a people's war, and everyone was in it.
>
> **—COLONEL OVETA CULP HOBBY,**
> first director of the Women's Army Corps

FORT HUACHUCA, ARIZONA, JULY 2012—The intelligence officer turned on her computer, logged into her email, and started scrolling.

It had been several hours since she'd checked her inbox. The full day of captain's and intelligence training had been strenuous, and Johanna Smoke leaned forward and placed her arms on the desk to let go of the weight that hours of academic pressure had created. When she reached the email with the subject line "change of orders" she stopped scrolling and stared at the words for several minutes. She blinked and read it again. Couldn't have been right.

When she opened the message Smoke was even more convinced that the email was a mistake. The orders were short: She was to report to Fort Knox, Kentucky, in September, where she would be assigned to the 3rd Brigade Combat Team. That unit would deploy to Afghanistan the following year.

She reached for the phone, but she hung up before dialing. The three-hour time difference between Arizona and her branch manager's office in Kentucky meant that her 5 P.M. plea for an explanation would end up an 8 P.M. voicemail. And the matter was too important to leave a message that might go unchecked.

She had just been accepted into Joint Special Operations Command at Fort Bragg, North Carolina. The application process had taken six months: she'd handed over records documenting high marks on physical fitness tests, copies of annual evaluations, her résumé, and a mental health assessment. And after jumping through every possible hoop, she'd made it. She was set to leave Arizona for her dream assignment right after training was over. Her husband, whom she had only recently separated from, was taking his career, despite efforts, in a different direction. When she found out that he wouldn't be waiting to greet her in North Carolina in September, she was relieved. The only reason he'd applied was because she did. Smoke made it clear that special ops was key for her. Her father had served in special ops during Vietnam, and her dad was her rock. When she had struggled in Iraq in 2009, her father's voice of reassurance and experience was the main one she looked to for guidance. There was no other person whose footsteps were more worthy of following. She knew that special ops would be a challenge, and she wanted to run toward it. She was going to serve in that elite Fort Bragg unit, she told her husband, whether they were together in North Carolina or not.

Smoke and her husband had been in the same Fort Drum, New York, unit when she deployed to Iraq. But in the war zone they rarely saw one another. After they arrived at FOB Hammer about eighteen miles east of Baghdad, their jobs took them in completely different directions. Her husband didn't want the two to be separated again. So he followed her lead and applied for special ops too.

But things quickly changed. The young couple, who had only been married for about three years, separated in March and filed for divorce in May. It would have been awkward if, during divorce proceedings, they'd been stationed together. The fact that she was going to Fort

Bragg, and he went to Fort Knox in Kentucky (his next duty station after special ops didn't work out for him), had been the perfect solution.

Now the words *Fort Knox* stared back at her from a cold, flat computer screen, and all she could feel was anxiety.

When Smoke called her branch manager early the next morning she was assured that the change in assignment was no mistake.

"You don't understand," she tried to explain, "Captain Smoke and I are no longer part of the Army married couples program. We don't need to be stationed together anymore. That's why this happened, right? Personnel thinks that, because I haven't changed my last name yet, we're still married?"

She abruptly sat down as she listened to the Army's reasons for disrupting her life. She was now part of a Women in the Army (WITA) program. She would be placed on a combat team so that the Army could get a sense of how women fared under such conditions.

To get a sense of how women fared? To get a sense of how women fared?

Smoke kept repeating that phrase to herself in disbelief.

Maybe, she thought, the Army should have asked her about how she fared after she returned from Iraq two years ago. Instead, she was being forced to participate in a program that, to her, seemed like a waste of time. She'd already done what WITA was just beginning to study. The change of duty came with questionnaires about her feelings in this new combat environment—completely stupid, she thought. She was told she'd need to attend group meetings to discuss how male superiors were treating her—also, she thought, a total waste of time.

WITA studies and reviews had been used for decades and were a good predictor of changes to come. The office often acted as a liaison between policymakers, coming changes, and women in the Army—testing potential shifts, like placing women in infantry units at the company level, before changes were made official. They wanted to develop a paper trail that proved the Army had documented all potentially negative effects.

By this time women on female engagement teams, like Rodriguez and Adams, had already been on the ground participating in combat—raids, enemy searches, firefights. Those women had done more than their male counterparts in combat ever could. They were also being criticized by men who didn't want women's roles to change, didn't think they deserved combat recognition, and had no idea how much women had already done to earn it—including women like Smoke, who had earlier been on the ground in Iraq in a combat role that hadn't included FET duties.

The Army was already making very significant shifts in the way it was using female soldiers. But since his decision in 2012 to eliminate a 1994 directive that had banned women from collocating with combat units, Defense Secretary Leon Panetta was forced to give the appearance that the military was controlling a transition that had already happened. And the pace of the DOD's public transition wasn't fast enough for many women who had for years been living and working through the hardships of combat. The 2012 Department of Defense move would only open a bit more than fourteen thousand combat jobs to women.

When Panetta later commented on the decision during a 2013 news conference he stated, "It's clear to all of us that women are contributing in unprecedented ways to the military's mission of defending the nation."

But his directive still left some two hundred thousand jobs officially closed to women.

In May of 2012 two female Army reservists, Command Sergeant Major Jane Baldwin and Colonel Ellen Haring, who had each served more than twenty years, sued the Department of Defense, stating that the policy of combat exclusion hindered advancement and retirement benefits.

Whether Smoke liked it or not, she, along with the thousands of other women serving in 2012, were operating in the world's largest fish bowl. Everyone—civilians, foreign military units, men who wanted jobs open to women, and those who didn't—was watching to see whether women could successfully transition into combat duties and serve side by side with men.

That combat transition had already happened for Smoke in Iraq long before she knew that a program called WITA even existed. She had been a military intelligence officer on the ground with the 2nd Brigade Combat Team, 10th Mountain Division, Light Infantry from

October 2009 to July 2010. Smoke got a Combat Action Badge for her service in the war zone.

The transition happened for other women during Operation Enduring Freedom and, before that, the Gulf War.

As she listened to her branch manager lay out the reasons why her participation in WITA was important, she began to feel Fort Bragg slipping out of her grasp. Her assignment to Fort Knox was going to happen regardless of whether she thought WITA was a waste of time. And the Army didn't care if its experiments were too little, too late. The military also didn't care if changing her orders meant she would have to endure a few uncomfortable moments with her soon to be ex-husband.

But Smoke did care. And she tried to tell her branch manager as much.

"Who else can I talk to? How can I get these orders changed so that I can go special ops like I'd planned?"

Her branch manager's answer: "Essentially, no one."

When she hung up, she was angry. She was resentful. She was a bit depressed.

But more than anything, she was tired.

She was tired of women being treated like an experiment. It was as if, Smoke thought, men wanted women to prove that they were worthy of being called fighters. And the willful ignorance of those in charge of this supposed transition prevented them from seeing that women already were.

This orders change was the latest manifestation of the military's misguided—and all too late—attempt to bring female equality to the ranks, Smoke thought. To her it felt fake, like an overreach.

She said nothing more about it.

FORT KNOX, KENTUCKY, SEPTEMBER 2012—The small home she rented when she got to Kentucky was nothing special. It was a white split-level with a fenced-in yard for her dogs. It was about fifteen minutes from the base and the best she could find on short notice. Once she'd spotted a home in the right location, she didn't bother looking further. She was only going to be there for a couple of years—long enough to get settled on the base and then serve a year in Afghanistan. After she returned from deployment she would reapply to special operations and go to Fort Bragg like she'd wanted to all along. Kentucky, she'd resolved, was just a pit stop.

The Army had given her a month between moving to Kentucky and reporting for duty to get her personal affairs in order. And about a week after she arrived, when she looked at the state of her living room, which had not a stick of furniture and was filled with so many unopened boxes that its cream carpet disappeared, she wasn't sure a month would be long enough.

Smoke knew no one in the area but her ex-husband, and she wasn't going to reach out to him for help.

She opened a few boxes of knick-knacks and, after realizing she had nowhere to place them, decided to tackle the shelving unit she'd bought just a few days before. And the only tool she had was the very small Allen wrench that was included in the box. She placed it in the screws, perfectly fitted for the tool, and put the unit together.

Then she tried to attach it to the wall. The Allen wrench didn't fit the larger screws that were supposed to secure the shelves in place. She tried three times, and each time the unit fell to the floor. After the third try she sat in the middle of her living room and broke down. She didn't care much about the shelf. But she did care that she was lonely and that her career plans had been stymied. And languishing in the middle of an incomplete living room, in a town where she barely knew a soul, was the perfect backdrop for her to beat herself up—something, in her quest for perfection, she did all too often. If she couldn't handle a set of bookshelves, she thought, how in the world was she going to handle being the only female officer in a combat unit? She worried about whether she'd get along with her command. She wondered about the kind of men who would be under her command. She wasn't used to feeling unsure about where her life was going.

Her phone rang. It was her dad.

Through sobs she explained that she didn't have any tools. The shelf kept falling down. She felt incompetent. She was alone.

Within two days a set of power tools showed up on her doorstep with a note carefully signed "Love, Dad."

She opened those boxes and got to work, putting her home and her life together again.

The highlight of her duty change was the fact that she would be going to the Middle East again. Preparing to deploy to Afghanistan gave her life purpose. She didn't waste her time filling out gender-integration questionnaires or going to group meetings. She had an important mission to prepare for. The crying bouts in that small house in Kentucky stopped.

And when she got to Zabul Province she didn't play combat as she felt the WITA program had encouraged; instead, she took on the most meaningful role of her career. She began calling herself "chief of staff" for a once-discarded woman who had become one of Afghanistan's leading freedom fighters.

CHAPTER 14

TEACHING OTHERS
TO FLEE

ZABUL PROVINCE, AFGHANISTAN, JUNE 2013—In that chasm between progress and destruction is where Johanna Smoke met Jamila Abbas for the first time.

A dilapidated white van sitting behind the guard station, to the left of everything else on the women's center compound, was the first thing that caught Smoke's eye as she walked onto the property. The missing front tire caused the vehicle to tilt slightly to one side. The outside of the van hadn't been washed since it was given to Jamila by a previous FET leader who had left long before Smoke had arrived. The van was one of the proudest gifts the woman had acquired for Jamila. It was meant to provide the feminist—whose male assistant was able to drive—with a way to visit women in the more remote areas of the province. It had also, temporarily, given Jamila the power to pull abused wives and young girls being forced into marriages with older men out of their homes during late-night escapes. Now the van sat, its smooth white paint interrupted with dull gray splotches where storms had repeatedly whipped sand against its sides.

Jamila waited by the women's center front entrance. Smoke followed the pathway, rutted and uneven, to the building's door. To Smoke's left, in the distance, she could see a greenhouse. Its sides were blown out. Dry tomato vines stretched across the ground. Cracks wove their way through the plaster façade of the women's center.

Smoke smiled politely at Jamila and introduced herself. Jamila looked at Edna Sahdo, Smoke's interpreter, and nodded, not really taking the time to meet Smoke's warmth with meaningful eye contact. She led the women to the back of the center, the part most damaged by a recent bombing. None of the women who used the center were there when the bomb went off. And none had been able to use the center since.

Smoke walked up to what had been a glass wall that made up the rear entrance. The clear wall once covered the entire back side of the center, allowing light to flow through to a large sunroom. Thin shards of glass hanging from the roof line were all that remained. Glass crunched underneath Smoke's boots as she walked into the center's destroyed back room.

Smoke turned to Jamila. "What happened?"

The woman looked at Edna and explained, "The insurgents. They bombed the government center a few months ago. Nothing has been rebuilt since."

"And the van?" Smoke again attempted to make eye contact with Jamila.

The center's director looked again at Edna, the translator, as she explained, "A former military woman gave the center that van. It worked for a while, but we have no money to keep up with the maintenance. It will not run. We can't repair it. We don't even really have money for gas."

Jamila took Smoke on a tour of the center. They walked an outer hallway that took the women along the perimeter of the entire one-story building. The hall was dotted with offices, one belonging to Jamila, another to her assistant. In the center of the building was a large conference room with a long wooden table in the middle and a couple of small sofas along the wall. Another room at the center of the building was used for classes. Sewing machines were lined up on small tables in the back section of that room—an area used for making crafts and designing clothing, which many of the women sold to make a living.

They ended the tour in the conference room, where Smoke spoke to Jamila and her assistant. In matter-of-fact tones the two explained the center's problems with funding and with reaching the women most in need. Smoke could tell that they had explained it all before: the lack of transportation, the immense poverty and dire needs of women in the poorest villages of the province's far north and deep south, places so far away that even the military was forced to use helicopters to reach them.

And like most of the FET women who had come before her, Smoke wondered how she would even begin to tackle the problems plaguing women in the province. Rebuilding the women's center, Jamila emphasized, would only be the beginning.

Smoke decided to be candid. She had no idea where to begin, and as she looked directly at Jamila, she made it clear that she was there to serve Jamila, to do the center's bidding—whatever that took. Jamila finally made eye contact with the soldier and smiled. It was the first time she'd felt that level of support from a FET member. As Smoke walked off the property she looked back at Jamila, who was standing at the front door. She smiled again, this time with worry. She wanted to make sure that everything she did fit into Jamila's goals for the women of Afghanistan. She still felt like the task was daunting.

Soon after their first meeting Jamila walked with Smoke and Edna into a back room of one of the main offices at FOB Apache, one that allowed for more private, intimate conversations. The Afghan woman pulled a small package wrapped in brown paper from her purse. She handed the gift to Smoke, who looked up, surprised, and thanked Jamila. The custom was a traditional one—Afghans often brought gifts to new friends and colleagues, people in their lives whom they respected. As Smoke peeled back the wrapper, Jamila began to thank the captain, who she called "Colonel Smoke," for her work. Over the past few days Smoke hadn't done much, but the small renovations she had started on the women's center meant a great deal. The captain had found a local contractor they could trust to get needed supplies and materials. Smoke had also created a mission for the engineering unit stationed at Apache to visit the center and assess the damage and how much time it would take to do a renovation. They were slated

to begin reconstruction on the center and its greenhouse and irrigation system soon. Smoke had done more in a few weeks than Jamila
and her assistant had done in months. It was a good sign that the two
women would be able to work well together.

Smoke thanked Jamila again for the gift—an orange silk scarf.

The three women sat around a small table to plan the next week's
mission. In the course of talking about women in the local villages,
Smoke casually mentioned marriage. She brought up her own engagement in passing and joked, as she had a few times before, that there
were plenty of eligible men for Jamila, who she knew was single after
having been married when she was younger. She had no idea why the
woman was no longer married. Jamila usually giggled. The thought
of marrying again wasn't something that occupied her time. The occasional jokes from Smoke made her, momentarily, feel good, as if she
were much younger.

But Smoke noticed that Jamila's usual giggle hadn't accompanied
the joke this time. Instead, the Afghan woman looked up at Edna.
There was no smile on her face. She nodded as she began talking to
the translator and telling her story.

A man wearing black showed up one day and asked for her husband.
Jamila remembered following Amir. She recalled that it had been a
slightly cold day and that the crisp air, as she walked back to her home
behind her husband and the man wearing black, had invigorated her.

The insurgents in the far-off distance forced her husband to his
knees and beheaded him. All four of her children were under the age
of eleven, and they had each seen everything. Jamila knew, all those
years ago, that she should have moved. She should have gotten her
children inside. For some reason she couldn't.

The three women sat for several minutes in silence. The small meeting room gradually filled with the sound of their sobs.

Smoke slowly reached for a Kleenex and handed it to Jamila. She
used the next one to catch her own tears—strangers united to defeat a
problem that went well beyond the fields of war.

BY 2013 JAMILA was waging her own feminist battle against Zabul's insurgents and had become a leader that the province's women ran to

for help to get away from abusive husbands, fathers, uncles, and the Taliban edicts those men cruelly followed. She could set women up in a new village or province and show them how to start their lives all over again. The activist's days of fleeing were over.

Zabul's women's center looked benign. It sat in the middle of a compound whose grasses had long since turned to desert. The compound was surrounded by a high stone wall, like so many places in Afghanistan that were owned by people trying to shield themselves from dangerous activity that existed only steps from their front doors.

Smoke was one of the war's most independent FET leaders—the product of a more informed command that had learned that denying supplies to military women hurt the overall mission and that getting Afghan women away from abuse and poverty was one of the best tools for defeating insurgents. And unlike Rodriguez, one of her Army predecessors, Smoke focused only on the FET mission.

Women came to Jamila's center for classes in sewing, gardening, and other skills that the province's poorest could use to create goods to sell and clothe and support their families. The center's underground mission was, at first, known only to them. In Zabul and surrounding provinces it was the only place women could send their daughters for freedom from the bonds of child marriage. Knowledge of Jamila's secret missions spread to women very quickly. It took men in surrounding provinces longer to figure it out. And the Taliban longer still. But once information about the underground shelter spread throughout Zabul, Jamila was a target.

One such mission came not long after Smoke arrived in the country.

An old, slightly rusted white van, which was usually broken down, had been recently repaired by someone, according to Smoke, with suspected ties to the Taliban. Smoke had facilitated the relationship between Jamila and the Taliban informant. Although he claimed not to espouse the group's sexist beliefs, he was being well paid to report on American activity. He was responsible for arranging the deaths of several US soldiers.

When he had entered the women's center Smoke was taken off guard. But she recognized him right away from a previous meeting and intelligence reports. She was terrified and glanced over the man's shoulder to make sure her guard, the woman who was always around Smoke and was armed when Smoke couldn't be, was standing close by. She couldn't ask the man to leave without causing offense or suspicion. She knew he was a wealthy, married womanizer. So her first thought was to cater to his ego. She had introduced him to Jamila and talked about how much they could use his help. The general smiled, drank tea, and listened to both women talk about the funding issues they'd been having.

Just days after that meeting the general had the van towed to a shop, repaired, and returned.

And now Jamila was using it to get women and young girls away from the extremist values brought to Zabul Province by the very insurgency the general supported.

One night Jamila's fifteen-year-old daughter ran into the center looking for her mother. Her daughter's friend, Haditha, followed. Haditha's father was going to marry her to a man who was generations older. The fourteen-year-old was scared, didn't want to be married, and wanted, instead, to stay in school.

They immediately hatched a plan. The girl would stay at the center overnight. Sending her home would be too dangerous—she might not come back. The next night they would drive her to another province with a girls' school.

As night approached, Jamila whisked fourteen-year-old Haditha into the van sitting just outside the women's center, near the outer wall of the compound.

Jamila's solutions to the problems of child marriage, abuse, and sexual assault weren't always the same, and taking girls away from their families only came after other attempts to mend bridges and develop more humane alternatives within families had failed. She was a mediator, family counselor, and crisis interventionist. And she had surely tried the same things with Haditha's family.

But Jamila also knew that sometimes the only real solution was to run.

It was pitch black outside. Jamila quickly pulled her scarf from around her shoulders and over her head. She turned to Haditha and tugged on the girl's head covering, pulling it as far over her face as possible. The two quickly climbed into the backseat of the van. As soon as they closed the van door her assistant started the engine.

Haditha was on her way to a new life.

CHAPTER 15

JAMILA'S CHIEF OF STAFF

The Afghan women set out early, walking in small groups toward the compound, some with their husbands, to avoid suspicion.

The morning air was slightly cool, and baby-blue burqas swayed softly in the breeze as the earliest participants arrived—sneaking to the meeting area hours ahead of the shura. In the small, rural district of a little more than sixteen thousand people, the women who knew each other paused to strike up conversations.

Some strolled along carrying children on their hips; others allowed their antsy little ones to run ahead. They were all fully aware that in this part of Zabul—a province reputed to be a lawless "wild east" of Afghanistan where the Taliban still had control—a group of women meeting at a health clinic that handed out birth control and was run, in part, by a man could be considered an act of rebellion. Registering to vote, a task many women had no idea was ahead of them, was practically a death wish.

At 10 A.M., less than a mile away, a helicopter landed in the middle of the Army's Special Forces outpost.

As its wheels touched down, two special ops soldiers briskly walked toward the landing pad—a small, square patch of black, rutted tarmac—followed by the outpost commander. Smoke, jumped from the passenger side of the chopper and walked to meet them. Ten of her FET members followed. Smoke moved her M4 rifle, the butt of which hovered just beneath her chin, to the right and reached out to shake each man's hand.

Two years after Rodriguez managed to elevate the status of Zabul Province's female police officers, the theme for women like Smoke, among the more recent to take on FET duties, was starting over—doing some of the same jobs again, often as if little to no progress had been made. Many of the previous leaders' accomplishments had all but disappeared by the time Smoke showed up.

That some strides for American military women had been made was clear: newer FET chiefs didn't need to fight nearly as much as early leaders did to gain respect from their male peers. By the time Smoke arrived at FOB Apache in Qalat City, she, unlike Rodriguez, didn't need to beg for vehicles, explain the necessity of female missions, or struggle to piece together a FET from only a small group of willing or qualified women. The hour-long helicopter flight from Qalat City to the special operations outpost in Tarnak Wa Jaldak, at Smoke's request, was a testament to that. The captain received almost immediate support from her chain of command when initiating FET operations—her mission plans only took about a week for approval.

But the fact that she needed such a large number of FET members to complete this mission told another story—one that pointed to less progress. It meant that there were few Afghan Female Police officers—who were supposed to be training to do the job American women were doing once our troops left the country—available to participate in missions. Officers like Bibi, one of the last holdouts trained under Rodriguez, were eventually pushed out, according to Smoke.

Bibi had led the AFP when Rodriguez stepped in as FET chief, and she had built a reputation for being tough. The insurgent forces who were watching didn't like her. The Taliban, along with other men in Qalat City near police headquarters, had worked to rid the province of all female police officers. They called headquarters, threatening to rape, behead, and bomb the women who worked there. They followed through on at least two of their threats and assassinated two women who worked on Zabul's police force in 2012, just before Smoke's arrival. But Bibi was among the few women who didn't quit.

In fact, her responsibilities expanded. She, along with other female officers in that part of Afghanistan, accompanied their male colleagues on missions throughout all of Qalat City and much of Zabul Province to ensure that bombs, weapons, and other contraband didn't get through. They also made arrests and found, underneath a few burqas, male insurgents hiding IEDs and other supplies that would have added to the violence plaguing Zabul if the AFP hadn't intervened.

Bibi and the women who followed her onto the streets of Zabul every day had picked up where FETs rotating in and out of the country left off. Bibi grew increasingly outspoken and, for her own safety, was moved to Kabul—the capital city was much more progressive than the rest of the country. So the dwindling ranks of AFP meant that on this heavily fortified mission, Smoke had to bring a large number of FET members with her. Her ultimate goal, like that of all US commanders in the field, was to eventually turn large operations like this one, along with day-to-day responsibilities, over to Afghan forces. But with only two Afghan female officers left in Zabul, that task was proving impossible. Redoing some of the work Rodriguez had already done, with a fresh crop of potential Zabul officers, became a large part of her mission.

Seven Afghan women spilled out of the helicopter. Six of the women who joined the conversation—a last-minute rundown of the day's mission—were Afghan female officers in training. The seventh was Jamila. They held tight to their headscarves and rushed to catch up with Smoke, her two AFP officers, the team of FET members, and the Special Forces men now standing in a circle next to a wall that was just steps from the helicopter landing pad. The top of the stone perimeter towered over Smoke, who leaned her right shoulder against it as the helicopter's wheels retracted and the chopper tilted south toward the FOB.

The Special Forces commander—his voice booming as he attempted to be heard over the retreating chopper—checked to make sure Smoke had everything she needed for the day. The helicopter's blades swooshed loudly as they sliced through the air, and the commander leaned toward Smoke, lowering his voice as the machine flew out of earshot. The group would remain on the ground no more than three hours—barely long enough to ensure that each Afghan woman and child (some of whom had already made their way into the shura) got the individual care and attention they needed, but short enough not to arouse Taliban suspicions.

During other missions the Special Forces commander may have added another layer of intelligence gathering to Smoke's operation. He would have handed over any information he gathered since the last time they talked and then reviewed the mission's intelligence goals.

In the weeks leading up to a mission Smoke and the Special Forces commander would call and email one another frequently so Smoke would already know some basic information about assumed Taliban threats. During one of those phone conversations the chief told Smoke about a bomb attack that US intelligence thought the Taliban was planning. The attack would have targeted an area at or near the Tarnak Wa Jaldak market, the one place in that small town that would have guaranteed a high casualty count. It was a main thoroughfare, the only place for the few thousand people in the area to purchase food. In this struggling community, located in Southern Zabul on the border with Kandahar and only a couple of hours from neighboring Pakistan, the market was the heart of its only business corridor. The entire province, including Tarnak Wa Jaldak, is an easy target for insurgent groups from Pakistan including Taliban and ISIS factions. Smoke's job was to find out as much as she could about specific local actors behind the plan—names, addresses, how long the attack had been planned—and the day the rumored attack may happen. She also needed to confirm where exactly in the market area the attack would take place. And she found out all of that through her conversations with women.

In the middle of that previous mission Smoke sat down in a clinic on a hallway bench between two women who had been waiting to be seen by the nurse who co-owned the facility with her pharmacist husband. Smoke introduced herself and told them why she and her team were there—to offer as much medical assistance as possible for the women and their children. First she asked the young mother on her right what brought her to the clinic that day. Headaches, the woman said. She took poppy, something common among women in the province, but the drug wasn't helping. Smoke smiled and reached her hand out to the three-year-old child who had been tugging at the bottom of the woman's burqa. The young mother looked down at the child as Smoke reached into her pocket and pulled out a packet of gummy worms. The little girl reached up for them, and the mother smiled.

The woman on Smoke's left also complained of pain, and Smoke turned to her and nodded, then assured them both that the military doctor, Major Shayna Thompson, would try her best to help them.

After a brief lull Smoke asked another set of questions, these much more critical: "Have you gone to the market today? What's the mood downtown been like lately?"

The young mother picked up her child before answering, brushing the little girl's hair out of her eyes before setting the child on her lap. The woman, at first hesitant about the question, said she had avoided the market all week because she had heard a rumor that the Taliban were planning to bomb it. She had also heard that the insurgent group had been working out ways to plant IEDs throughout the town center. The other young woman confirmed the bomb scare but said that she had to venture out the previous Wednesday, desperate to gather food for her family. When she got there, she said, the outdoor market was virtually empty, save for a few shop owners and one or two women. That was highly unusual for the middle of the week.

Smoke paused before asking another question, waiting to see if either woman would offer more information on her own. Sometimes intelligence collection in Tarnak Wa Jaldak—a poor district with few resources that forced its residents to compete with each other for everything they could get—involved playing off each woman's need to appear smarter than the other. If Smoke was quiet long enough, she had learned, there was a good chance the women would start talking again—each trying hard to give Smoke a more meaningful nugget of data or local fact than the last. Winning Smoke's favor could put them at the top of the list when it came to getting extra food, blankets, and medical attention for their families, the mothers thought. To the women in poverty-stricken Tarnak Wa Jaldak—who competed fiercely for supplies, attention, and extra rations—American military women like Smoke represented a lifeline, one that could fix some of what was wrong with their crumbling homes and villages. Military women brought food, wellness, and a means, in some cases, of connecting to the outside world.

She asked the women when they normally went to the market—what day of the week?

They usually felt free to go any day of the week, each woman said. That week they had not.

"How did the rumor start?"

One woman had heard it from other women in the village. The young mother had heard it from her husband.

"Sounds scary. How do you cope? Had rumors like that ever spread before?"

The women confirmed that they had been afraid, perhaps more than usual, to leave their homes that week. And that rumors as specific as that one rarely came up. If they did, they likely became reality.

The list of needs for these women was overwhelming—homes had no running water, and Taliban forces were bombing irrigation systems, leaving farmers and their families with destroyed crops.

But the list of intelligence needs for the Special Forces team she was working with was also long.

Smoke had to be two different people—a nation builder who brought medical care to hurting women, held sick babies, and helped repair facilities that the Taliban had destroyed as well as an Army captain who manipulated some of the same women she was helping in order to gain intelligence. The duality often made her feel guilty. The fact that she couldn't do enough to help Afghan women get out of desperate situations made her feel even worse. But she also knew that filling intelligence reports is what, ultimately, was going to change these women's lives. They were participating, without knowing it, in their own liberation.

That day's intelligence report was also filled with information from others in the clinic. She got the names of suspected insurgents who may have been involved in the threat. Smoke also found out the day of the week that the attack was likely to happen. One of the women talking to Smoke confirmed that the coming Thursday was the day she planned to avoid going to the market. She had heard repeatedly that IEDs had been planted and would be detonated on a Thursday. Smoke memorized what she could and, moments later, casually made her way out of the clinic and into a secluded area by the back wall of the compound. She turned over several pages in her notebook and jotted down all the information she had retained. That afternoon the intelligence officer typed up a report for Special Forces and forwarded it to them as quickly as possible. Special Forces then used that information to curtail an attempted attack and takeover of Tarnak Wa Jaldak the following week.

But that was several weeks ago.

Now she was preparing for the biggest shura mission she had run, and the Special Forces commander knew of no impending threats.

Smoke and her team headed off the base, walking toward an underdeveloped park, the beginning of a half-mile march to the clinic. The lead Special Forces soldier turned left and headed down a quiet road surrounded by unusually lush greenery—a contrast to the desolate, dry landscape that covered much of the country. The rest of Smoke's team filed in behind him, making sure to walk as closely as they could in the bootprints he left behind to avoid potential IEDs. Walking through downtown may have been quicker, but the comparatively brief hike would have also been much more dangerous and could have stirred up activity among Taliban operatives who may have been watching.

Shah Joy (another shura location) and Tarnak Wa Jaldak were among the poorest districts in the country. Immense poverty had made some women especially hard. Their conversations, Smoke recalled much later, were often clipped, cold, and distant. They fought for everything they could get their hands on and were petty toward other women they thought were getting more.

In 2010 the US military, NATO, and the Afghan government had decided to stop putting money and troops in Zabul, focusing instead on more densely populated provinces such as Helmand and Kandahar, despite the growing Taliban threat surrounding Qalat City, Zabul's capital. For years the Taliban crossed the province with little fear of retaliation. Insurgents had completely overtaken at least one of the province's eleven districts. At the end of 2010 there were thirty thousand additional US troops in Afghanistan, none of them in Zabul; instead, they were concentrated along the Helmand River valley. By the time Smoke landed in Zabul in 2013 the southeastern province ranked between thirty-second and thirty-fourth out of thirty-four provinces in terms of education, poverty, and its care for and treatment of women.

This was Smoke's first women's shura—a meeting among local women that always included medical help and sometimes voter registration. She would learn from her interactions that day to brace herself for the worst physical abuses and the most aggressive behavior. Some women would snatch food, blankets, and water from her; others would yell about the female next to them getting an extra bag of rice. She started developing debilitating headaches from the stress. It was hard not to become jaded.

When her team arrived at the clinic, more than a hundred women already filled the space surrounding the one-story building. Some sat along the sidewalk. Others leaned against the high wall outside of the compound. Even more stood in the grassy area near the compound's front gate.

Smoke turned to her translator, Edna, to address the crowd.

She explained that all the women would need to be searched. They would need to line up against the back compound wall, lift their arms, and allow members of the AFP to frisk them. Jamila, the feminist and women's center director, reinforced the message, stating that the safety and security of the shura was their first priority. The Afghan leader's reassuring voice prompted shura participants to stand up, some taking their children's hands, others allowing their young six- and seven-year-olds to play.

A small woman in a baby-blue burqa hesitated before taking the last few steps to fill an empty space in the quickly forming line. Smoke watched as the two qualified AFP officers and the other trainees took charge of the search. The captain wanted the Afghan women to interact with one another as much as possible. The FET was there to guide, stand guard, and jump in where needed.

Two Afghan female officers and a third trainee stood only steps from the compound entrance and broke the long search line into three shorter ones. They made quick work of the searches and pointed each woman toward one of three trainees, who guided them to the grassy area inside the compound, where the women sat down and waited for Jamila's lecture—an inspirational speech on voting rights and registration, fighting domestic violence, and spreading feminism.

The hesitant woman approached the front of the line. An AFP officer ordered the woman to lift the blue cloth that covered her body. The petite female refused. The officer ordered the woman to hold her arms out to the side, which she did. The policewoman felt as best she could along the outside of the covering and then ordered the woman once again to raise her burqa. She raised it slowly to reveal, much like the other women, a colorful dress underneath. But instead of pulling the burqa up to her forehead and folding it back to reveal her face, she held it just above her chest so her body could be searched. After the second pat-down the woman lowered her burqa back to the ground and found a place to sit in the grassy area among a sea of colorful dresses and bare faces—the only woman not fully revealed.

A few other women were still arriving, accompanied by their husbands. The FET stopped the men from entering the compound, asking them to sit outside with the other husbands instead—the shura was for women only. Large trees that had been planted in the median shaded the men's faces from the sun. Their wives were searched and then walked inside the compound and headed toward the clinic.

Smoke surveyed the crowd of women, nearly all of whom had removed their burqas. Being in the presence of females only meant they were free to reveal their faces, fan themselves to cool off in the heat, freely breathe in fresh air. Smoke had already done the military equivalent—taking off her rucksack, helmet, combat protection, and M4 rifle and leaving them near the compound entrance with her FET security team. She wanted to show the women that she trusted them, that she had no doubt of her safety in their presence. The move ultimately signaled to the women that they were also safe with her.

The captain stood in the middle of the crowd and looked around from woman to woman for any potential threats—anyone who may be acting strangely, not mixing with the crowd. She noticed the small woman sitting in a corner near the back of the crowd. Her face was the only one on the compound still covered. She sat with her legs bent at the knee, crossed at the ankle slightly in front of her body. The woman's hands were in her lap. The mesh face covering of her baby-blue burqa was tilted toward the sky.

Jamila's voice boomed over the din of the crowd. "You're fine. You're safe," she said after all the women were seated. "Your men think you are here to get yourself medical treatment. And we'll do that, but that's not it. Your men think you are here to take a class. We are actually here to register you to vote."

The activist started each shura the same way, whether among the aggressive crowd of women in Tarnak Wa Jaldak or the women in Shah Joy. And the response, no matter how outwardly aggressive or timid the women initially appeared to be, was often the same.

The crowd would fall silent. Women would turn to one another, wondering, for a moment, if the announcement was a mistake. Within seconds questions that revealed immediate fears would arise from the crowd:

"What if my husband finds out?"

"What if the Taliban in our village finds out?"

"How will we register?"

"Where will we go?"

"Who will keep us safe?"

The litany of questions from women in the more than thirty districts that Jamila, Smoke, and her FET visited throughout Zabul were understandable. Women all over Afghanistan were wrenched between two systems: one run by a corrupt government that claimed it wanted women to vote but did very little to protect the females who tried and another in which the Taliban cut off women's fingers if they were stained with blue voter registration ink. The second was the same world in which husbands sometimes beat their wives if the women came home with voter registration cards.

Jamila's response to the litany of questions was often the same: "You are safe here. Your husbands will never find out. You can do this. This is nothing. You've got this. You've walked here five miles. It's in you."

And the women would follow.

During a shura in Shah Joy, the district northeast of Tarnak Wa Jaldak, closer to Zabul's northern border, a woman who began the day too intimidated to make eye contact not only registered to vote but shook the hand of an AFP officer who provided security for her to do so. "Thank you," she said, "for being brave enough to help us to do this. Thank you for what you do."

Coaxing her into the registration site, in this case a room right next to a doctor's office inside the district's medical clinic, hadn't been easy. Before the shura began, the elections official who accompanied Smoke's team had set up two folding tables in the room—one with a lamination machine and the other with a clipboard, short registration forms, and cards.

The woman sat on the floor against a wall in a far corner of the clinic and stared straight ahead. Her face was plump, her skin heavily tanned, the deep-set wrinkles in her forehead hardly changed as she allowed her eyes to follow the paths of women who walked into the room next to the doctor's office that she didn't really understand and was afraid to move toward. Her hair was tinted with henna. The mostly gray style was parted down the center and pulled into a bun near the nape of her neck. On both sides of the part, three inches of salt-and-pepper hair slowly faded into strands that were dyed copper orange. When she raised her hands she revealed the yellow-orange henna that stained her palms and fingernails.

Smoke, who had been giving candy to some of the children who were growing impatient as they waited for their mothers, looked up and saw the woman sitting alone against the wall. She walked over to Jamila and inquired about whether the activist knew the lady in the corner and whether anything was wrong. Smoke wanted to find out if there was anything more this gentle creature with the henna hair needed—additional medical attention, extra food, blankets.

Jamila approached, and the woman looked up, her burqa falling, most of it cascading around her shoulders.

The woman revealed that she hadn't seen the doctor or registered to vote. She couldn't move because she was afraid to do either. Jamila gently touched the woman's elbow and lifted her arm to help her rise.

She said that she would walk with her into the doctor's office and that she didn't have to register if she didn't want to. "We'll just walk into the voter registration room," Jamila said to the woman, "and see what the other women are doing. Let's just see what it's all about."

The FET doctor, Shayna Thompson, gave the quiet woman a brief examination, and Jamila stood by her side. After they walked out of the doctor's office they turned to the right and approached the small room that had two folding tables inside. An elections official stood, waiting for women to approach the tables to fill out a registration form and get inked. The lady with the henna hair stopped in the doorway. For a few moments she watched the baffling activity unfold in front of her—she saw one woman pick up a registration card, another sign a document, and a third dip her thumb in blue ink.

The woman leaned back, as if she was going to turn and run away. Jamila stopped her and whispered in her ear: "You can do this."

The woman with the henna-dyed hair fell silent for a moment, then revealed two of her biggest fears: her husband could find out, and so could the Taliban. She couldn't dip her thumb in ink. If she did that, her husband would know what had happened. She also knew who the Taliban were in her area.

Jamila remembered that Smoke had brought wet wipes to the shura and reassured the woman that they could use those to wipe the ink off her thumb. She explained that for some women who were especially in danger, the elections board was willing to make exceptions. It wasn't necessary that she get her thumb inked, Jamila explained. She could simply sign the paperwork next to a specific voter registration number. Then the elections official would give her a voter registration card with a corresponding number. As long as that was also signed, that was enough.

The woman walked, with Jamila, past the station with the ink well. They continued to the elections official. Once Jamila explained that the woman was nervous, the official pulled out a sheet of paper with a list of numbers. She pointed to an empty spot near the bottom, one of the last registration numbers available on the page. The woman picked up a pen and, showing her henna-tipped fingernails, slowly, methodically signed her name. Her hand shaking, she placed the pen on top of the ledger and waited for her card. The elections official carefully compared the registration numbers to ensure that she was giving the new voter the corresponding card. The official asked the woman to sign again.

The woman with the henna-dyed hair, who was approaching middle age, had for the first time exercised a basic right. She couldn't find the courage to look up while walking into the clinic that day, but she walked out of the Shah Joy shura looking Smoke directly in the eye. She had a smile on her face. She pulled her bright purple burqa back over her face and allowed it to cascade all the way to the ground to cover every square inch of her body. She slowly approached Ghol, one of the AFP officers who had frisked her earlier that day. When she reached the officer she raised her burqa, flipping it back again to fully reveal her face.

She reached her right hand out to Ghol, pushed by a newfound sense of bravery, one the woman imagined AFP officers summoned daily simply to do their jobs. She thanked the officer for having the courage to go to work every day. Then she restored her burqa and began her miles-long journey home.

But women in areas like Tarnak Wa Jaldak, where it wasn't even safe for the US military to walk through the town center, were living through much worse. And those conditions created a cynicism. Some women took opium to cope with the depression brought by long stints of seclusion or the pain that they had no idea how to treat. In other cases mothers drugged their children to keep them calm during the day. Opium acted as a babysitter for the few women who could sneak outside their homes to work and as a disciplinarian for mothers too young and inexperienced to handle the responsibility of multiple kids. Smoke could see the effects of drug use in the listless eyes and blank stares of at least one baby during that first shura in Tarnak.

Smoke had struggled to find an elections official to accompany her team to the area. Her calls and email requests went ignored. No elections official inside the compound during the shura meant that, unlike the convenient registration room in Shah Joy, women would need to leave the compound in order to register. It also meant that voter registration for the more than a hundred women who showed up in

Tarnak Wa Jaldak would prove more dangerous than in any other district Smoke's FET would visit.

Jamila's plan to register women would sound simple to most Americans. She would walk the women to the boys' school across the street and take them through the front door and into that local voter registration site. But the site was run solely by men. Taliban surrounded the area. And there would be no American military protection for the crossing. All the soldiers they could find would be protecting the shura. Election officials who refused to come to the Tarnak district told the activist that the plan was too dangerous—it would never work.

Jamila insisted that it would.

The women once again walked to their destination in small groups to avoid suspicion. But this time they had to move quickly.

Jamila walked with three women off the compound. They turned sharply to the right to avoid being seen by the few husbands sitting on the street corner at the other end of the road waiting for their wives. Trees that lined the street along the front of the compound helped conceal the feminist warrior and her followers. Out of the corner of her eye Jamila saw one of the men look up, and she began to walk even more quickly. They followed the tree line, which thinned slightly and then gathered into a dense cluster in the middle of the street.

The group reached the front door of the boys' school. Despite the lack of protection, the women never waivered. They defied Taliban law in plain sight. Jamila opened the door, and the three women filed in. They were met by a long table behind which sat three men. Jamila walked up to the man closest to the door.

"We are here to register these women to vote," she said.

Silence. The men stared. One looked past Jamila at the three women behind her.

"They need identification," he said.

"They have it." She turned to the women, who each produced an ID card that identified them by name, address, and description.

Reluctantly the first man grabbed a sheet of paper and asked the woman standing directly behind Jamila to sign her name. The other women walked up to the table to do the same. They inked their thumbs and received cards. They waited for them to be laminated and then quickly tucked them into pockets covered by billowing burqas.

The trip back had to be equally quick. They made sure to stay as much as they could in the shadows. It was only a matter of time, Jamila knew, until she was caught.

She was aware, Smoke recalled of Jamila, that there were enemies all around her. Taliban spies who didn't want progress for women frequently watched her. Jamila regularly received text messages that were death threats. Harassing phone calls eventually forced her to stop answering her cell after 7 P.M. She was constantly sent emails that demanded she close her women's center. The center was bombed twice, once when she was in it. The American military traced the phone numbers to Pakistan. Even some Afghan government officials who sat across from her during meetings on progress for women, Jamila knew, were her enemy. They smiled to her face, then implemented programs behind her back that impeded progress for females in Afghanistan.

"I know that the Taliban is going to kill me one day," Smoke recalled the activist saying. "I know I'm going to die. But I'm not going to stop. I will die doing this."

When Jamila reached the compound she dropped off the first group of women directly inside the clinic. Before gathering the next three to make the trek again, she noticed Smoke.

In the lush green of the grass behind the medical building, children were sitting in a circle. And the intelligence captain was doing something that no one would have ever expected. With a large smile on her face, she tapped the first child on the head, then the next, and the next. Then she yelled "goose" in Pashtu and started to run! A ten-year-old boy, wearing a long tan-and-gold outfit, giggled, jumped up, and ran around the circle after Smoke as fast as he could. She slid into the empty spot the child had left behind. Safe!

A few minutes earlier Jamila would have encountered a much different scene. The youngest children were crying; some of the slightly older boys had grown rowdy. Some kids had been there for several hours before the shura had started. And the candy Smoke had given them only kept their attention for a fleeting moment. It took a few seconds for the kids, who had never heard of the American standby duck-duck-goose, to pick up the rules of the game. Suddenly they were laughing, having fun.

The best way that she could conduct her FET mission, Smoke later explained, was to facilitate Jamila. And sometimes the best way to do that was to take care of the children so the mothers could get on with the job of progress. By the time the shura missions were held, some of the most important parts of Smoke's job were done: she had trained her FET, coordinated the mission with the local AFP force, ensured a slot for Thompson on the chopper, stockpiled supplies to give away to women and their children (food, blankets, and small, solar-powered radios so women could keep up with the outside world from the confines of their homes), and developed a plan to gather intelligence. She made sure female shuras covered three missions at the same time, all of which supported the larger American military goal of defeating the Taliban: intelligence gathering, winning hearts and minds (and improving the condition of women and children) through medical care, and supporting the advancement of local women through voter registration. The last part of the American military mission aligned with Jamila's goals. The activist had been paired with many FET chiefs, but her relationship with Smoke was the strongest. And voter registration was something, Smoke knew, that only Jamila—who had been an activist in Zabul long before the American military landed there—could handle effectively.

"I often felt like I was [Jamila's] chief of staff," Smoke said after she had returned from Afghanistan. "My job was to bring what she needed to make sustainable change among the local female population." For the women, Smoke said, it was about survival.

Jamila admired Smoke's inventiveness, her compassion, and her patience.

She gathered the next group of women, and the four of them took the surreptitious walk through the shadows and across the street to the boys' school.

But this time the men behind the table refused to register the women. When the man closest to the door asked for identification, the women could not produce any—not uncommon in Afghanistan.

Jamila refused to move.

She knew that voter registration was a numbers game in Afghanistan—some precincts cheated to make it look like they had more registered voters than they did.

"You don't really care about these women having identification cards," she said to them. "You simply care that they are women."

Jamila looked directly into the eyes of the man closest to the door. Her face was unencumbered by a burqa, unlike the three women behind her. Instead, she sported a multicolored scarf, which she draped over her hair, around her neck, and down her shoulders. The man stared back, unmoved at first by her defiance. She finally broke the silence: "Just do it," she said. "We're going to stand here until you do."

Jamila returned to the compound with three more successfully registered voters and would continue the risky journey, three women at a time, until she had registered the more than one hundred participants. When she walked into the clinic to pick up the final three women to take across, the last of the shura females were being examined. Smoke was inside, helping to prepare the children for shots and physicals. Most of the kids were now reunited with their mothers or lined up to see Thompson or the nurse who co-owned the clinic. The woman in the blue burqa, the one who refused to remove it even when she was being frisked, still hadn't been seen.

Smoke stood in the waiting area of the clinic, surrounded by children, with the afternoon sun soaking through the vast windows on the outer wall of the building. She held the baby of one of the women, who was being seen by the nurse. A few children surrounded Smoke, some tugging at the shirt of her uniform, and others reaching for her arms in a gentle plea for her attention. The infant was small and motionless in Smoke's arms, swaddled tightly in a red blanket. Its eyes were shut, its tiny head tilted and turned slightly toward Smoke's chest. The captain gently shook the child, but the baby didn't even feel as if it was breathing. She stopped moving and waited to see if the baby would stir. She was hoping to feel anything—a slight movement in the child's arms or legs, a deep sigh coming out of the child's mouth. Nothing. She put her hand on the baby's chest to feel for a heartbeat, her large hands gently covering the baby's small torso, and stared into the child's face. Nothing. In a panic she quickly lifted the baby's face to her ear. Smoke listened, blocking out the noise of the other active children around her. Finally the captain felt and heard the faintest of breaths. The three-month-old baby had been a victim of her mother's opium abuse. The mother had not only been taking the drug herself but also regularly giving opium to her baby to stop it from crying.

Thompson called into the exam room the woman who refused to remove her burqa. The surgeon wasn't sure what to expect.

After the woman sat on the examination table, Thompson asked her to remove her burqa. Slowly she lifted it past her ankles, her knees, her stomach, and to her chest. She paused before lifting the burqa the rest of the way over her chin, eyes, forehead, hair, and, finally, off her body.

And there it was: a young face that had yet to shed the last ounces of baby fat usually lost during the transition from late teens to early twenties. A dark red spot covered the right side of her chin, her left eye was swollen shut, the white of her right eye was red, and her right cheekbones were blue and bruised.

Thompson looked closely at the woman's face. She gently placed her hand on the fleshy area between the woman's chin and cheek—one of the few spaces free from bruising. She took care not to touch any spots where nerve endings must have been raw as she gently turned her face to the right, toward the light from the nearest window, so she could take a closer look.

Thompson asked the young mother what had happened.

Her husband, she said, looking for a moment at the translator, and then the ceiling. The bruised woman offered no further explanation.

She heard Thompson mention the phrase *domestic violence*, a term she had never encountered before and didn't understand. The reluctant patient had risked her life simply by walking into the clinic. She just wanted something for the bruises on her face, something to make the pain go away, she said.

"What choice did they have?" Smoke stated much later when discussing physical abuse and other vestiges of Taliban influence, including the alarmingly high rate of drug use. "The abuse is just another aspect of life they have to deal with."

CHAPTER 16

WHEN RADIO
CHANGES A WAR

Nestled in a small corner in a secluded back room of a nondescript, one-story stone building, Jamila Abbas waited. She patiently listened, headphones fitted snugly over her ears, for her name. Through the thin scarf that covered her dark hair and draped just below her shoulders she could hear a slightly muffled version of the radio host's baritone voice. He announced the week's upcoming programs—all male-centered talk focused on the much-anticipated Afghan elections. Sitting across from him, Jamila watched his lips quickly move as he rattled off the radio station's call-in number and followed that with a message encouraging Zabul's men to express their views. They could call in every day, the host explained, but that day. That day, for the first time in the station's history, was reserved for Zabul's women.

Although this was the first time the feminist was delivering her message to Qalat City's young mothers, wives, and teen girls on the local radio station, Jamila knew that the booth she sat in was regularly occupied by the American military to send targeted messages meant to intimidate the Taliban. Members of Smoke's unit periodically took over the airwaves to push out propaganda to the province's insurgents. And she also knew that if those same insurgents heard *her* voice over their radios—telling women to register to vote and encouraging abused wives to leave dysfunctional homes for safety in other provinces—they would immediately seek her out.

Her first crime, in their eyes, was working with the American military. This was the fifth month of her partnership with Smoke, and the Army captain had used Jamila as a bargaining chip to get her on the air. During an afternoon meeting with the 3rd Brigade Combat Team, Smoke heard details about an upcoming radio mission. The combat team used programming to, among other things, get a better sense of what the local community was saying about the Taliban. Smoke immediately saw an opportunity. She approached her commander after the meeting to pitch an all-female radio program, with Jamila at the helm. Radio was the perfect medium, she explained, to reach rural women—many of whom are stuck at home all day without their husbands and had no form of entertainment other than what is pumped out over the air waves. Part of the FET mission is to ensure that information reaches as many women in the province as possible. Jamila, she assured her command, could do that.

Smoke also had to convince the men in her unit who were already using several radio slots to step aside and make room for a female talk show. The mission would be the same—to rid the area of insurgents—but the methods for accomplishing the mission would be very different. Instead of pumping out messages intended to instill fear in the enemy, Jamila's approach would empower women to turn against the enemy and toward their own interests.

Afghan officials and station executives were already working with American and coalition forces to produce radio ads that supported the FET mission, which was, in part, to train more women to be police officers. "The elections are coming," the ads said, "make sure that your women stay safe when they go to the polls, and support the training and development of female police." But the success of these ads, in the face of Taliban threats and violence, was meager. What coalition forces needed was an activist like Jamila who could speak directly to women about their fears, push the importance of education, and lead by brave example. Smoke appealed further to coalition forces and radio managers operating in the area who needed access to government officials. Jamila, who worked closely with the government in Qalat City, would bring them. "Help us get on the radio," Smoke negotiated, "and we'll bring you officials."

Getting on the air was a bold move. But for the Taliban the feminist's larger crime was—and had been for years now—the message itself. She was telling women that they had rights in a world where the actions of husbands, fathers, brothers, and sons—supported by the militancy of the Taliban—told women that they didn't. And since her return to Zabul, the province of her birth, Jamila kept finding more meaningful ways to slowly move women from complacency to action and break with the Taliban's extreme version of traditional law. In 2010 she and dozens of other women marched through the dusty streets of Qalat City in a demonstration against the Taliban's ongoing mistreatment of female workers and mothers in the province. Jamila organized the rally, during which women covered themselves with extra care to avoid detection. Jamila, who normally wore just a scarf, covered her entire face, revealing only her eyes. That year the Taliban had beheaded a woman for daring to step out of her home and work for Zabul's government. Another woman was shot for working with an American development company. Insurgents talked of a hit list with the names of women who were next to be killed if they continued to defy authority.

So by the time she sat next to the radio host in a small booth in Qalat City just ten minutes outside of FOB Apache, threats from insurgents, for Jamila, were nothing new. She had to keep working. Her activism was the only means she had of facing down the militancy that had killed her husband.

The last time she fled was thirteen years ago, she was desperate for a place where she could finally put down roots. She left Tajikistan early one morning, after she had remained there long enough, she thought, for the men who killed her husband to have forgotten about her existence. She left the home she had built for her family with her daughter on her left hip, her three sons walking on her right, each holding the next's hand, with the youngest holding hers. They traveled for several days by car, by horse, by donkey. They stayed in the homes of strangers. Walking into the unknown terrified her. Most of her children were too young to understand the consequences. She didn't know whether she would be greeted by friend or insurgent. She looked for homes where there were women and children. When they finally reached Zabul she and her four children showed up at her brother's doorstep—family, comfort, stability, and the chance to begin again is what she was looking for. All those things, plus a room where she could lay her head down at night, is what he provided for as long as she needed. After a year she and her children were smiling again. Jamila stopped feeling sick and nervous all the time. She had also saved up enough money to purchase her own home. Eventually she and her children moved out, making the decision to remain in Zabul province.

And as she fought to rebuild her life, she also fought to save the lives of other women who were, she quickly learned, even less empowered than she was.

The morning of Jamila's first radio program, Smoke, along with another member of the captain's FET, met her and the manager of the local women's center outside the gates of FOB Apache. Just as they had for so many local missions, they snuck Jamila into the backseat of a military truck. Traveling through the streets of Qalat City for the activist, even for just ten minutes, wasn't safe. Smoke encouraged Jamila to wear body armor. As always, the woman refused. "If it's time for me to die," Smoke remembered Jamila saying, "hopefully I've done enough."

Sitting in a small booth in a tiny radio station on the outskirts of the Army's FOB, the activist heard her name.

"Jamila runs a local women's center," the host's muffled baritone hit her ears. "This is the first of what will be many appearances. Jamila, welcome. Why don't you tell the female listeners out there about yourself?"

Confidently the plump woman leaned toward the microphone. Her voice, with its wavering timbre, crackled slightly: "My name is Jamila," she said. "I am here to tell women about their rights." With a few short words she began her latest act of defiance.

CHAPTER 17

AN UNEXPECTED RUN-IN

DAYCHOPAN DISTRICT, ZABUL PROVINCE, JANUARY 2014—High in the mountains of Southern Afghanistan, Johanna Smoke followed Afghan soldiers over rocky terrain and past the jumble of barbed wire that spanned several feet across the dry sand.

She was on foot, as were several of the men on the 3rd Brigade Combat Team, 1st Infantry Division mission, and the weight of her gear combined with the heightened threat of IEDs, which were much harder to spot in arid, unfettered land, slowed her gait. With each step she glanced down at her boots, quickly scanning the earth immediately around them for slightly disturbed gravel or sand—any signs of explosives in this vastly barren terrain. Smoke and her translator were the only women among the more than one hundred infantrymen working the four-day mission, and by midmorning the small group she had been marching with finally made it to the remote ANP headquarters.

Often described as "desolate" and "rugged," much of Daychopan, aside from its small pockets of farms and struggling orchards, had been abandoned. Once considered too dangerous for development, the Afghan government cut funds to the district. There was little to no business activity and few of the markets that, though meager, dominated downtown life in other districts across the province. To the Army, the area meant frequent reports of rocket-propelled grenade (RPG) fire. To the Afghans who lived there—in small pockets of isolated communities spread across the desert—it meant a heightened fear of insurgent attacks.

During Smoke's mission she would be the only female soldier attending the all-male shura, and she would see the level of fear that still existed in the hearts of those living in the district.

The police headquarters was one of the smallest and most remote police compounds in the country. Its only building was stone with one story and an open courtyard in the square structure's center. Offices for the Afghan policemen who regularly worked the outpost were sprinkled in rooms around one side of the building's perimeter, and catty-cornered from the main entrance were rooms filled with bunkbeds and lockers where the policemen, even those whose families lived elsewhere, slept. Attached to the wall that surrounded the compound, reaching high above its front-facing far corners, sat narrow watchtowers. In between, two members of Smoke's combat unit (dubbed Combined Task Force Duke) stood guard, sniper weapons slung low across the fronts of their bodies.

Smoke walked behind a member of her unit's security team underneath the black tarp that sheltered the police compound entrance from the searing sun. She cut a sharp left around another set of barbedwire fencing curling its way across part of the entrance and walked through the opening of the headquarters building. When she reached the courtyard she saw several Afghan men sitting under an awning to her right. The dark covering shaded the group of twenty Afghan elders, sitting on their knees, only the small mats they had brought with them protecting their shins from the ground underneath. The men had gathered, much like men in other shuras before them, to talk about security in the district and the upcoming elections, which inevitably made villagers a target for Taliban reprisals. Smoke's commanding officer stood in front of the group, his back to the police headquarters building, a few rusted chairs sitting in front of him. The men directed their attention to the commander. They were anxious to hear about the US military plans to keep their families safe.

When Smoke wasn't talking to the Afghan men, she was observing them. And the fact that not one had a female with him confirmed what the military already knew—that Taliban dominance in the region was high and that efforts to pump up security were overwhelmingly needed.

But beyond being an intelligence gatherer, on missions like this, Smoke was there as an example of female accomplishment. The commander wanted her to talk to the men participating in that shura and show them that women could serve, just like men, even under threatening circumstances. Just as Smoke stood guard, so too could their wives, sisters, and daughters. In the most isolated parts of the country, where the number of Taliban fighters nearly surpassed the general population of those sparsely inhabited communities, police officers were needed. And the US Army didn't mind leaning on reluctant husbands and fathers in an attempt to get local women to fill a void that was rolling back American military strategy.

But even as she maneuvered across rugs partially shaded by the tent's thick black tarp—walking around the men who remained seated in order to remove herself as a potential distraction from the rest of the shura—Smoke's focus never veered from intelligence collection. Even the smallest of atmospherics, she knew, were worth noting.

As she approached the edge of the tent a man who sat lounging on the steps of the police barracks caught her attention. Smoke couldn't, at first, see his face, but his stature looked familiar. His hair was a brownish red, he was heavy set, and his legs, even with bended knee, were long enough to span the last few risers of the building's front stairs, allowing his feet to touch the ground. He looked down at his large hands as he threw small bits of orange peel to the ground. Puffs of dust plumed at his ankles. He raised his head only to smile at the man to his right as he stuffed bits of fruit in his mouth. His reddish beard, Smoke noted, was unmistakable.

Although he was an ANP criminal investigator, he was a suspected operative. He had never actually killed an American soldier. He was careful not to link himself to attacks that took out US service members at FOBs or blew up convoys during patrols. He never talked about his links to the Taliban. In fact, the high-ranking Afghan government official appeared to be working with allied forces. He seemed to do everything right.

But according to the military intelligence officer, the US Army had suspected for some time that he had been working for the Taliban as an operative, feeding the insurgent group the locations of service members along with mission schedules and targets. And in return, Smoke said, the Taliban paid him lucrative sums of money. What the Army couldn't figure out was where this operative would show up next. He seemed to randomly appear, sometimes during US missions, like the one Smoke was on, that focused on antiterror tactics pinpointed at protecting local communities.

Smoke slowly walked out of the tent's protective shade and nodded toward her translator, who joined her as she approached the investigator. He, along with the men around him, stood as soon as Smoke was close enough to reach out her right hand and introduce herself.

As she shook his hand, she gave her name, told him that she knew of his work on criminal investigations, and wanted to introduce herself. Although they had never met, he recognized her name immediately.

He had heard of the great work she was doing for Zabul's women's center and for the woman who ran it, Smoke recalled him saying.

And like any good intelligence collector, Smoke made her target comfortable by giving information about herself first. With a tone that implied she was straining to make casual small talk instead of probing for more details than she was about to give, Smoke told the suspected operative about her work to rebuild the women's center. She also mentioned that the woman who ran the center needed transportation to their FOB and wondered if he'd be able to help.

He flashed a broad smile and then proceeded to give her information that the US military would use to track his whereabouts for the next several months. She had given him all the prompting he needed to fall into a role that came easily to many Afghan men. He became the all-knowing male and Smoke the passive female he was eager to impress.

Just in case she needed to contact him about providing transportation for the director of the women's center, he gave her multiple cell phone numbers. She was encouraged to use them at any time to contact him. He has a daughter, he mentioned. He reassured her that he's a strong supporter of women's rights. Smoke thanked him.

"How often are you in that area near Qalat City?" she asked. "Where do you usually travel?"

By the time the conversation was over, Smoke had learned the areas of the district where the criminal investigator traveled most frequently. She found out where the suspected operative lived, how often he visited Qalat City—the town in Zabul where her base, FOB Apache, was located.

As he walked her through the barracks to show her how some of the men he worked with lived, she had managed to draw from him details about his schedule for the next several weeks. After her translator relayed Smoke's questions, she also wrote down key words from the man's response, ones that the captain would later use to recreate the exchange with as much accuracy as possible in her intelligence report. From the conversation, Smoke figured out the suspected operative's patterns of life—daily travel habits that can tell an intelligence field operative plenty about how to track someone.

After an hour of talking, Smoke's heart rate began to return to normal. During all that time she was reading his face, his gestures, any indication through his body language that he might be getting irritated, suspicious of all the questions she had been asking. She found none. After the second hour she got nervous again, afraid that perhaps she was spending too much time with him. She was relieved when, out of the corner of her eye, through the open doors of the barracks, she saw the men who had come to the shura begin to disperse. She thanked the operative for his time and walked out of the compound sure that soon the soldiers who were left on this last day of the mission would need to return to the base.

Smoke stood to the right of the outer compound wall waiting for the chopper that would transport her team back to FOB Apache.

The captain turned her head as gusts of wind blew small rocks and soil against her helmet. She could hear the blades begin to slow as she walked away from the compound and toward the chopper, which landed right outside the barbed wire for the return flight. Choppers never landed this close. The primary landing zone usually forced long treks, like the mission's early-morning march. Smoke ducked under the blades knowing, from the commander's announcement just moments earlier, that FOB Apache had been attacked. There were no details.

By the time the chopper landed in Daychopan, members of the base's quick-response team had already been alerted of the shooting. Those soldiers, who were notified during emergencies on and around the FOB, had likely already rounded the corner just outside the motor pool where the shot soldier had collapsed.

As Smoke boarded the helicopter and strapped in, she looked directly into her commanding officer's eyes, studying his expression for some sense of reassurance. The swoosh of the blades grew louder as the chopper slowly lifted off the ground. Smoke and her translator shifted forward with the momentum of the Chinook as it departed Daychopan with little security. There were gunners on high alert on either side of the Chinook, but the dozens of infantrymen who had arrived ahead of the officers to provide mission security were long gone. The confidence Smoke was looking for in her commander's eyes, the reassurance she leaned on during tough missions, was gone. The bird they occupied flew into uncertainty. No one knew whether the base shooting was an isolated incident. No one knew yet who was responsible. There could have been other attacks planned across the country, including on the small compound they occupied for their mission in Daychopan. The longer the unit stayed on the ground, the more vulnerable it was to attack. But air strikes were also a possibility. And the frequent RPG attacks in this deserted southern section of the country prompted some chopper pilots to refuse to fly this far into Daychopan territory.

Members of the quick-response team ran through the motor pool, ducking behind vehicles to avoid gunfire. It took the team more than an hour to find and gun down the killers—two Afghan soldiers who had been stationed on the base to train and learn from the US military. In the middle of the search another soldier, a member of the team, was shot and injured.

During the two-hour ride back to Qalat City Smoke thought about the information she had gathered that day. She had spent most of the mission next to a man the military had been trying to pin down but couldn't. She had gathered more than the usual atmospherics that filled FET intelligence reports.

Instead, this report would give key information on the location of a man who for years had been on the military intelligence watch list. Afghan locals had reported seeing the operative talk to insurgents. Her biggest worries were whether she would make it back to the base that night and whether the man she had spent most of her time talking to that day would turn her into a target.

The team had returned to FOB Apache too early to land—the threat level was still too high. The Chinook circled the FOB for more than thirty minutes. Smoke looked down and saw the combination chain-link and mud fence that circled the perimeter and was reminded of how small the base actually was. She ran down the list of people she knew who had been left behind while she participated in that day's mission. She also thought about the Afghan military members who worked, slept, ate, and recreated on the base with American soldiers every day, the ones who had become like brothers to everyone. She had developed tight relationships with soldiers on both sides. She prayed that the dead soldier and the two Afghan guards in danger weren't among them.

Smoke would later learn the details of the attack: an argument had started between two soldiers on guard duty—one American, the other Afghan. As the argument got heated, the American soldier began to walk away. The Afghan soldier followed and opened fire. Soon after, another Afghan soldier joined the shooting.

The American's body was found only moments before the chopper arrived at the FOB. He was barely out of his teens.

CHAPTER 18

THE SMALL VICTORIES
WOMEN LEFT BEHIND

The message resonated throughout Qalat City and slightly beyond:

"Afghan local and national elections are coming. Women, you must register to vote."

In their two-room homes in rural villages along the outskirts of the city young mothers flipped on small radios, some of which had been given to them just months before by the American military. Most of them had not left their homes for weeks. Others, whose husbands allowed them to occasionally leave, hadn't for days. Stepping outside of the small shelters that made up their confined worlds was dangerous. Mothers attending a shura meeting—a mission for Smoke and a necessity for Jamila to spread her feminist message and ensure the health and well-being of the females of Zabul Province—was a rarity. Many of their husbands hadn't even known that their wives had attended. Raising children who, by American standards, weren't much younger than the people they called mother was their main responsibility. Listening to the radio was their primary form of entertainment.

Through the pop and crackle they could still hear Jamila's voice. The mothers sat on dirt floors covered with large, colorful rugs as young children ran between the wives and the tiny boxes that allowed temporary escape. The babies who hadn't been subdued with opium cried. The mothers listened: "Women, call me with your issues."

Unlike her first appearance on the radio—when she was interviewed by the local host so the public could get to know her—by January 2014 Jamila acted as her own host. She introduced the topics and encouraged the audience to participate. The show was geared toward women, but men called too. She encouraged dialogue among anyone who was willing to listen to what she had to say about women's rights. The show defied insurgents and supported the FET mission. She talked about women working outside the home, women voting their own interests, women getting help to conquer drug addiction. The responses her show generated at any given moment showed the US Army the level of Taliban threat. If plenty of people called in and spoke freely, the military mission may have been making progress. If few felt free to speak, insurgent presence may have been higher than usual. On this day both men and women flooded the phone lines.

A male caller: "I support women having the right to vote."

"But," the man on the other end of the line continued, "I don't want my daughters traveling to areas where they won't be safe. If the Taliban is there to keep our daughters and wives from voting," he asked, "how do we keep them safe?"

"That's an issue that the local chief of police is working to solve," Jamila informed the man. "They are trying to recruit more women to serve as officers on the police force and to protect polling stations." She invited the man to tune in for a subsequent program, during which women from the local police force would speak along with Zabul Province's police chief.

A female caller: "Violence from men in the home is a problem for many women in these villages."

Jamila: "The women's center can help."

Jamila frequently explained how her work at the center saved families, marriages, and lives. She intervenes to help couples and families stay together, she explains, but only if their homes can become functional ones. She works first to educate men who themselves likely grew up in households where their fathers—or some other older male figure—dominated with violence and control. If it's possible to change the husbands' behavior, that's always her first goal. The last resort, she explains, is for women to leave their families. But if needed, she can help wives and daughters in dire situations escape to other provinces. Sometimes just fleeing to the next village isn't far enough.

Women on the outskirts of the city looked to their radios for the last few seconds of the show—before their husbands returned home from work. During that one hour when Jamila's voice resonated through their villages they could feel that someone was—for the first time—speaking directly to them, nurturing their desires to be informed and to hear the stories of other women in their province.

A few miles away Smoke stood near the back of the booth watching Jamila sign off.

The soldier so often thought back to the start of her relationship with the activist whose voice was now a regularly welcomed guest in the homes of hundreds of desperate Afghan women. When they first met, Jamila rarely initiated conversations.

Now, months later, Smoke and Jamila had made an art form out of civil disobedience and peaceful resistance and turned their work into the ultimate military mission. But future opportunities would be limited. Smoke's time in Afghanistan was running out. More and more, as the end of her deployment neared, she worried about Jamila's future and whether the women had accomplished enough.

Before they left the radio station the two women sat with the station's manager and looked through the following week's programming schedule. Jamila's call-in program never aired at the same time twice. Having a set time slot was too risky. The Taliban might figure out the feminist's routine and show up at the station with the intent of killing her. Jamila's life was constantly threatened. She and Smoke had seen firsthand how, with one fatal blow, insurgents could devastate an entire family or rend a once-peaceful peaceful village. Constantly changing the show's time slot was the only way to keep her safe. And even that wasn't a guarantee. One week Jamila's voice was heard on a Tuesday morning. Another, a Wednesday afternoon. A few weeks later it was on in the evening on a Sunday. Some weeks Jamila wouldn't show up at the station at all. Instead, Smoke and her translator Edna would record Jamila speaking during a shura, edit excerpts, and ship that to the station to air. Other weeks the women would broadcast a shura live. Their goal—and the most vital part of this mission—was to keep the Taliban guessing.

That day the three looked through the programming schedule and decided Jamila's show could safely air the following Thursday. Jamila would take calls at the radio station. Members of Zabul's female police force were slated to join her.

Quickly Smoke and her FET moved the Afghan woman from the back door of the station to the military vehicle waiting outside. Before exiting the building Jamila lifted the edges of a scarf that hung just below her shoulders to cover the exposed parts of her face. Air and wind hit her eyes, the only part of her body exposed to the outdoors. The woman squashed her body as low as possible into the backseat, and the truck took off for FOB Apache.

BIBI KHALA SCHOOL, QALAT CITY, APRIL 2014—Smoke stood on the first step outside the cream-colored, one-story school building behind a handful of twelve-year-old girls, some of whom fidgeted and squirmed as they waited for the provincial governor. The students' lavender head coverings and starched white headscarves, pink undercoats, and deep-red dresses were explosions of color against the gray sky and concrete sidewalks. The tallest girl in the front looked down at the notebook paper in her hands the entire time, never once raising her head. She wanted to get all the words right in front of the province's highest-ranking politician.

The rest of the youngsters stood up straight and raised their voices in unison as the man in the long brown overcoat and traditional headdress stood in front of them. "Nari, nari, mananaaah. Nari, nari, mananaaah!" The song was a symbolic thanks to the head of Zabul Province for the computer lab that the American military had spent several months revamping—a strategic gesture to a man who had nothing to do with the lab's development. But Smoke hoped the cute faces and earnest singing would go a long way toward engendering a political commitment to girls' education long after she was gone. If the governor's image was associated with the lab and the school, there was less of a chance for Taliban retaliation. As long as he felt connected to the school, he might also feel obligated to continue to fund it.

It was the day before Smoke was scheduled to leave Afghanistan for good, and to her left, standing just on the other side of the group, was Smoke's replacement. The new FET leader's job would be to build on the changes that Smoke spent the last ten months making. But Smoke knew that, often, building on change in a country like Afghanistan meant rebuilding—especially when the surrounding community didn't always want those changes. Just down the road from FOB Apache, po-sitioned beneath a palace once occupied by Alexander the Great, sat a shining example of American hubris—a multi-million-dollar town that nobody in Afghanistan wanted. The Taliban didn't need to destroy it; the people of Qalat City did that themselves—neglecting it out of fear, rejecting everything about it that was fresh, new, and could make them a prime target for insurgents.

The US government spent millions to create what many must have thought would be ideal: miles and miles of newly paved roads and a home for the provincial governor that lacked security. He never moved in; instead, the façade of his home collapsed. The buildings fell into disrepair. The development is an example of what Smoke called "unsustainable American thinking." Soldiers sometimes leave be-hind—in spite of the lives lost attempting to build a legacy of change and progress—a testament to a Western mindset that doesn't fit the traditions of other cultures, lifestyles, or desire for safety that many Afghans wanted to establish where they already lived. Just as larger military units sometimes struggled to build social projects that some residents of rural southern Afghanistan—with very little money and even less education—could easily sustain long after the units left, FETs struggled to find sustainable and empowering projects to leave for Afghan women. Often nearby water wells that FET units built were destroyed, sometimes by the Taliban but even more frequently, accord-ing to Smoke, by women in villages whose only chance to leave their homes was when they got to walk a few miles to get water. The jour-ney looked to Americans like an illogical chore. To Afghan women it looked more like a rare opportunity to connect with friends and leave the stifling confines of their compounds during the only moment that was socially acceptable and likely to be safe.

During her time in Afghanistan the captain had realized that the only way to make temporary social changes permanent was for FETs to leave behind more than just vans and repaired irrigation systems; they also had to leave behind the funds that these Afghan women needed to make those changes last.

In September 2013 Smoke had sat with Jamila and the Afghan woman's assistant at the women's center conference room table to hatch a plan that would make the repairs they had started as permanent as possible. Finance was a topic Jamila rarely had help wading through. Her women's center was a government-supported organization. And Jamila's official job was considered a government position. But the title of *women's center leader* was just that—a title, with very little meaning to some of the men who ran provincial and national operations. Although the center, like all government institutions, was supposed to get funding from the local and provincial council, it didn't. Jamila's life, though better than it had been, was still a fight. She struggled while sitting on government boards and in council meetings, often as the only woman there, to explain why a women's center should be thought of as more than a token symbol of progress and should be taken seriously enough to get regular government funding. And as she spoke she knew that some of those smiling male faces—nodding and professing to agree—were among the same people who were actively stopping funds and progress from coming to her center. And even as she struggled to explain to men in local and provincial government why a women's center should be taken seriously, she struggled just as hard to stave off the Taliban, who saw her center as a threat to insurgent dominance. But fighting them, their bombs and destruction, also took money.

Smoke thought she had found a solution—a Spirit of America grant. Not only would it provide immediate funds for much-needed repairs; it also had the potential to be a continued source. The group decided that Smoke should write Spirit of America a letter:

The women's center successfully supports local females and their children, with socioeconomic-based programs and training . . . the center has received substantial support the past few years from previous military units, Provincial-Reconstruction Teams, and USAID grants. Unfortunately, this support has not been sustainable. . . . She [Jamila] does not receive a substantial budget for operations and management from the Afghan government.

She asked the organization for $10,000. Within two weeks Jamila had received enough money to fix the center's crumbling plaster and walkway, repair the greenhouse, and reestablish the compound's irrigation system. And they had created ties to an NGO that Smoke banked on helping the center long after she was gone.

Smoke used the same sustainability approach in her work for the girls' school that she stood in front of the day before she left Afghanistan.

The young girls sang in unison one last time "nari, nari, mananaaaa." The provincial governor, standing next to the school's principal—a short, slightly stout woman wearing a loosely draped scarf—clapped, as did the rest of the small crowd, which included a few fathers and the governor's assistants. One man pulled out his phone and took photos of the girls as they projected the last beats of their simple song. A wide, toothy grin stretched across Smoke's face.

As she walked away from the school that day, she glanced at the roof. It was flat, metal, black. The main things that distinguished it from the condition it had been in when she arrived in Afghanistan were the shiny panels that were slanted toward the back of the building and provided the solar energy needed to keep the school's computer lab running. Accomplishing that mission, next to her work with Jamila, was one of the most satisfying moments of her military career.

It had started with a long wait outside the school compound. Smoke had gathered soldiers from an engineering unit to help her FET complete the mission—the same unit that helped during Smoke's first repair missions at the women's center. A few soldiers stood guard on the roofs of the compound's two main buildings, scanning the horizon for potential threats. The rest of the men sat along the low, concrete wall that surrounded the school and its adjoining yard. The solar panels, they knew, were in bad shape, capable of providing only enough power to keep the school running for three hours a day. Most of the panels had broken long ago. The few that did work stored and distributed power inconsistently. Poor working conditions like the ones at Bibi Khala School weren't unusual in Zabul Province, especially at educational facilities intended for girls. There were only a handful of such schools in the province, and often one small building catered to girls in elementary through high school.

But facilities with barely functioning electrical systems meant no heat, no air conditioning, and spotty, infrequent attendance. Schools were only open a few months every year. That world—one that valued boys' education over girls'—was a dysfunctional one that Smoke learned to conquer early on during her deployment.

After the Army captain repaired the women's center from the ravages of a Taliban bombing, her reputation grew as a FET soldier who could create and carry out missions that contributed to the well-being of women and girls in need. And Bibi Khala School, which had just opened five years before, was already in trouble. A US-led provincial reconstruction team (PRT) had built the school, considered the premier example of girls' education in the province when it opened in 2009. It had upgraded electrical systems and had been stocked with enough supplies for fifteen hundred female students along with computer, biology, and chemistry labs. The United States provided the school with dozens of computers, modems, and printers. The school's small staff—a principal, an IT specialist, and a few underpaid teachers—had a hard time maintaining the equipment they had been given. Its headmistress had known Jamila for years, and the women's center director introduced the headmistress to Smoke. Much of what the PRT had done was, over the years, gradually undone.

From Smoke's first missions with Jamila she had learned the best way to navigate the counterintuitive and complex system of labor contracting and supply distribution in Afghanistan—vet frequently, trust very few local contractors, and be prepared to get supplies through a convoluted network of contacts.

When she walked into the Bibi Khala computer lab on the first day of the mission she saw just how much the staff was struggling. What she thought would be a relatively simple operation to repair solar panels was clearly turning into a large-scale assignment: the computers were so old that they were no longer compatible with modern-day software, there was no internet connectivity, and there was no paper for students to print or write on. She reached out to Spirit of America for another grant.

On a sunny afternoon, the mission officially began. The electrical engineers who had been sitting on the concrete wall outside the compound jumped into action. One soldier crawled along a ladder that stretched from the roof of one compound building to the roof of another, making the small chasm between them passable. He needed to get to the second roof, where other dilapidated panels waited for repair.

Days later the FET returned, this time with truckloads of black computers, sleek flat-screen monitors, and reams of printer paper. Local children, boys and girls alike, gathered as soldiers unlocked the sand-colored truck gates that barricaded the sides and backs of the desert MRAP vehicles. The youngsters pointed and questioned as soldiers unloaded computers and placed them on school grounds. Inside, two-person wood desks, each with its own narrow bench behind it, sat in obedient rows. The stations—made of lightly sanded wood and wrought iron—dotted concrete floors, filling one of the school's eight cavernous classrooms.

Smoke hunched over boxes that sat on the floor, unwrapping the new equipment as another FET member stood at one of the desks behind her, swapping out old equipment. Another soldier from the engineering team unwrapped a small monitor and placed it at the center of the desk, the anchor of the computer station that two students would share.

Dawby, who appeared to be in his seventies, had been around for as long as the school. He was Bibi Khala's maintenance manager. He had a gray beard and slowly shuffled behind soldiers unlocking doors. Outside the soldiers gave him pointers on how to check and maintain the solar panels. The edges of his dark brown coat, which covered a blue kaftan and matching loose pants, flicked up in the wind. The soles of his shoes dragged slowly against the concrete, leaving a faint echo in his wake.

Now, the day before she left Afghanistan for good, Smoke walked away from the compound, the voices of her girls singing in unison to celebrate the opening of the remodeled computer lab still resonating in her mind. She headed back to FOB Apache hoping she had done enough to sustain the children's needs. She prayed that her replacement would be able to build on the changes she had made.

She was confronted again with one of the biggest frustrations of nation building in Afghanistan: there rarely seems to be progress. Future military leaders will be lucky if they aren't reconstructing parts of this same school again in another five years.

PART TWO
THE WARS AT HOME

CHAPTER 19

PROMOTE OR PERISH

SHEENA ADAMS

CAMP PENDLETON, CALIFORNIA, MARCH 2012—She typed as quickly as she could in order to add her ideas to the report before she forgot them. Forgetfulness is something the Marine found herself constantly battling after her return from Afghanistan. The brain injury she had sustained during an IED blast was slowly diminishing some of the mental acuity she had once taken for granted.

FETs can be used, she wrote, long after the wars in Iraq and Afghanistan are over in countries like Somalia and Nigeria, locations where the United States is not participating in ground combat but where women are struggling for equality and insurgencies are making it impossible for them to gain it.

The long, narrow, gray trailer that housed her small desk and beat-up chair (that was once comfortable but was now starting to exacerbate what she recently found out were slipped disks in her back) defined the boundaries of her new world. She spent much of her days trying to figure out how to save and reshape the FET program. She wanted it to be sustainable, to outlast what many saw as its current usefulness.

When she wasn't inside the trailer, she was on the concrete lots outside, training women in combat tactics and the importance of relationship building for FETs as they prepared to take on what she had only recently left behind in Afghanistan.

In many ways she had gotten her long-held wish. She was far away from the confines of the helicopter hangar. That bay and its adjacent flight line were among the most open spaces on the base, yet during the months she worked the line the repetition of helicopter inspections and the job's distance from the combat experiences she had craved made her feel more caged than the small trailer where she now spent most of her days. She was no longer in combat—the only thing she regretted. But she was helping to shape combat missions. And that was enough of a connection to keep her uplifted.

Adams was still typing—filling her report with data to show how much help women in sub-Saharan Africa needed—when her phone rang. It was me.

The first time I talked to Adams she was battling multiple fronts—the possible end of the FET, the deteriorating physical conditions that combat had thrust onto her body, and a gender-biased Marine Corps that was making her fight to keep her job.

"Hello." I could only faintly hear her voice on the other line.

She walked outside of the trailer for a better connection. Of the three struggles, her dedication pushed her to talk about the FET program first.

"These units can not only help women; they can help men and kids," Adams explained of her expanded FET protocol.

And until the Pentagon fully opened combat roles to women, Adams's expanded FET program would be one of the few paths available for female Marines who wanted to make an impact on ground conflict in Afghanistan. Just the month before that first phone conversation the Pentagon finally admitted that women were participating in the ground conflicts in Iraq and Afghanistan. It struck down part of the 1994 regulation that barred women from collocating with units whose primary missions were ground combat. But that back-door admission did very little to expand opportunities for Adams or the hundreds of other women who had already given their strength and heart to the FET. It did nothing for the women she was training and sending to Afghanistan to continue the FET mission.

If the Pentagon had very loudly and publicly proclaimed the FET's existence when the program started in 2003, women would likely have gotten better access to mental healthcare. Less than half of women surveyed between 2010 and 2011 said that the Department of Veterans Affairs met their mental health needs either "completely" or "very well." Pregnant women have an even harder struggle, with mental illness, including PTSD, ranking twice as high for those female veterans, according to a study by the National Institutes of Health. After serving in Iraq and Afghanistan, women reported experiencing flashbacks, nightmares, and other symptoms common among combat troops. Some of those same women also reported being dismissed by the VA and commanders who didn't understand that females were actually participating in intense battles in the Middle East.

Recognition from the Pentagon would also have given women more opportunities to excel at promotions boards. Talking frequently about FET achievements early on—as they were happening—would have shown that the military's combat strategy was logically evolving and that the services understood the critical role women could play.

There were other avenues to the battlefield for women. And the females who chose them also were not recognized as having served in combat. Major Mary Jennings Hegar was one of the four females suing the Pentagon to open all roles to women. As a helicopter pilot, she had received a Purple Heart after her chopper was shot down during a medical rescue mission. Enemy bullets and glass from the front of the chopper pierced her right arm and leg. She convinced her team, on which she was the only female, to continue the mission.

Adams had lived among other combat Marines and Afghan women for seven months in Helmand Province. And those had been among the most meaningful months of her life. She had circumvented part of a military structure that had tried, no matter how unintentionally, to limit her ambitions.

She swiftly became the kind of leader that other FET members—or "the girls," as Adams called them—could readily lean on for strength. The FET mission had given her an unexpected voice, and she continued to use it.

Adams now spent several hours each day writing new FET protocols. She hoped to pen a standard operating procedure that would take female engagement teams to countries in sub-Saharan Africa and Asia—where there was no significant US military presence but where she knew females could help save nations from insurgent threats by empowering the country's women. When Adams wasn't writing, she was training other US military females on current FET protocols and procedures that would prepare them for life on the ground in the worst parts of Afghanistan.

In just a short period of time she had already tweaked the protocol to adjust what women did on the ground in Afghanistan. She had developed a shorter training program—one that could be done in two weeks instead of several months. The program also introduced the idea of women keeping a foothold in their regular military occupational specialty (MOS) and just coming together when needed for FET missions. The FET assignment wouldn't be permanent; several women would be trained in combat skills. When needed, a few of the women would be pulled from their regular jobs to go on FET missions—similar to the way FETs were assembled for some Army units under Rodriguez in 2011.

But Adams was also trying to save the FET program just as the Marine Corps was considering killing it—not because it wasn't working but, more likely than not, because internal support was lacking. The program was touted by men and women on the ground as a success, but in 2012 the Marine Corps decided to turn FET duties over to Afghanistan. There were plenty of indicators that Afghan security forces weren't ready—not the least of which came from the FET leaders themselves. Afghan women were still getting death threats for becoming police officers in remote areas of Zabul Province, making recruitment a challenge. When Smoke showed up, she had to repeat much of the training that Rodriquez had already done because of the AFP's turnover rate. She worked with Jamila to push out radio messages not just to encourage voting but also out of a pressing need to recruit women for the police force.

A January 2012 assessment from NATO's International Security Assistance Force (ISAF) showed that 149 FETs from fourteen countries were struggling with "employment, institutionalization, ad-hoc requirements, standardized training [and] national caveats" and that, in addition, US FETs especially struggled with a "lack of institutional proponency." In other words, the teams were being destroyed from within the US military by many of the obstacles that leaders like Rodriguez and Adams constantly fought to overcome: a lack of sufficient transportation, restrictions that kept female soldiers from leaving FOBs, and insufficient time for proper training. ISAF recognized the heavily entrenched discrimination that was killing any chances the FET program had of surviving, despite the intelligence and mission boon that the teams continually provided.

The boon to intelligence collection was obvious in 2010.

That year Major General Michael T. Flynn had coauthored the report detailing what was failing about intelligence collection in Afghanistan and what could improve it. He referenced the lack of sufficient intelligence staffing in the field and touted the work by FETs, among others, to fill those gaps—collecting atmospherics and grassroots-level data as well as building in-person relationships and trust among residents throughout Afghanistan. Those practices led to more information about enemy targets. That was a model, the report stated, that needed to be expanded, not diminished.

FETs had helped Afghan women circumvent gender restrictions in order to vote, get medical care, and build businesses. These women, both Afghan and American, had become expert at finding a way where often there was no way. The same US FET presence, Adams preached, could help push back Taliban-like insurgent groups in other countries.

Her strongest argument: in regions where women don't face restrictions as severe as those in Afghanistan, FETs are still vital. Insurgents in Africa have used sexual violence and trauma against females as weapons of terror. And women and young girls in those countries

may view men in uniform—including American men—as an enemy.
No one would blame women in rural Nigeria, for example, for being
uncomfortable if male forces approached them. One of the worst kidnappings of girls in the country's history was perpetuated by the uni-
formed extremist fighters of Boko Haram—a group that has pledged
its support and dedication to the Islamic State.

April 14, 2014, at the Chibok Government Girls Secondary School
started like any other day. Some girls were sitting in classrooms taking
notes. Upcoming graduates were studying and preparing for exams
that were just around the corner. That day ended in a way that no
one in that town likely would have imagined, with militants raiding
the school, abducting hundreds of students, and setting the building
on fire. Reports soon emerged that some of the girls were raped and
forced to carry the children of their captors. Sadly, the nightmare for
many of their families continues, as 195 girls are still thought to be
somewhere in the forests of Nigeria.

The parallels between what happens in Afghanistan at the hands
of the Taliban and in Nigeria at the hands of Boko Haram are strong:
both terrorist organizations recruit young boys as fighters, both
groups attack schools in order to ruin educational opportunities and
advancement for young girls, and females are sometimes rejected by
their families and villages after they've been attacked. Many of the
kidnapped girls in Nigeria have also been forced into marriages with
older men—in this case their captors.

The women of Chibok could have used the community support
and gender empowerment of FETs long before Boko Haram—a militant group whose roots go back in Nigeria more than a decade—kidnapped girls for having the audacity to sit in a classroom. Education
for girls under Boko Haram is forbidden, just as it is under the Taliban.
Boko Haram has destroyed more than a thousand schools throughout
the country. In areas that the terrorist organization hasn't hit, poverty
and lack of educational funding from the government keeps girls out
of school. FETs have battled and succeeded in helping families overcome many of those problems in Afghanistan by building schools and
providing microloans to women so they can pull themselves out of

poverty. They also developed relationships with women who provided information used to prevent some attacks from happening.

In Afghanistan, teams worked with Army engineers and provincial reconstruction teams to rebuild schools destroyed by the Taliban. And FET leaders like Smoke learned to develop strategic political relationships that would encourage the Afghan Army to continue to protect girls on their way to school long after the US military left.

Those same strategies could have prevented the hashtag #bringbackourgirls from becoming a worldwide trend. As of 2017, three years since the girls were kidnapped, more than six have been killed. After negotiations only twenty-one girls were released. Limited US military assistance, which has included drones and some boots on the ground, doesn't include a strategy to empower the extremist group's most vulnerable target—women and girls.

The terror group al-Shabaab, which has links to both al-Qaeda and Boko Haram, gained a foothold in Somalia by doing many of the same things that the Taliban did to gain support in the more rural communities of Afghanistan. It preyed on the poverty and desperation of the residents by promising food and stability—basic necessities that appeal to starving young men who need to support their families. And that desperation has been used to manipulate them into the ranks of the terror group. For more than a decade al-Shabaab's goal has been to take control of the entire nation, and the group has attempted to do that, in part, by suppressing its women.

Throughout the country's southern regions—the only areas where al-Shabaab has consistently maintained control—the insurgency has instituted practices intended to control and terrify women, including public stoning for adultery. The same social ills that make it virtually a death sentence to be a female in Afghanistan—religious extremism, lack of education, and poverty—have infected Somalia. In 2011 the country was ranked the fifth-most dangerous place to be a woman on the planet (behind Afghanistan, India, Pakistan, and the Congo), according to a report by the Thomson Reuters Foundation. Women are routinely raped and sexually assaulted, and girls as young as four are forced into the abusive ritual of genital mutilation. The death rate for women during pregnancy is one in twelve. And young girls in the most impoverished areas—just like in Afghanistan—have their childhoods and opportunities for education snatched from them way too soon.

Female soldiers in Somalia are fighting back.

Women from Uganda are taking on expanded roles in the African Union Army as gunners and patrolling Somalia's streets in combat tanks. The UN has been calling for more female forces to fight sexual violence and promote peace and security worldwide since 2000. Female engagement teams could bring the skills they've gained in Iraq and Afghanistan to reach women in the southern areas of Somalia, where conditions are the most desperate. The same three-pronged strategy—reach women, gain intelligence, and train the weak Somali National Army—could work to support the African Union Army and the UN as they fight against al-Shabaab.

IN 2012 ADAMS was not only pushing the Marine Corps to more fully support female engagement but was also fighting to save her career. Her seven months in combat prevented her from putting time in on her regular job as a helicopter mechanic, and that made getting promoted difficult after she returned from Afghanistan. Taking on a risky combat tour was usually a career boost for men. But for Adams, volunteering to lead a FET and then leaving again to have a baby proved detrimental.

A phone call came to her home just after her son was born.

Her command was aware that she was interested in being promoted. But she was also told that her chances, essentially, were dwindling. The paperwork she had filled out before going on maternity leave, indicating that she wanted to go before the promotions board, was now nowhere to be found. And the sergeant who helped Adams work on her promotions package rotated out of the unit. The board was scheduled to meet during her absence. Because her FET unit deployment pulled her away from her regular duties, the promotions board, she was being told, would question her ability to fall back into the skill set the military had hired her for. It had been nearly a year since she had acted as a helicopter mechanic. When Adams hung up the phone, she was shaken. The sense of stability and accomplishment that the military had once given her had been destroyed.

The day of the boards Adams, who was at home feeding her newborn, wasn't even on the list to compete for one of the few promotion slots available. She was approaching the ten-year mark, and becoming a staff sergeant after ten years in the Marines was mandatory. If Adams didn't get promoted, her military career would be over. Despite her struggles, when Adams returned to work from her maternity leave, her immediate focus was on saving the FET. Her goal was to make the combat experience more meaningful for her sisters in arms, even if the changes she was trying to push through didn't help her.

On March 20, 2012, Adams stood on the grounds of Pendleton saying good-bye to two Marines she had worked with in a previous unit and who she had just trained to go to Afghanistan.

At the end of the training session the twenty-three women who had gathered for one last day of instruction began to disperse. Adams had tapped the two women she was especially close to on their elbows and asked them to quickly follow her to an empty area just outside the gray trailer where she worked.

She reached into her right pocket and pulled out two bracelets—small, green, intricately braided. She looked each woman in the eyes for a few seconds before she began to speak.

"Stay safe," she said, handing each woman a bracelet as she began her good-byes. "You guys were amazing during training. Email me as soon as you guys get there and are safe. Let me know."

With large smiles the two women embraced Adams, holding onto their friend as tightly as possible. When they separated, Adams's eyes welled. She had known the two women, one of whom was her best friend, for years. They were tough. She kept reminding herself of that fact during those last days of training. She was happy they were getting what they wanted—the chance to make a difference during ground combat. She was also worried about what they would encounter. She had helped the women become engagement team candidates. She was proud of the way they had grown during training. But, seeing them off, she felt like a parent pushing her children into a world that she wanted desperately to protect them from.

As they parted, the women thanked her for the training and placed the bracelets on their wrists. They weren't to be removed until the Marines made it home from combat.

Adams had passed on a tradition that one of her commanders had passed along to her. The bracelets, made from the same cord used in parachutes, were given from one combat fighter to the next. The ritual sealed friendships. In times of struggle the bracelets helped ground troops who were lucky enough to get one strengthen their resolve. It was Adams's way of saying, *I made it through, and so can you.*

The two Marines boarded a bus for the first leg of their journey to the country from which Adams had only recently returned.

The next week Adams and her husband boarded a plane for their journey to Washington, DC.

Long before lawsuits, Adams had been part of the fight for full combat equality. And now she was taking her story all the way to the Obama administration.

HOME OF JOE AND JILL BIDEN, WASHINGTON, DC, MARCH 26, 2012—The Marine slowed down once she reached the reception hall of the small Victorian home, allowing her gaze to linger on the vertical stripes of the cream-and-lemon-colored wallpaper that decorated the open area near the crisp, white staircase. As she approached the first step she looked to her left, turned the corner, and walked through an arched doorway.

She glanced up at the wall and stopped moving. The last thing she expected to see during an event honoring fifty successful women—all representing some form of progress in the military, business, education, and industry for the Women's History Month reception—was a photo of herself.

For a moment she was frozen, unable to process the fact that as she waited to hear from the vice president of the United States and his wife, standing in their home, on the grounds of the Naval Observatory, she was looking at a scene from her own FET career reflected back at her.

She slowly ran her fingers along the right side of the glossy frame, shifting the photograph ever so slightly left, and redirecting the light that bounced off the glass, allowing her to see the familiar image a bit better.

Adams was, very briefly, back on the unpaved streets of Afghanistan, reliving a series of moments that had been captured with one flash and shown many times over—the *Daily Caller,* the *Chicago Tribune,* NBC News, Pinterest. It was one of her favorite memories:

> The little boy had been about six. His hands were covered in the pale orange henna often used by Afghan women in rural areas to polish their nails and decorate their palms; his eyes were outlined with traditional black makeup (likely a homemade mix of soot and oil), thought by some rural mothers to protect their children's eyes from evil spirits. He and his friends had surrounded Adams. One girl, the tallest in the little bunch, stood in the back; four other boys—small, smiling, their white and brown clothes covered in a thin layer of sand—flanked Adams (three on one side with their friend and one on the other). The Marine had been on patrol in Musa Qal'ah when they ran up to her—a familiar face who always brought warmth and fun. She removed her helmet and squatted in the middle of the crowd, allowing her weapon to rest naturally across the front of her body, its scope pointed toward the ground. She tilted her head back and slowly blew a sugary bubble that captivated the little boy in the middle of the crowd. His mouth was open wide with astonishment. He reached his right hand, with its tiny, henna-soaked fingers, in the bubble's direction.

The photographer snapped. It seemed an unlikely wartime moment.

Adams felt her arms and face flush cold with goosebumps as other women walked by and glanced at the photo and then at Adams standing in front of it. The Marine remembered the joy of interacting with Afghan children. Kids in the most war-torn parts of the country were hard, burdened with worries about raids and insurgents' bombs and battles that left their homes crumbling and families impoverished. But they were also children—open, playful, endlessly energetic, and still capable of finding wonder in bubble gum. Thinking about their well-being, during the war in 2010 and now, reminded Adams why FETs were so important. At its core the program was about nation building and ensuring a country's progress by bringing equality to its women and educating its children.

The wall was lined with other female engagement photos, and she walked slowly past them all.

In the open reception hall, just on the other side of the staircase, Vice President Joe Biden stood on a small platform beside his wife, hands tucked behind his back, waiting to speak. His dark blue suit popped against the deep maroon of Jill Biden's dress. Adams stood a few feet away to his right with four other FET women—one small corner in the crowd of honorees standing in front of the couple. Adams's focus was fully on the Second Lady, whom she had met the year before when Jill Biden visited Marines at Camp Pendleton as part of her effort to reach out to veterans and military families. Adams had spoken to the Second Lady about the FETs and their work in Afghanistan. The Marine wasn't at all surprised when her unit commander recommended that she fly to Washington for the Women's History Month event after Biden's staff called asking for the best representatives of the FETs to attend. By that time she had been named Marine of the Year, had received a Combat Action Ribbon, and had been one of many service members invited by the NFL to attend the Super Bowl. Reporters for several newspapers and magazines had interviewed her, and her story had been told all over the country. She was getting used to the calls.

During her Women's History Month speech the Second Lady, according to a report on the White House site, talked about the collective "courage, strength and resilience" of all the women in the room. Then she turned to her right, shifting the crowd's attention to Adams, Corporal Mary Walker, Sergeant Jamie Isaacson, and Captain Angela Nelson—other FET females in attendance. Raising her right hand in their direction, Jill Biden spoke of the FETs' heroic efforts in Afghanistan. She emphasized the work the women had successfully accomplished with the country's female population. Adams helped one woman start a business. The women gathered information from the previously unheard voices of mothers and wives. They helped empower women to educate their daughters.

"These women," she explained of the FET members in a video created during the event and posted on the White House website, "are a whole new generation of pioneers."

The honorees turned their attention to one another just after the speeches ended. As Adams traveled deeper into the crowd, she glanced to her right and saw a member of Congress walk past. To her left were women from Lockheed Martin.

She stopped briefly to talk to a group of women she'd never met before, one of whom inquired about what she'd done in Afghanistan. She wanted to know what Adams's duties, outside of her connections to Afghan women and children, had been.

"You were just a female Marine, right? You didn't see combat—you just dealt with women and children?"

The woman paused, nodding very casually and smiling at Adams as if she already knew the answer to her question. Her goal, apparently, was confirmation that her assumptions had been correct.

As Adams explained the firefights she'd been through and talked about the explosive device that tore her vehicle apart, she watched the smile on the woman's face slowly fade. The eyebrows of a few other women raised as Adams kept talking.

They clearly had not expected to hear about combat. Adams could feel her face turn red. The last thing she wanted was to make people feel uncomfortable.

Even in a room full of strong, trailblazing women, there were some who weren't prepared to hear the truth about females in combat. Adams was asking civilian architects and artists, politicians and engineers— many of whom had accomplished firsts in their fields—to comprehend things they couldn't begin to imagine. Her work, some of her proudest achievements, existed in the dark caves, blown-up streets, embattled mountains, and crumbled schools an entire world away. That fact distanced her, just a little bit, from many of the women in the room.

Their silence, after she finished speaking, wasn't an attempt to shun her, she realized. It was an attempt to understand. And perhaps push back—even if unintentionally—against an unexpected and somewhat frightening answer.

"A lot of people don't understand that I was a female grunt, and they look at me like I'm crazy," Adams said years later. "They respect us for what we did, but they don't understand us. They don't want to hear what you did."

She excused herself from the conversation and mingled with others, taking care not to give too much detail about her combat work.

Before she left the Bidens' home at Number One Observatory Circle in Washington, she and three other FET members were whisked off to a separate room that was dark except for a few large camera lights pointed at a small chair. Behind the chair was a black backdrop.

Adams sat down, and a member of the White House staff stood beside a camera in front of the Marine to record her thoughts on the female engagement teams and women taking on expanded combat roles.

"I don't like to be considered anything different," Adams said in the video, parts of which were posted on the White House website. "A Marine's a Marine. But we are able to do something by cultural aspects in Afghanistan that males aren't able to do. . . . [The female engagement team] is everything I ever wanted when I joined."

The next day Adams and her husband headed back to their home in California and to their three-month-old son.

Adams returned to her narrow, gray work trailer feeling uplifted. She sat at her desk and again worked quickly to write a new protocol she hoped would allow women to fight for other women in troubled spots all over the world.

CHAPTER 20

LAWSUIT—PUSHING AGAINST THE BRASS CEILING

SAN FRANCISCO, CALIFORNIA, NOVEMBER 27, 2012—The combat fighters showed up in skirts and high heels and crisp colorful blazers. One wore an American flag pin in the left lapel of her dark blue suit. Each stepped up to the podium to explain her unique experiences on the ground in Iraq and Afghanistan.

Of all the statements made that day, Army Staff Sergeant Jennifer Hunt's best captured the urgent need for the lawsuit the group had just filed against the Pentagon and was now gathered to announce. The way the Army views male wartime experiences, she explained, is inherently different from its judgment of her experiences and those of the other three women with her who also fought in war. When it comes to advancement, she said, men "still get looked at more favorably for having that combat arms experience. I would have absolutely no chance to make up that . . . bonus that he gets from having that position open to him."

Hunt's blond hair is straight and cascades down her back as she speaks. Her mouth and jaw pull slightly to one side with every syllable, perhaps a lingering effect of the injury she received during her time in Iraq. Her Humvee rolled over an IED, lodging shrapnel in her arms, face, and back.

For that she earned a Purple Heart. The statement she made during a *Washington Post* interview days after the group announced its lawsuit was even more to the point: "The shrapnel that tore through the vehicle that day didn't stop because I'm a female."

One suit had already been filed in May by two female Army reservists—a colonel who had served nearly thirty years and a sergeant major who had served more than twenty. The fact that the military closed off combat opportunities to women, the lawsuit said, meant fewer promotional opportunities, smaller paychecks, and less money for retirement.

Hunt's suit—the one she filed with Air National Guard Major Mary Hegar (named as the lead plaintiff), Marine Corps Reserve Captain Zoe Bedell, Marine Captain Colleen Farrell, the American Civil Liberties Union (ACLU), and the Service Women's Action Network—was about recognition for the life-threatening fights women were already waging.

Their goal was to declare the policy barring women from combat— which boiled down to sanctioned discrimination and was in direct conflict with what was happening on the ground—unconstitutional. Continuing to fall in line meant propping up the DOD myth that women weren't in the very roles that they had been in for more than a decade. The policy had turned women into fighters of convenience for men—ones willing to put their lives on the line for combat missions when men needed them but who also got no credit or benefit for displaying acts of courage. The policy also meant that women weren't threats to male careers. Female fighters were denied access to promotions that would have pushed some of those same men who needed their help out of contention for spots as officers and high-ranking enlisted men in infantry units. The Department of Defense seemed content with women continuing to lurch forward, broken and used, while quietly and obediently allowing the public to believe the lie that they weren't sending their daughters as well as their sons off to die.

During the November news conference announcing the suit Ariela Migdal, senior staff lawyer with the Women's Rights Project of the American Civil Liberties Union, said, "The servicewomen who have been spending the last ten years trying to accomplish missions in Iraq and Afghanistan are coming back and seeing there really is a brass ceiling."

In 2011 the military was about 15 percent female. That year there were close to 150,000 troops on the ground in Iraq and Afghanistan; enlisted women were about 3 percent of frontline units.

The year the lawsuit was filed, Rodriguez had already served on the frontlines in the Panjwai District of Kandahar Province in Afghanistan. Near the end of her deployment she was trudging through villages in a district that was once the epicenter of Taliban recruitment and risking roadside bombs and firefights to reach out to village elders and reinforce the face of the US Army as a nation builder intent on strengthening women and communities. By that point in the wars about 150 women had been killed in combat and about 860 injured.

Service for Bedell and Farrell, two lawsuit plaintiffs who ran FETs, closely paralleled that of Rodriguez.

They were on the ground in Afghanistan in 2010. Bedell was in charge of forty-seven women assigned to multiple units throughout Helmand Province. Similarly, Farrell managed up to twenty women during her tour. And like Rodriguez, they experienced restrictions that hindered them from doing the jobs for which they were deployed. Bedell's and Farrell's teams had to return to their respective FOBs in the middle of longer missions, they said, because women technically weren't supposed to be participating in ground combat. To get around that rule, unit commanders shipped women back early, told them to stay on the base overnight, and then, much like Rodriguez frequently had to, wait for a convoy to pass through on which they could catch a ride back to the field to complete the missions (like Rodriguez, the women were forbidden from driving themselves outside of the FOB). Bedell and Farrell say that restriction put them in even more combat danger. The more they traveled, the greater their risk of encountering an IED or ambush attack, all "for a legal façade," Farrell wrote on an ACLU site blog. "And in some cases, commanders were forced to reschedule major operations due to the lack of an available Female Engagement Team."

After Bedell returned to the United States in 2011 she left the regular Marine Corps and joined the reserves out of frustration. She felt that her FET work in Afghanistan wasn't being recognized or appreciated. She saw officer advancement happening much more quickly for male combat Marines than for women like herself. She encountered sexual harassment, and so did her FET females, she said, and she felt helpless to do anything about it.

WOMEN IN THE RANKS

Perhaps the key to understanding why the military has struggled with equality for women is to examine the reasons why women were integrated into the regular Army. One of the earliest surges of enlistment for women came during World War II. The Women's Army Auxiliary Corps (which eventually became the Women's Army Corps) was created in 1942 for the sole purpose of freeing up men to fight. Women took over the noncombat jobs that men would have been working if they weren't needed in combat. More than 150,000 women joined a gender-segregated Army, the first women—aside from nurses—to do so. Before then women were contracted to work *with* the Army but didn't actually wear a uniform or join ranks. Both the military and the public resisted the idea. It took six years of women working as bakers and telephone operators and, in the case of nurses, performing duties incredibly close to the front for the government to integrate women into Army units with men in 1948. It took another twenty years for the government to allow women to serve in the National Guard and rise to the highest enlisted ranks. In 1972 the Army finally opened all jobs aside from those involving combat or physical risk to women.

In 1978 the Women's Army Corps (WAC) was disbanded, and the handbook "What Do You Do with a WAC?" (created by the Racial Equality and Equal Opportunity Division of Fort Knox, Kentucky) was released to units during the change.

But the move toward greater gender integration in the 1970s pointed out an even more dangerous contradiction in the military's treatment of females. That decade was the first in which weapons training was made mandatory for female recruits. Female soldiers had been sent to Vietnam for thirteen years as nurses without even the most basic of combat skills training. It wasn't until 1977 that the Army made basic training equal to that of enlisted men mandatory. And unlike the guerilla warfare of the Middle East, where the frontlines are no longer clear, the frontlines in Vietnam were much clearer, and women were often crossing it. More than seven thousand women served in Vietnam as nurses, and at least one died from enemy fire. More than twenty-one thousand Army nurses served during World War I, and at least four hundred died. More than twice that number of nurses served during World War II, and more than two hundred died during the war.

And even as women started serving in Vietnam as nurses in 1956 (and during both world wars before that), the highest officer ranks remained closed to them. It wasn't until an act of Congress was signed in 1967 that women were allowed to get promoted to general. And even today achieving the highest officer ranks is very difficult without credit for combat duty. As of 2013 only 7 percent of the top officers in the military were females, according to a CNN report. That included just one female general in the Marine Corps.

Despite barriers to service, women have come a long way in a very short period of time.

By 1993 the DOD allowed women to fly helicopters for the first time during combat missions—even though those women still weren't considered combat troops. And in 1994 President Bill Clinton struck down the regulation that forbade women from joining units whose missions involved some combat risk. It was the most significant change for women the military had seen, opening thirty-two thousand jobs to female soldiers and leading to the first DOD mandate to integrate basic combat training based on gender.

I entered one of the first gender-integrated basic training classes in the US Army's history under the new mandate. I landed in Fort Jackson, South Carolina, for training in February of 1995, only months after Clinton signed the regulation that eased job restrictions for women in the service. The new regulation stated that placement for females should no longer be based on whether units took on missions that involved some level of danger or combat risk. It required, instead, for the military to bar women from serving in units whose primary directive was ground combat. In other words, women were allowed to serve in units that may encounter some amount of danger but not units whose primary mission was ground warfare. Actions in Desert Storm and Desert Shield practically forced Clinton's hand. Units on the ground during those conflicts were using women during critical missions, and the traditional frontlines of war were already starting to disappear. The Gulf War was the first modern war during which two women were taken hostage. Fifteen women were killed on the ground. Some of the tactics used during those wars influenced new basic training protocols.

Fort Jackson in 1995 was ground zero for studying how gender integration in basic combat training could affect military readiness, the conditioning of male soldiers, and women's ability to handle the stresses of dangerous combat-like conditions around allegedly more aggressive men. The military also wanted to know how training should be altered, if at all, now that women were formally taking on riskier assignments.

During basic I trained side by side with men. Males and females ate together, learned to fire weapons together, were split into two-mile running groups based on speed (not gender), and did push-ups and sit-ups daily together. We learned how to break apart, clean, and reassemble our weapons together. No one got pregnant (as was rumored would happen as soon as the women hit the ground in South Carolina), and there were no conflicts based on gender. In fact, the opposite happened. When faced with challenging circumstances— like going through live fire drills at night as ammunition rounds flew overhead or climbing up and rappeling down walls during obstacle courses—we propped each other up. Every morning we had to run at least two miles to prepare for basic training's final physical fitness test. That daily run, for me, was the hardest part.

Participating in live fire didn't scare me—in fact, it gave me an adrenalin rush. I remember screaming with exhilaration once I finished crawling under the barbed wire that was the last obstacle on the live-fire course. As I stood, I looked up at the night sky and could see red flashes of live rounds flying in quick succession overhead. I followed the man in front of me as we both ran the last few feet to the end of the course. The faint outline of our drill sergeant grew larger as we reached the finish line. To my right was another recruit, a male. After I stopped running I turned to him and saw sheer terror in his eyes. I asked him what was wrong, but he didn't respond. He was immobile with fear. Far above his Kevlar helmet I could see red tracer rounds still streaking the night sky. I could hear loud pops in rhythmic succession as bullets rapidly discharged from their weapons. I glanced behind him and saw other recruits who had started the obstacle course after us, both men and women, stand up and run in our direction. To me that night was the successful culmination of so many things we had learned during an especially intense week of training—how to low crawl on our stomachs face down through the mud, falling into the prone position, moving with speed while protecting our battle buddies during enemy fire. I was proud of myself and the soldier beside me for getting through. Neither of us was injured; we had both finished. The idea that I might get shot—a very remote possibility during training courses like this but not unheard of—didn't shape or alter my determination. And it didn't dampen my sense of accomplishment once I was finished. In fact, it intensified it. As much as I was thrilled, the man next to me was terrified. I could feel it. I patted my fellow recruit on the back and told him he would be fine.

But basic training's two-mile run—part of the physical fitness standards required to graduate that had to be completed in under twenty minutes—was, for some reason, my biggest obstacle. I've never been much of a distance runner—sprints were always where I shined. Add a stop watch, and that's when I freeze. But in spite of my fears, I pushed myself to move up to the next-fastest running group. I was determined to make it out of basic training, and if I didn't pass the physical fitness test, that wasn't going to happen. My first day in the new run group I started to flag. It was my turn to get a pat on the back and be told I could do it. The men who ran with me didn't complain about a woman joining their group; instead, they congratulated me on moving up and told me, when I needed to hear it, to keep going. When my breathing become irregular because I was getting nervous about moving so much faster than I previously had, they could tell. I could hear guys behind me calling out tips: "Rivers, loosen your hands! You're running too tight. Relax. Relax your shoulders." "Rivers, breathe. You can do this." And I did. During the two months I was in basic I cut more than a minute off my run time. My drill sergeants noticed my improvements—not just in running but in my ability to help fellow soldiers. I got up early each morning to help the women in my platoon prepare their battle gear—cover their Kevlar helmets, tidy up and pack their rucksacks. The drill sergeants noticed. I excelled against other soldiers in an informal competition that involved drill and ceremony (those sharply shouted commands like left face, right face, right flank, eyes right). As drill sergeants rattled off the names of movements, soldiers executed them just as quickly. Those who got commands wrong were picked off one at a time and pulled out of formation. It came down to me and one other soldier—an older male who had prior military experience. The drill sergeant commanded: "Right face. Left face. Right flank!" My competitor got the last command wrong, and I was the only soldier left standing. I eventually became platoon leader.

The men on the ground who have worked with women are much less likely to perpetuate doubts about females' ability to achieve. If they start with doubts, those are often erased once the mission is finished. They see women propping up their brothers-in-arms when needed. And the men on the ground prop up their sisters in return. There are always exceptions, but in my experience it was more frequently the officers, soldiers, and policy makers far removed from the fields of work, training, and battle—enlisted men in units that didn't frequently deploy or soldiers on the ground who had never worked with women in any intense capacity—who supported regulations that restricted female service.

The baby steps of those Fort Jackson experiments—considered groundbreaking in the 1990s—seem like obvious ones now. When I saw a man who needed help, I gave it. When men saw that I needed help, they gave it. In times of intense struggle, gender difference never played a role in the group I was with. The question of whether the person next to me could protect me during battle maneuvers, finish the live-fire course, or pass their marksmanship test—those kinds of thoughts always played a role. Those Fort Jackson studies were the final steps toward the normalization of gender integration in Army basic training.

To women who have served on the ground in Iraq and Afghanistan—and many of the men who have served with them—the importance of opening all combat jobs to women in 2012 seemed just as obvious.

The regulation signed by Clinton was a point of progress some twenty years ago. But as conflicts beyond Desert Storm and Desert Shield continued to push women closer to the front during wars, the groundbreaking 1994 change quickly became outdated. It actually solidified the rule that has kept women from full combat recognition since. And it eventually became the ultimate example of how the military wasn't willing to back one of its basic principles to "train as you will fight."

By 2012 in Afghanistan women were doing nearly every combat job that men were. But they weren't going through the same training as men in infantry units. Infantry training is much more intense than the basic combat training I received and that all soldiers receive, no matter their jobs.

And until women like Bedell and Hunt returned from war and were confronted with noncombat environments that restricted their ability to move up, females who had served before them had simply accepted the restrictions for what they were. But previous generations of women hadn't been on the frontlines in the same way that women involved in the lawsuit had.

More than anything, the wars in Iraq and Afghanistan have shown us how the nature of combat means everyone is a grunt and that all service members, no matter how far from the action they think they might be, actually are on the frontlines.

In February of 2012 the Pentagon made it clear it would eliminate parts of the 1994 regulation, specifically those that didn't allow women to collocate with direct ground combat units and that excluded women from a few units below the brigade level whose primary directive was combat. In doing that, the Department of Defense admitted that "the dynamics of the modern-day battlefield are non-linear, meaning there are no clearly defined front line and safer rear area." But Bedell, Hunt, Farrell, Hegar, and plenty of other women wanted more. The Pentagon ruling would only open 14,000 jobs to women. Their November suit demanded that women have access to the remaining 240,000.

CHAPTER 21

MILITARY MESSES UP
YOUR LIFE

MARIA RODRIGUEZ

FORT LEAVENWORTH, KANSAS, DECEMBER 2012—Even after nearly
a year apart, Maria Rodriguez and her ex-husband easily fell into a
smooth routine. It was as if the major had been living with Chris and
the children for the last seven months instead of Skyping as frequently
as time would allow during her stint in Afghanistan.

They had all moved back in together. Chris and the kids followed
her to Kansas for another career advancement—she was selected after
her work with the 1st Stryker Brigade, to attend the Army's Command
and General Staff Officers' Course, another step on her way to the
higher officer ranks. Her goal was to make lieutenant colonel within
two years. The course was a bit less than a year long, and Chris and
Rodriguez had found a house that perfectly accommodated their unconventional family of four. The major was anxious to get to know her
daughter, now almost a preteen, and son, whom she almost no longer
recognized.

She rented the home, and Chris, who was finally getting used to
being a stay-at-home parent after leaving contract work and raising the
kids alone, slept in the finished basement apartment. Rodriguez and

the kids occupied rooms on the second floor of the house. The first floor was where everyone lived. The two parents dated other people. And they were comfortable enough with one another to talk about their separate lives and to give support when either needed it. When they moved to Kansas in July for the start of Rodriguez's course, they briefly talked about marrying each other again. It wasn't a lack of love that had led to their divorce, and Chris was now settled enough to give Rodriguez the support she needed.

But they knew that if they made a go of it again, there would be more pressure to make it work this time. Not only would failure be heartbreaking for them; it would also have adverse effects on two people they never wanted to hurt, who were now old enough to know disappointment. They dropped the conversation, not for lack of interest or for fear of getting involved again but because they thought they had plenty of time to work things out. Perhaps they would circle back to the conversation when Rodriguez finished school.

But on December 20, not long into the flow of their daily routine that included carpools and kids and homework and laughter, Rodriguez's entire world changed.

Late one afternoon she walked into a house that seemed too quiet and thought immediately that something was wrong. She glanced around the living room, past the sparkly bulbs that hung on the Christmas tree the family had finished decorating days before, but she didn't see the telltale signs that Chris had made it upstairs. There was no newspaper strewn across the sofa, no shoes kicked off for comfort. She hadn't seen her ex, who usually started his day by midmorning, since the night before. She sent her kids to their rooms and approached the basement steps. She paused for a moment at the top of the stairwell and listened. Nothing. She heard nothing. She knocked on the door and softly called his name. Still nothing.

She slowly pushed her way into the dark space. The room felt cold.

Straight ahead she saw the shadow of his still body. His arms and legs stretched from one side of the bed to the other. Chris had long ago been diagnosed with diabetes. The illness was, in part, what kept him from returning to the battlefield. She tried, but she could find no heartbeat.

She acted quickly, calling for an ambulance and the police. She was terrified. But in crisis she catered to her intellect first: *What's the solution? What's the quickest way to get there?*

That matter-of-fact approach made her a successful wartime leader. There was no leeway to show fear during combat missions. The slightest emotion could lead to bad judgment that might end a raid before it started. And the only person she was ever fully able to show her emotions to was now gone.

She looked at him and thought of the most meaningful moments of their lives together: their wedding day (they had eloped), trips with the kids to Disney World, his pep talks when she was on the frontlines in Afghanistan. She heard his voice telling her that everything would be okay. She saw his grin, which was bright and carefree and accompanied the jokes he told to cheer her up. Her eyes welled, and she felt the warmth from tears that rolled down her face. She wondered how she would tell her children their daddy was gone.

By the time the police arrived, her eyes were red, her eyelids slightly swollen. As a military police officer, she knew that the cops had to question her. She answered each inquiry as thoroughly as she could.

After the memorial service ended, after family members returned to their lives and her kids returned to school, she sat alone on a white sofa in the living room of the home she had shared with her best friend. She wasn't sure what the future held, but she knew it wouldn't be in Kansas.

She stayed at Fort Leavenworth just long enough to finish the officers' training course. In June she packed up her home and moved her children to Georgia. It would be a fresh start for her kids. And for her, she hoped, a career advancement.

CHAPTER 22

STATE OF THE UNION

SHEENA ADAMS

US HOUSE OF REPRESENTATIVES, WASHINGTON, DC, FEBRUARY 2013—
The Marine sergeant stood in the First Lady's box, and the din of conversations from members of Congress below became, for her, a distant echo. She reached her right hand forward and felt the hem on the skirt of her dark blue uniform rise slightly as she shook the hand of Michelle Obama. The statuesque woman towered over Adams, flashed the smile that she has become known for, and asked about Afghanistan.

"Tell me about the FET. You built a school there, right?"

In the presence of the First Lady's physical strength, which she had always admired, Adams squared off her shoulders and straightened her back to stand a bit taller. She heard herself confidently speak—as if she was both experiencing and witnessing the moment—about the importance of educating Afghan girls as one of the factors that motivated some of the women who volunteered for the duty. It was one of the factors that had motivated her.

Adams glanced at the two parents from Chicago who stood between herself and the First Lady, inviting them into the conversation as she told Michelle Obama about the medical facilities she helped build in

Musa Qal'ah. The young couple had lost their daughter after a shooting at a South Side Chicago park, and the First Lady had returned to Washington from the funeral just the week before.

Michelle Obama nodded, staying engaged as Adams explained more about her time in the desert and the outreach program that had allowed her to take medical and health supplies to women who had no running water. "Most of the women," she said, "were forbidden from leaving their homes because of Taliban occupation." Out of the corner of her left eye Adams saw Apple CEO Tim Cook, who sat one row behind her in this small section of the second-tier balcony within the chamber of the US House of Representatives. The Marine could hear buzz and bits from conversations within the group of about two dozen. Michelle Obama shot Adams another warm smile and turned her attention to the young couple. Jill Biden, who was seated on the other side of Michelle Obama, stepped in.

She delicately maneuvered around the First Lady and reached her hand out to Adams: "It's good to see you again."

The combat Marine's gestures were sure in this small world within a world, different and distinct from the rest of the House as the entire chamber waited for the president to enter.

Adams leaned forward, tilting her small frame slightly right against the low wooden partition that defined the balcony's edge, and returned Biden's gentle handshake. She had made progress in her push to expand FET operations since the two first met the year before, and Adams quickly shared key aspects of the protocol, anticipating the Second Lady would soon move on to connect with other State of the Union guests. Biden remarked about how the military was changing its attitude toward women in combat. Adams had, without trying, become the public and political face of that change.

As Biden moved on, Adams lowered herself into her chair and removed her voice, for just a moment, from the group's casual conversations.

Her eyes drifted across the chamber to the oversized American flag that hung on a wall behind the podium from which the president would soon speak.

Sitting in the first row on the House floor, directly in front of the podium, was General Martin Dempsey, then chairman of the Joint Chiefs of Staff and a man who supported the full combat recognition that Adams and those female engagement teams long ago deserved.

Just the month before, Dempsey had written a letter to Secretary of Defense Leon Panetta stating that "the time has come to rescind the direct combat exclusion rule for women and to eliminate all unnecessary gender-based barriers to service."

He sent the letter two months after four servicewomen came forward and filed a lawsuit against the Pentagon over combat exclusions. He was the first chairman of the Joint Chiefs to make such a statement.

Next to Dempsey sat Supreme Court Justice Elena Kagan. Near the aisle, Chief Justice John Roberts.

Within seconds the sergeant at arms' voice quickly cut through the steady, low hum of the chamber.

"Mr. Speaker! The president of the United States!"

Adams started clapping and quickly stood. She craned her neck slightly but could see very little of the man whose words might include mention of FETs' work in Iraq and Afghanistan. The sea of politicians rushing toward the chamber's center aisle and hands reaching out to connect with the president temporarily obstructed her view.

She continued to clap as she waited to catch her first glimpse. The crescendo of applause was overwhelming. Random cheers burst from different parts of the House floor.

President Obama finally emerged from the throng of senators and representatives. From above, Adams noticed his slightly graying hair. She watched him slowly progress toward the podium and continued to clap when the president paused for brief chats with the Joint Chiefs of Staff and members of Congress and the Supreme Court. Obama moved with grace, was patient, and had a warm smile that, even from where Adams stood, resonated.

At the podium's microphone Obama—flanked by sleek, black teleprompters—thanked the joint houses of Congress. The applause began to ebb.

"Mr. Speaker, Mr. Vice President, members of Congress, fellow Americans," the chamber fell silent. "Fifty-one years ago John F. Kennedy declared to this chamber that the Constitution makes us not rivals for power but partners for progress. 'It is my task,' he said, 'to report the state of the union. To improve it is the task of us all.' Tonight, thanks to the grit and determination of the American people, there is much progress to report. After a decade of grinding war, our brave men and women in uniform are coming home."

Cheers erupted from the House floor.

Behind the president Vice President Joe Biden and House Speaker John Boehner rose. Adams saw the Joint Chiefs of Staff remain seated. They were the only people in the room not standing to applaud.

Adams knew the reality that separated the officers' views from those of the commander-in-chief who stood before them. Afghan troops weren't ready to take the lead in pushing out Taliban forces. The government in Afghanistan was still corrupt. Women were left with little political power or economic options. Too many girls still did not have safe passages to school or safe schools to attend. Troops may have been coming home, but it was not because commanders on the ground thought the time was right.

The applause died down, and the president continued.

Adams glanced at two female entrepreneurs in the row directly behind her when Obama spoke about job growth—a nod to the hundreds of people employed by small business owners like the two the First Lady invited to the speech. Entrepreneurs across the country, the president explained, found innovative ways to help raise employment and boost an economy that had been suffering.

Adams was anxious to hear more of Obama's words on the wars and women in combat. Forty minutes into the speech the moment she had been waiting for arrived.

"Tonight we stand united in saluting the troops and civilians who sacrifice every day to protect us. Because of them, we can say with confidence that America will complete its mission in Afghanistan." The president's voice rose as he referenced defeating the core of terrorism.

The Joint Chiefs of Staff, led by Dempsey, gave Obama a standing ovation.

"As long as I am commander-in-chief we will do whatever we must to protect those who serve our country abroad, and we will maintain the best military the world has ever known. . . . We will draw upon the courage and skills of our sisters and daughters and moms because women have proven under fire that they are ready for combat."

Adams never cries. Marine Corps boot camp knocked any inclination to do that right out of her. The brain injury she suffered sometimes made it hard for her to tap into her deeper feelings. But as Obama spoke, she was moved.

She shifted in her seat. The blues, yellows, and reds of the Combat Action Ribbon she received for holding her own during a thirty-six-hour firefight stood out among the many badges and awards that lined the front of her uniform. She had been the Marine with a spotty record of service and was greeted with skepticism and resistance by unit commanders when she requested FET duty. The president's State of the Union reference to FET accomplishment gave her more validation than she had imagined possible.

Being a FET leader hadn't been difficult or crazy. It had been a privilege for her to walk into the homes of other women and collect their stories, help their children, and fight the Taliban. It had been her attempt to carry out the president's promise of progress.

But there was a sharp contrast between the president's clean narrative about women in combat and the fight to keep the FET program alive. There was a messiness in trying to build on a system that the military erroneously thought it no longer needed.

Adams's struggle to keep her job revealed a harsh reality. Women who had proven themselves on the front lines were making progress for future fighters. But the battle for combat recognition had done little for their own advancement. Dempsey's letter declaring that the military should erase all barriers to combat jobs for women also stated, "to implement these initiatives successfully and without sacrificing our warfighting capability or the trust of the American people, we will need time to get it right." That declaration signaled progress but changed nothing in 2013 for women like Adams. The fourteen thousand combat jobs that had been "opened" essentially gave a nod to low-level Army, Navy, Air Force, and Marine Corps positions women had already occupied. The Defense Department's move to scrap the

1994 collocation ban simply rubber stamped what FETs had already been doing for ten years.

Both fights—to expand the FETs reach and mission and to save her career—were still waiting for Adams when she returned to California.

"I want to thank Michelle and Dr. Jill Biden for their continued dedication to serving our military families as well as they have served us," the president stated near the end of the State of the Union address. First Lady Michelle Obama and Dr. Jill Biden looked straight ahead toward Obama and smiled as Adams and the rest of the House stood. Applause filled the storied chamber.

"Thanks, honey," the president stated. "Thank you, Jill."

The women remained seated. Adams and the rest of the joint sessions of Congress continued to applaud.

After her return to California, Adams realized that the last group of FET women she trained would be the last she would ever mentor. The Marine Corps ended the program. By July Adams's military contract expired, and she left the service for good.

CHAPTER 23

AND THEN YOU WIN

JOHANNA SMOKE

FORT KNOX, KENTUCKY, JANUARY 2016—Johanna Smoke sat at her dining room table and fidgeted for a moment, hesitant to pick apart the war's faults. She paused for an extended period of time before responding to the question. She'd had plenty of conversations with her father about the parallels between Vietnam's failures and the war in Afghanistan. Her father had served as a Special Forces commander in Vietnam, and when she was still on the ground in Afghanistan he had been one of the few people she confided in. She called him after especially long days that felt directionless—ones during which insurmountable issues of security, poverty, and training made her wonder whether any of the current efforts would be enough to support the American mission or be worth the continual deaths of American soldiers.

"We never learned from Vietnam," she recalled her father saying on many occasions. "We are doing the same things. . . . Occupation with a different spin."

That was fine for her father to say. But for her to speak openly now about an Army in which she still served to a writer who could make those feelings very public—she feared that may be a step too far.

"I support my commander-in-chief," she made clear during our conversation. She also acknowledged that her father was right on many levels. US efforts could have been more strategically aligned with the reality on the ground. Political goals should have evolved when the need to maintain troop levels became obvious. "I don't think we should have left Afghanistan. I don't think we left Afghanistan for the right reasons. The US presence should have sustained. We were starting to evolve and starting to learn from our mistakes. We had units that had civil affairs capacity to make a difference at the community level to suppress the Taliban and national problems. We left this black hole in the Afghan culture and country where people became reliant on military support. And now they are facing those repercussions. And now ISIS has taken over, and we're starting from scratch. . . . I was not ready to leave. My commander was not ready to leave. My unit was not ready to leave."

What she feels more comfortable talking about are the positive military changes that have evolved since her dad's war. Deployments for all soldiers are shorter, and those deployments, thanks to the work of FET leaders like her, have included a greater number of women. The FET program pushed the Pentagon to recognize the combat work women were already doing just as well as men. And lawsuits by six military women—two of whom had been FET leaders—pushed Smoke into an infantry unit she hadn't expected and forced Leon Panetta, defense secretary from 2011 to 2013, and Ash Carter, who took over directly after him, to publicly admit how the military had already been using its female service members.

After Smoke returned to Kentucky in 2014 from Afghanistan, where she was assigned to the 3rd Brigade Combat Team, 1st Infantry Division as part of an Army effort to see how women would work with infantry units on the ground, she watched with the rest of the nation as pressure mounted for Carter to open all roles. The efforts, she thought, were overdone and a few years too late.

"I was sick and tired of all the gender integration discussion and the politics behind it," Smoke recalled much later. By that time she had already fought in combat in both Iraq and Afghanistan. "Male commanders and leaders have been putting women in the toughest jobs during Operation Iraqi Freedom and Operation Enduring Freedom, so why the need for a program to mandate it?"

Smoke was understandably disheartened. Women had been sacrificing and dying as infantry troops in all but name for years. The idea that she was supposed to be happy about getting recognition for something she and thousands of other women had been doing for more than a decade was almost an affront. But mandating it went beyond validating what women had already done; indeed, it helped women begin to break through the long-standing brass (and Kevlar) ceiling.

On December 3, 2015, Carter announced that all combat roles would be open to women by January of the following year: "They will be allowed to drive tanks, fire mortars and lead infantry soldiers into combat," he said when making the announcement during a news conference. "They'll be able to serve as Army Rangers and Green Berets, Navy SEALs, Marine Corps infantry, Air Force parajumpers and everything else that was previously open only to men. And even more importantly, our military will be better able to harness the skills and perspectives that talented women have to offer."

In April of 2016 women would accomplish a flurry of firsts in the Army.

On April 7 a woman enlisted for the first time in an infantry occupational specialty, helping to break the Kevlar ceiling for enlisted (nonofficer) women.

On April 28 the first women graduated from Army Ranger School. One of them took another step toward breaking the brass ceiling: she graduated from the Army's Maneuver Captains Career Course, making her the first official female infantry officer in the branch's history and giving her the skills needed to command a frontline unit. But the Army was still having a hard time keeping pace with the accomplishments of its determined women, and as of May 2016 she was stuck in a training brigade waiting for an assignment to an infantry unit—something that wasn't slated to happen until the summer of 2017. And the first woman to enlist in an infantry specialty didn't head to basic training until 2017 either, giving the Army time to fill higher-ranking infantry positions with women. About two dozen other female soldiers followed in their footsteps in 2016, graduating from West Point, Officer's Candidate School, and ROTC (Reserve Officers' Training Corps) with commissions as infantry and armor officers.

And in January 2017 three enlisted women became the first to officially join a Marine Corps ground combat unit.

But Carter's words also ensured that these officers and enlisted soldiers would get better access to services than some women had in the past, especially those suffering from PTSD while dealing with issues men generally don't—pregnancy, caring for children, and balancing household duties. All units—combat or not—will know that females have seen combat and that their nightmares can be triggered by those stresses and need treatment just like any man's.

A moment that Rodriguez could only dream about when she was on the ground in Afghanistan training women to fight as part of FET units—and pushing back against a lack of institutional support for female engagement—had come. And it had been during her lifetime.

Female soldiers are doing what "only male soldiers were allowed to do in Iraq and Afghanistan for a long time," Rodriguez said a year after her return from Afghanistan. She recalled those FET deployments and her previous expectations for women in combat: "Now we have . . . female soldiers [attached to] infantry platoons and an infantry battalion. We would get excited about that. [We would think] in a couple of years it would be female soldiers *in* the infantry."

There would be no Army Ranger opportunities if not for the FET. And no viable lawsuit without female engagement. These women sacrificed. They put their lives on the line for so long without asking for credit. They forced the Pentagon to erase the military's unequal treatment of women—one that presented a public face of safety for females and supported the myth of a frontline that only men crossed and that women stayed far away from. But the reality had been different for decades: women were getting hit by IEDs, dying, attacking the Taliban while crossing into enemy territory. They were changing the nature of intelligence collection for the better and ensuring wartime progress but without the same opportunity for advancement.

FETs in Iraq and Afghanistan were, as Rodriguez said, placing bricks in a foundation. And they built that sturdy foundation, as Smoke so clearly articulated, without a mandate. The first women to graduate from Army Ranger School stood on it.

FETs did "good and created opportunities," as Adams often said during my interviews with her. But they did so much more than that. They forced the military, known for being ahead of the civilian world on issues of integration, to rid itself of its last nod to legal discrimination.

Cracks in the Kevlar and brass ceilings were evident.

EPILOGUE

I am here as a soldier who has temporarily left the field of battle
in order to explain . . . what civil war is like when
civil war is waged by women.

—**EMMELINE PANKHURST,** suffragist, Great Britian

FORT BENNING, GEORGIA, AUGUST 20, 2015—Everyone wanted to capture the stories of the two women sitting behind microphones at a long table at the front of the room.

The sound of camera shutters filled the small space.

First Lieutenant Shaye Haver, an Apache helicopter pilot, leaned forward and glanced to her left, giving the other female at the table, Captain Kristen Griest, a military police officer, a brief two-second opening to tackle the reporter's question first. She turned back to her microphone and allowed her voice to flow:

"To the other females who plan on coming, I hope that they come with a strong mind. That's what it takes to get through here."

The men who sat on each side of Griest made her small frame look almost childlike by comparison. The dark stubble on her shaved head matched theirs in length and texture. She leaned in only slightly to give her views and sat very still as she spoke. Her eyes were wide, her voice, at first, slightly hesitant:

"I just came here to be a better leader and to improve myself and I did that. And for other women who have that same goal in mind, just keep that goal in mind. Just don't lose sight of it. And just keep reminding yourself why you're there."

Their tired expressions were the first tangible signs of progress the public had seen of the military's multiyear promise to open all combat roles to women. To see if women could meet the physical and mental standards imposed on those seeking combat jobs, the Army decided to conduct a sixty-one-day experiment. It placed nineteen women in Army Ranger School to see if they could make it. No one expected that any of the women would. Haver and Griest were the only two left standing.

FEW SOLDIERS, MALE OR FEMALE, even meet the standards to get into Army Ranger School.

Griest and Haver watched several women drop out during prequalification training—a course of physical tests (push-ups, sit-ups, and a five-mile run) meant to weed out those who are unsuited before the actual two-month Ranger course starts.

After that, peer evaluations—assessments given after each phase of training by fellow squad members—have the potential to make or break a cadet's future in the course. The weakest link in the group— the one considered the slowest, the least valuable to team cohesion, who weighed everyone down or made little to no contributions to the successful completion of a training mission—is generally given a low peer score. A failing score in phase one can get a soldier kicked out.

And performance on the Darby Queen—a two-mile obstacle course—could be the most revealing part of the first phase of training.

The cadets had to trudge through mud, crawl under barbed wire, and run through shoulder-high, mucky waters. And between each of the twenty-six obstacles cadets completed push-ups, leg lifts, and mountain climbers while drill sergeants sprayed water in their faces and counted an endless number of repetitions that soldiers had to complete with rhythmic precision. The sergeants' goal was to break each soldier down and then build them back up into fearless leaders who could confidently rush a squad into live combat.

Griest's face was splattered with mud. The cadet jogged in place, first row, right, in the all-male squad. She and the handful of other cadets behind her looked straight ahead, focused on the tall wooden obstacle that awaited them. Its rungs were menacing. The ropes that hung from the sides were an intimidating reminder of how difficult it would be to get to the top of the multistory structure.

"You can't ride in my little red wagon!"

The group yelled cadence as they waited.

Griest was among the first to tackle it—the tallest and most difficult of the twenty-six obstacles on the course. She jumped on the thirty-foot-high rope that led to a small number of rungs at the top, determined. She knew she had to complete at least twenty-three of the twenty-six obstacles in order for that day to count. She would lose points for each obstacle she missed. Failure would have meant starting all over.

"Hurry up!" the drill sergeant directed his screams straight at Griest as she reached the first knot in the rope. "Hurry up, Ranger. Sometime today!"

She flung her left leg over the first rung and used it to hoist her body over the small ladder and onto the platform. Another soldier climbed over behind her, and they both ran across the wooden floorboards to a net on the other side.

They scurried across it, only to be greeted by another drill sergeant.

"Get off my obstacle!" His voice was louder and more booming than the first's. She avoided looking directly at him and just kept moving. "Let's go!"

A member of her squad jumped onto the rope at the end of the obstacle and lowered himself to the ground, picking up the pace as the sergeant's words grew louder. Griest quickly lowered herself behind him and jumped the last couple of feet.

She hit another obstacle flat on her stomach.

Griest pushed herself across a dry trail covered with woodchips—face down, head first, with her hands behind her back, using only her feet to move her body forward. This time it was the US Army Ranger Creed that she and the man she was paired with recited as loudly as possible.

"I accept the fact that as a Ranger my country expects me to move further, faster and fight harder than any other soldier," he said. She repeated the words, gasping for breath. "Never shall I fail my comrades. I will always keep myself mentally alert!"

Her forehead was only inches from the ground. Her mouth hung open. She was panting between syllables. She grimaced each time her boots slipped, failing to push her body as far forward as she wanted to go.

Griest stood beside her partner, holding a small black knife in her right hand. She tilted left and leaned into his gut. In a flash the male cadet maneuvered himself onto her shoulders. She scooped him up, quickly righting her upper body and straightening her legs. "Run!" With the drill sergeant's words ringing in her ears, she moved. Wood chips shifted under the weight of her body, which was carrying the full weight of a man more than a foot taller than her.

On the other side of the course Haver took on a different challenge.

Her hands were in the air, beside her shoulders as she completed several squat repetitions.

Each time the drill sergeant yelled, "One, two, three," Haver yelled "Ranger!"

Her voice stood out among the cacophony of the other men and women in her group.

A pair of cadets in front of her, one male and one female, get tapped out. A drill sergeant yells at them because the male cadet allowed his hands to fall below his shoulders. The two are forced to move to the end of the line. Haver and her partner move up one spot.

In a ditch Haver laid on her back at the center of a line of men doing the same. On the other side of that ditch another squad laid in the dirt. The two groups of cadets are so close that their boots are almost touching each other.

Haver holds her legs straight in the air and raises her shoulders off the ground; the only thing stopping her from sliding further into the ditch are her stomach muscles. Her neck is shaking. Her brows are furrowed. She looks to her right and her left and sees the men struggling as much as she is. That knowledge motivates her and gives her the mental strength to keep going. The drill sergeant starts counting, and she starts kicking her legs—slowly at first, then just enough to keep pace. The man to her right stops. She keeps kicking.

As dusk falls and night slowly takes over the Georgia horizon, eight women realize they've made it through the Darby Queen, day eight of training. They fall in line, spent, and head back to the base.

There were plenty of men who had their doubts about Griest's and Haver's ability to make it through the training and, more importantly, to have the backs of their male counterparts as they did it.

But the women proved repeatedly that they were more capable than some of their male counterparts. Lieutenant Michael Janowski recalled one such moment. During a twelve-mile ruck march it was Haver, not the other men in his squad, who saved him.

At mile six he started to flag. His pace slowed. He announced that the team's automatic weapon was too heavy for him to carry any further. He was about to give up. He had pushed himself to exhaustion. Haver was also exhausted. But when Janowski called for help, she reached out and grabbed the weapon. Haver carried it, along with the thirty-five pounds on her back, for the rest of the march. She, like the rest of the men, had no water to drink for the entire maneuver.

But it was the swamps of Florida—the last phase of Ranger school— that almost brought Griest to her breaking point.

The cadet slowly lowered herself into the cold, snake-infested waters. The 105-pound ruck on her back started to pull her down. The thick, black swamp, which was chest high at its deepest point for the men who had crossed before her, reached the tip of her chin. She grabbed the rope that had been stretched across the river, tied to trees on either side, and used the slippery guide to pull herself through the same water that had killed four cadets in 1995—all of whom suffered from hypothermia.

It took Griest and her squad two hours to complete the half-mile march between the swamp's maze of trees and shoulder-high weeds.

This is the phase when more than 30 percent of the cadets who remain either quit or fail. Those who are lucky get to start the last phase again and hope they pass the second time around—their last chance.

As she began to march away from the shore Griest reminded herself why she was there: to be a better leader, to be a stronger soldier. She had dreamed of attending Ranger School since the day she learned it existed during her time at West Point. She had graduated in 2011 and waited four years for the barrier against females to fall. There was nothing so tough, she reminded herself, that could make her quit now. Under the growing weight of her ruck she marched on. Her gait was a bit faster, her stride a bit wider, more confident.

The school is among the Army's most grueling. It prepares soldiers to lead troops into battle and includes mock raids of homes, mountain drills, combat leadership training—all tasks that Smoke, Rodriguez, and Adams had been doing in Iraq and Afghanistan long before the school opened its doors to women. People who were shocked to see women meet Army Ranger School standards either didn't know or didn't believe what women returning from war had been recounting. The real question shouldn't be whether women can make it through Army Ranger School but whether the school can effectively prepare soldiers for what's really happening to women on the ground in Iraq and Afghanistan—which, for women like Adams, who suffered a traumatic brain injury after her vehicle was blown up by an IED, can be much more gruesome.

No amount of training can prepare someone to watch other Marines (or soldiers, or airmen) get blown up—which Adams did.

In the face of doubt from some of their peers, social media taunts stating that standards must have been lowered, and government scrutiny, Haver and Griest met Army Ranger standards. And along the way they earned respect from the men in their squad, getting higher peer evaluation scores than many of their fellow graduates, according to data released by the *Army Times* three months after the women graduated. Two of the nineteen women who started in the school graduated. Only ninety-four of the more than three hundred men made it through.

That training milestone solidified what real-life experiences already told us—that women can fight, lead, and excel under the stresses of combat. And in places like the Middle East—where cultural restrictions have drastically changed war tactics—real life tells us something that training can't: that women participating in combat are essential to war strategy.

In 2015 requests came for female Marines on the ground during deployments in Afghanistan. When there were no FETs to send,

Marine units at Camp Pendleton returned to the very ideas Adams had touted three years before: shorter training times and assignments that sent women not just to Afghanistan, but to other countries that were in need of the special skills FETs had to offer—training women in gender-restrictive countries and engaging with female populations to gain useful information. That year they started sending FETs back to the Middle East.

FORT BENNING, GEORGIA, AUGUST 21, 2015—"Company! Attention!"

The graduates moved in unison, signaling the ceremony's official start. A collective stomp echoed and trailed off into the woods behind them.

"Rangers!" The ninety-four men and two women yelled an affirmation of the title they'd worked for sixty-one days to achieve.

In the bleachers, in front of the grassy area where the soldiers stood, a small group of friends and family members had gathered—all bonded by the fact that in some way their sons, daughters, and fellow soldiers were a part of history.

"You have people who will question the standards of Ranger School," said graduation speaker and 1985 Army Ranger School graduate Major General Scott Miller.

"Tell the truth about what you see and what you do. There's an Army depending on us for correct information. Ladies and gentlemen . . . standards remain the same. A five-mile run is still five miles. The times don't adjust. A twelve-mile road march is still twelve miles. . . . The swamps remain intact. There was no pressure from anyone above me to change standards. . . . Many of those who began with you did not finish. . . . You're leaving Victory Pond here today with a small piece of cloth on your shoulders. But more importantly you carry the title of Ranger from here on out. . . . Congratulations. Very well done. When I shake your hand, I know there's something very special behind that handshake. Rangers lead the way."

Guests milled around the parade grounds, taking selfies, hugging graduates, reconnecting with fellow soldiers they hadn't seen since their own graduations.

The two female graduates beamed, posed for photos, and shook Miller's hand as he walked by to congratulate them. Their achievements made them instant celebrities among the crowd—soliciting compliments and questions from the friends and family members of other guests.

In the middle of the chaos Haver's father pushed a large, silver safety pin through the gold-and-black Ranger tab and onto the sleeve of the woman's camouflaged uniform. Griest's mother did the same for her daughter. They hugged, and as the melee died down, the relatives returned to their seats so that the final moments of the ceremony could begin.

Haver and Griest lifted their voices with the rest of the Ranger Class of 8-15 to recite the Ranger Creed. The last part especially reflected the leadership demonstrated by the two women who, according to the men who served with them, were ready to pick up the slack when others in their squads fell behind.

"I will never leave a fallen comrade. . . . Readily will I display the intestinal fortitude required to fight on the Ranger objective and complete the mission, though I be the lone survivor."

Some of the graduates would become leaders in the 75th Ranger Regiment—an elite infantry unit that participates in joint special operations and raids. It was the ultimate ranger assignment they had all been training for.

Haver and Griest would return to their units—each with an extra badge, but no extra combat duties.

The 75th Ranger Regiment still refused to open its doors to women.

In September the Pentagon officially lifted the Army Ranger School's gender ban.

In October a third female—Major Lisa Jaster, an engineer—graduated.

As part of the ceremony Jaster's husband, an officer in the Marine Corps Reserves, pushed the traditional large silver safety pin through his wife's uniform. With a proud smile, as Jaster stood with her arms loosely wrapped around their two children, he pinned the black-and-gold Ranger tab to the shoulder of her right sleeve.

Haver and Griest, who returned to Fort Benning for the ceremony, watched with broad smiles. As soon as Jaster's husband stepped back, the two women raced toward her. The three friends, who all attended West Point, embraced for several seconds—putting an endcap on a grinding experience of scrutiny and doubt and support and pride.

A history-making club that only a few could understand.

NOTES

As detailed in the Preface, this book is the outgrowth of a multimedia project I started for *USA TODAY* in 2009, and most of the information recounted in this book comes from diary entries and extensive interviews with the women featured, other women who spoke about their experiences mainly on background, a male military intelligence source who worked with FETs (but wished to remain anonymous because of the sensitivity of the information he disclosed), film documentarians of the experiences of women in the military, and Afghanistan's Zabul Province police chief. Interviews were conducted by phone, in person, and by email.

Much of the information contained in the chronology, unless otherwise noted, was culled from four primary sources: *Women in the Army*, army.mil/women; *Restrictions on Assignments of Military Women: A Brief History*, a report from the National Women's Law Center; Megan Eckstein, "Timeline: Women in Combat Roles," *USNI News*, September 21, 2015; and William Abbatt, *The Female Review: The Life of Deborah Sampson, the Female Soldier in the War of the Revolution*, a reprint of the original book by Herman Mann (Applewood Books, 1916).

Quotes used at the beginning of each chapter were pulled from two primary sources: Simon Sebag Montefiore, *Speeches That Changed the World* (Metro Books, 2013) and brainyquote.com.

CHRONOLOGY

x   *acknowledged for her service through a military pension:* "Cathay Williams," National Park Service, nps.gov/people/cwilliams.htm.

xi   *Bragg said much later:* "Janet Harmon Bragg: Pioneering African American Aviator," Smithsonian Institution Archives, https://siarchives.si .edu/blog/janet-harmon-bragg-female-aviator.

xi   *A racially segregated Army also denied the commercial pilot entry into the WASPs:* Ibid.

xiii   *Captain Linda Bray leads her military police unit:* Michael R. Gordon, "Noriega's Surrender: Army; For First Time, a Woman Leads G.I.'s in Combat,"

New York Times, January 4, 1990, www.nytimes.com/1990/01/04/world/noriega-s-surrender-army-for-first-time-a-woman-leads-gi-s-in-combat.html.

xiii *modern-day war in which women were held hostage:* "Abused Gulf War POW Describes Her Ordeal; Flight Surgeon Says It's All a Part of War," *Baltimore Sun*, June 29, 1992, http://articles.baltimoresun.com/1992-06-29/news/1992181107_1_cornum-gulf-war-prisoner-of-war.

xiv *Team Lioness: Lioness*, documentary film, Room 11 Productions, 2008.

xvi *She's one of the best in the company:* Dave Phillips, "For Army Infantry's 1st Women, Heavy Packs and the Weight of History," *New York Times*, May 26, 2017, www.nytimes.com/2017/05/26/us/for-army-infantrys-1st-women-heavy-packs-and-the-weight-of-history.html.

PREFACE

xvii *President Bill Clinton's late 1996 cruise missile and air attack:* "U.S. Attack on Iraq," C-SPAN, September 3, 1996, www.c-span.org/video/?74762-1/us-attack-iraq.

xviii *International Security Assistance Force directive:* Gina Maria O. Jones, *Female Engagement Teams: Making the Case for Institutionalization Based on U.S. Security Objectives in Africa*, School of Advanced Military Studies, US Army Command and General Staff College, 2013.

CHAPTER 1. THE FIRST RUN

12 *The insurgent group's first political move was to assassinate Najib:* Terrence White, "Flashback: When the Taleban Took Kabul," *BBC News*, October 15, 2001, http://news.bbc.co.uk/2/hi/south_asia/1600136.stm.

14 *A few years later some of those same people would long for the former leader's return:* Ali M Latifi, "Executed Afghan President Stages 'Comeback,'" *Aljazeera*, June 22, 2012, www.aljazeera.com/indepth/features/2012/06/2012618134838393817.html.

CHAPTER 3. THE BEGINNING OF FEMALE ENGAGEMENT

27 *The Ar Ramadi operation was one of the bloodiest battles in Iraq: Lioness*, documentary.

30 *Our intelligence apparatus:* Major General Michael T. Flynn, Captain Matt Pottinger, and Paul D. Batchelor, "Fixing Intel: A Blueprint for Making

Intelligence Relevant in Afghanistan," report from the Center for a New American Security, January 2010.

34   *Parliamentary candidate Salama al-Khafaji:* "A Face and a Name: Civilian Victims of Insurgent Groups in Iraq," Human Rights Watch, 17, no. 9 (October 2005), www.hrw.org/reports/2005/iraq1005/iraq1005.pdf; Anthony H. Cordesman and Emma R. Davies, *Iraq's Insurgency and the Road to Civil Conflict*, vol. 1 (Westport, CT: Praeger Security International, 2007).

35   *survived several assassination attempts:* "Pascal Warde: Serving in Politics and Surviving Assassination Attempts in Iraq," Religion and Ethics Report, ABC, www.abc.net.au/radionational/programs/religionand ethicsreport/pascal-warda-iraqi-politics-and-surviving-assassination -attempts/7034314.

CHAPTER 4. THE SURGE IN AFGHANISTAN

36   *he announced the largest surge in the war's history:* "President Obama on the Way Forward in Afghanistan and Pakistan," The Obama White House, December 2, 2009, www.youtube.com/watch?v=oZLVqhsLgIw.

37   *the number of troops on the ground:* CBS News, "The War in Afghanistan: A Timeline," *CBS News*, December 1, 2009, www.cbsnews.com/news/ the-war-in-afghanistan-a-timeline; "Timeline of the Major Events in the Iraq War," *New York Times*, August 31, 2010, www.nytimes.com/inter active/2010/08/31/world/middleeast/20100831-Iraq-Timeline.html ?mcubz=1#/#time111_3262.

37   *drone strikes were failing:* Spencer Ackerman, "41 Men Targeted but 1,147 People Killed: US Drone Strikes—The Facts on the Ground," *Guardian*, November 24, 2014, https://defence.pk/pdf/threads/41 -men-targeted-but-1-147-people-killed-us-drone-strikes-the-facts-on-the -ground.439795.

38   *Western values . . . that Afghans strongly espoused under the Daoud government:* "Timeline of Women's Rights in Afghanistan," PBS.org, October 25, 2011, www.pbs.org/wnet/women-war-and-peace/uncategorized/ timeline-of-womens-rights-in-afghanistan.

CHAPTER 5. ALWAYS WANTED TO BE A COMBAT FIGHTER

46   *lost their lives in Afghanistan in 2010:* Iraq Coalition Casualty Count, icasu alties.org.

CHAPTER 6. THE LONG MARCH

53   *The three-day battle, waged from December 7 to 10, 2007:* Noor Khan, "50 Taliban Killed After Musa Qala Fight," *Washington Post*, December 12, 2007.

53   *roadside bombs had killed three thousand:* Gregg Zoroya, "How the IED Changed the U.S. Military," *USA TODAY*, December 18, 2013, www.usa today.com/story/news/nation/2013/12/18/ied-10-years-blast-wounds -amputations/3803017.

54   *"suicide missions":* Rebecca Leung, "GIs Lack Armor, Radios, Bullets," *60 Minutes*, October 31, 2004, www.cbsnews.com/news/gis-lack-armor -radios-bullets-31-10-2004.

54   *In three hundred attacks on Marine MRAPs:* Tom Vanden Brook, "New Vehicles Protect Marines in 300 Attacks," *USA TODAY*, June 28, 2007, http://usatoday30.usatoday.com/news/world/iraq/2007-04-18-marines -new-vehicles_N.htm.

CHAPTER 10. BREAKTHROUGH

104   *according to a 2013 Oxfam report:* Louise Hancock, "Women and the Afghan Police," Oxfam, September 10, 2013, www.oxfamamerica.org/ explore/research-publications/women-and-the-afghan-police.

105   *In 2010, 2,777 civilians were killed in Afghanistan:* Laura King, "U.N.: 2010 Deadliest Year for Afghan Civilians," *Los Angeles Times*, March 10, 2011, http://articles.latimes.com/2011/mar/10/world/la-fg-afghan-civilian -deaths-20110310.

105   *provided billions to the Afghan Security Forces Fund:* "FY2005 Supplemental Appropriations for Iraq and Afghanistan, Tsunami Relief, and Other Activities," CRS Report for Congress, May 12, 2005.

CHAPTER 12.
BUSINESSES MORE IMPORTANT THAN BOMBS

129   *Sergeant Robert Bales walked a mile:* James Dao, "Soldier Is Expected to Plead Guilty in Afghan Massacre," *New York Times*, May 29, 2013, www .nytimes.com/2013/05/30/us/staff-sgt-robert-bales-to-plead-guilty-in -afghan-massacre.html.

CHAPTER 13. VERY OLD CONCEPT, VERY NEW MISSION

135   *women are contributing in unprecedented ways:* "Women in Combat" news conference, with Defense Secretary Panetta and Joint Chiefs of Staff Chair General Martin Dempsey, C-SPAN, January 24, 2013, www.c-span .org/video/?310586-1/women-combat.

CHAPTER 17. AN UNEXPECTED RUN-IN

168   *the Afghan government cut funds to the district:* Ben Brody, "At Remote Afghan Base, U.S. Troops Locked in Battle for Hearts and Minds," PRI .org, August 6, 2011, www.pri.org/stories/2011-08-06/remote-afghan -base-us-troops-locked-battle-hearts-and-minds.

CHAPTER 19. PROMOTE OR PERISH

192   *Boko Haram has destroyed more than a thousand schools:* "10 Countries Where Girls' Education Has Been Under Attack," ReliefWeb, March 10, 2017, https://reliefweb.int/report/nigeria/10-countries-where-girls -education-has-been-under-attack.

193   *After negotiations only twenty-one girls were released:* Hilary Matfess, "Three Years Later, a Look at the #BringBackOurGirls Catch-22," *Daily Beast,* April 14, 2017, www.thedailybeast.com/three-years-later-a -look-at-the-bringbackourgirls-catch-22.

193   *Limited US military assistance, which has included:* Warren Strobel, "Obama Sends U.S. Troops, Drones to Cameroon in Anti-Boko Haram Fight," Reuters, October 14, 2015, www.reuters.com/article/us-nigeria -bokoharam-usa/obama-sends-u-s-troops-drones-to-cameroon-in -anti-boko-haram-fight-idUSKCN0S823F20151014; Adam Taylor, "MAP: The U.S. Military Currently Has Troops in These African Countries," *Washington Post,* May 21, 2014, www.washingtonpost.com/news/world views/wp/2014/05/21/map-the-u-s-currently-has-troops-in-these -african-countries/?utm_term=.a30599d29ed1.

193   *The terror group al-Shabaab . . . gained a foothold in Somalia:* "Who Are Somalia's al-Shabab?" BBC News, December 22, 2017, www.bbc.com/ news/world-africa-15336689.

193   *control and terrify women, including public stoning for adultery:* "Rape Victim Stoned to Death in Somalia Was 13, U.N. Says," *New York Times,*

November 4, 2008, www.nytimes.com/2008/11/05/world/africa/05 somalia.html.

193 *according to a report by the Thomson Reuters Foundation:* TrustLaw, "FACT-SHEET—The World's Most Dangerous Countries for Women," Thomson Reuters Foundation News," June 15, 2011, http://news.trust.org//item/?map=factsheet-the-worlds-most-dangerous-countries-for-women.

193 *The death rate for women during pregnancy is one in twelve:* "Child and Maternal Health," Unicef, Somalia, www.unicef.org/somalia/health_53.html.

194 *Women from Uganda are taking on expanded roles:* "Somalia—Uganda Women of African Union Troops Fight Al Shabab for Somalia Peace, Rights, Women," WUNRN, November 17, 2016, http://wunrn.com/2016/11/somalia-uganda-women-of-african-union-troops-fight-al-shabab-for-somalia-peace-rights-women.

194 *The UN has been calling for more female forces:* "Landmark Resolution on Women, Peace and Security," OSAGI, www.un.org/womenwatch/osagi/wps.

195 *becoming a staff sergeant after ten years in the Marines:* "MCBUL 5314 Enlisted Career Force Controls (ECFC) Program," Marines, September 16, 2015, www.marines.mil/News/Messages/Messages-Display/Article/897415/mcbul-5314-enlisted-career-force-controls-ecfc-program.

CHAPTER 20. LAWSUIT—PUSHING AGAINST THE BRASS CEILING

201 *"still get looked at more favorably":* Laird Harrison, "SF Lawsuit Demands Combat Roles for Women," KQED, November 27, 2012.

202 *"The shrapnel that tore through the vehicle that day":* Craig Whitlock, "Four Female Service Members Sue over Pentagon's Combat-Exclusion Policy," *Washington Post*, November 27, 2012, www.washingtonpost.com/world/national-security/four-female-service-members-sue-over-pentagons-combat-exclusion-policy/2012/11/27/460cf994-38da-11e2-83f9-fb7ac9b29fad_story.html?utm_term=.aebd6b6a375a.

202 *Ariela Migdal, senior staff lawyer:* James Dao, "Servicewomen File Suit Over Direct Combat Ban," *New York Times*, November 27, 2017, www.nytimes.com/2012/11/28/us/servicewomen-file-suit-over-direct-combat-ban.html.

203 *That year there were close to 150,000 troops:* Alan McLean and Archie Tse, "American Forces in Afghanistan and Iraq," *New York Times*, June 22, 2011, www.nytimes.com/interactive/2011/06/22/world/asia/american-forces-in-afghanistan-and-iraq.html.

203 *Bedell was in charge of forty-seven women:* "Women in Combat: Zoe Be-
      dell at TEDxHarvard Law School," TEDx Talks, YouTube, May 2, 2014,
      www.youtube.com/watch?v=qsyJl98XGqk.

203 *Farrell managed up to twenty women:* Colleen Farrell, "Let My Marines Do
      Their Jobs," ACLU, July 1, 2013, www.aclu.org/blog/womens-rights/
      let-my-marines-do-their-jobs.

203 *The more they traveled, the greater their risk:* Ibid.

204 *"What Do You Do with a WAC?": Combat Integration Handbook,* 1st ed., Sep-
      tember 2016, p. 4, http://wiisglobal.org/wp-content/uploads/2014/02/
      Combat-Integration-Handbook_Sept.20161.pdf.

CHAPTER 22. STATE OF THE UNION

216 *Obama . . . thanked the joint houses of Congress. The applause began to
      ebb:* "Watch President Obama Deliver the 2013 State of the Union Ad-
      dress," *PBS NewsHour,* February 12, 2013, www.youtube.com/watch
      ?v=bvK-o6u82tI&t=13s.

216 *"Fifty-one years ago John F. Kennedy declared:* "Remarks by the President
      in the State of the Union Address," White House, February 12, 2013,
      https://obamawhitehouse.archives.gov/the-press-office/2013/02/12/
      remarks-president-state-union-address.

EPILOGUE

225 *to capture the stories of the two women:* "Trailblazers: Two Women Pass
      Army Rangers School," CBS Evening News, August 20, 2015, www.you
      tube.com/watch?v=52wWxY9PgdA.

225 *And for other women who have that same goal in mind:* Matthew Cox, "Two
      Women Make History by Graduating Army Ranger School," Military
      .com, August 21, 2015, www.military.com/daily-news/2015/08/21/two
      -women-make-history-by-graduating-army-ranger-school.html.

226 *A failing score in phase one can get a soldier:* Michelle Tan, "Army Stats:
      Women Performed Comparably to Men in Ranger School," *Army
      Times,* November 11, 2015, www.armytimes.com/news/pentagon
      -congress/2015/11/11/army-statswomen-performed-comparably-to
      -men-in-ranger-school.

227 *US Army Ranger Creed:* "Ranger Creed," Army, www.army.mil/values/
      ranger.html.

INDEX